St. Louis Community College

Forest Park
Florissant Valley
Meramec

Instructional Resources
St. Louis, Missouri

GAYLORD

The Social Role of Higher Education

Garland Studies in Higher Education
(Vol. 7)
Garland Reference Library of Social Science
(Vol. 988)

Garland Studies
in Higher Education

Philip G. Altbach, Series Editor

This series is published in cooperation with the
Program in Higher Education, School of Education,
Boston College, Chestnut Hill, Massachusetts.

The Social Role
of Higher Education
Comparative Perspectives

edited by
Ken Kempner
William G. Tierney

Garland Publishing, Inc.
New York & London
1996

Library of Congress Cataloging-in-Publication Data

The social role of higher education : comparative perspectives / edited by
    Ken Kempner, William G. Tierney.
            p.   cm. — (Garland reference library of social
    science ; vol. 988. Garland studies in higher education ; vol. 7)
        Includes bibliographical references and index.
        ISBN 0-8153-1765-4 (alk. paper)
            1. Education, Higher—Social aspects.   2. Educational anthropol-
    ogy.   3. Comparative education.   I. Kempner, Kenneth Marc,
    1947–   . II. Tierney, William G.   III. Series: Garland reference
    library of social science ; v. 988.   IV. Series: Garland reference library
    of social science. Garland studies in higher education ; vol. 7.
    LC191.S6566   1996
    370.19—dc20   96–16423
                                                            CIP

Printed on acid-free, 250-year-life paper
Manufactured in the United States of America

Contents

Series Editor's Preface

Higher education is a multifaceted phenomenon in modern society, combining a variety of institutions and an increasing diversity of students, a range of purposes and functions, and different orientations. The series combines research-based monographs, analyses, and discussions of broader issues and reference books related to all aspects of higher education. It is concerned with policy as well as practice from a global perspective. The series is dedicated to illuminating the reality of higher and postsecondary education in contemporary society.

Philip G. Altbach
Boston College

Chapter One
Academic Culture in an International Context

Ken Kempner and William G. Tierney

Institutions of higher education are socially constructed realities that in part develop from their own sociocultural histories and traditions. The content and structure of colleges and universities also are shaped by the external cultural environment and a nation's place within the "international knowledge networks" (Altbach et al. 1986). How national and international cultural contexts affect the role of higher education in a society and their institutions of higher education provide the focus for this book.

For the purpose of this text, we define organizational culture by way of five key terms. *Organizational mission* provides meaning and definition to the organization's participants. As the overarching ideological apparatus of an organization's culture, the mission underscores the social relations at work in an organization. *Symbolism* pertains to the manner in which things get done, the signals employed to display particular meanings, and the communicative framework for the organization. *Strategy* relates to the unique decision-making structure of the organization. The organizational structure, the style of the leadership team, and the avenues employed to create plans to reach decisions all highlight the culture of the organization. The *environment* situates the organization within specific local, national, and international contexts. A social constructionist view emphasizes the interpretive and dynamic nature of the organization's environment. Finally, analysts of organizational culture investigate how *knowledge* gets constructed. Whose interests are served and who are silenced by the definition and manner in which knowledge gets constructed are key areas of investigation. These five terms—mission, communication, strategy, environment, and knowledge—provide key areas for studying academe from a cultural perspective (Tierney 1994). Although we will touch on all of these themes, for the purpose of this book the authors focus most of their attention on (a) how environments get defined and how they shape universities, and (b) how knowledge and academic work interact in national contexts. Our intent is to highlight these areas in order to develop a comparative perspective about particular facets of academic culture.

Because culture and knowledge do not flow only from the dominant, core countries to the periphery, the contributors to this book focus upon unique cultural circumstances and how higher education institutions and the faculty and students within them are affected by these circumstances. Both developing and newly industrialized countries have rich cultural traditions that contribute to innovations in learning and research unique to the social and cultural moment of a country and its institutions of higher education. Unfortunately, the contributions to knowledge from the periphery, and those making these contributions, are not always valued in the international networks. The knowledge and the scientists constructing this knowledge from the periphery are often considered too parochial, nationalistic, or "local" compared to the more worldly "cosmopolitans" of the core, to use Gouldner's (1954) terminology. As Marcos Valle (1994) has noted, however, the goal of knowledge production should be to "decenter the periphery" and make the superhighway a "two-way street." Valle encourages social scientists, in particular, to reconceive the notion of what constitutes the core by accepting the knowledge produced in the periphery into the core.

Insuring that knowledge flows to and from the core and questioning whose and what ideas actually constitute the core are at the essence of comparative research. Comparative research is helpful because it allows scientists to look back upon themselves from a holistic perspective, best accomplished by standing on the outside looking in. Merely looking, of course, is not sufficient to explain social reality, and it is for this reason the contributors to this volume focus upon culture as a key to understanding a nation's system of higher education. We propose here that a comparative and cultural perspective is helpful in recognizing the place of higher education in a nation's development, and how knowledge is created, defined, managed, and valued. Through individual and comparative case studies, the contributors to this book offer illustrative examples of how the cultural context of each country shapes the structure, function, and place of higher education in a particular society.

The authors question in each chapter the social function of higher education and how knowledge is constructed and disseminated in a specific country or between countries. Because, as Fay (1987) notes, "we live in a world in which knowledge is used to maintain oppressive relations," the authors are guided by the perspective of "critical postmodernism," as proposed by Giroux (1992) and applied to higher education by Tierney (1993). Critical postmodernists combine critical and postmodern theories by framing their investigations in a cultural perspective that addresses the inherent oppressive nature of social reality. From this perspective the effects of culture are central to understanding what and whom are valued and devalued in a society.

To understand how culture affects the role of higher education in a society and how culture both enables and restricts new ways of thinking, transmitting, and constructing knowledge, the contributors to this volume draw upon their comparative research in developed and developing countries. Rather than offer merely a "travelogue" that chronicles *what* a nation's educational system is, the authors consider *why* the system looks as it does. Similarly, rather than evaluating education only by assessing inputs and outputs of institutions, the contributors to this volume are guided by the perspective that culture is a key to understanding why a nation's educational system is structured as it is.

Educational inputs and outputs have meaning only when considered in relation to the larger cultural context that defines a nation's social structure and its educational system. Understanding culture is necessary to accomplish comparative educational research in order, as Noah (1986, 154) suggests, to "help us understand better our own past, locate ourselves more exactly in the present, and discern a little more clearly what our educational future may be." To truly understand why the present looks as it does, what the "future may be" in education, and how knowledge is produced, Kelly and Altbach (1986, 312) note that comparative education must be guided by a larger, more integrative understanding or "world systems analysis." This larger analysis enables a greater recognition of the dependent relationships among nations not only in the typical realm of economics and politics but also of education and the creation and exchange of knowledge. Assuming the flow of knowledge and culture is only from the developed to the developing nations denies the dignity of "other" cultures and enables only "First-World" solutions to

"Third-World" problems. The interdependency of knowledge creation and exchange should not be bound by nationalistic or geographic boundaries.

Certainly, there are strengths and weaknesses to our predominantly single case inquiries in this book. While all the authors attempt to be comparative, we are each trapped by our parochial focus on the nations we know the best, even though we have attempted to view them from "offshore." While our perspectives may limit the integrative and comparative view of culture we seek, we attempt to overcome these limitations through the number of languages we speak and the different cultures in which we have lived. This book provides cultural interpretations from the perspective of our accumulated knowledge, however parochial it may be, because we all recognize the limitations of our own personal lenses. Yet, to provide a deeper interpretation of educational systems than mere functional explanations of inputs, outputs, or budgets can offer, we have all attempted to look deeper into a nation's educational system for cultural explanations that define structures and policies. Of course, the individual chapters here cannot suggest definitive explanations of the cultural effects on a nation's entire system of higher education. The chapters do, however, attempt an assessment of how specific aspects of higher education are influenced by unique social and cultural circumstances. Even though "national culture" is a social invention, the authors attempt to understand how national and international cultural circumstances give the form to academic institutions. The distinctive strength of our mutual efforts is this recognition of the cultural complexity responsible for defining a nation's education system. Yet our equally distinctive weakness is our inability to explore the greater depths of this complexity than a single chapter, or single volume, allows.

Although all the authors in this volume have attempted to understand higher education by probing beyond surface-level explanations, there are many layers left unexplored and await further analysis. We have not, for example, looked at concepts within a particular culture; we have, of necessity, forgone some of the comparative assessment of the whole. In a number of the chapters, however, we have sought a greater comparative integration by joining international colleagues: a Japanese author with a U.S. author (Makino and

Kempner), a Brazilian with a Chilean (Valle and Figueroa), a U.S. author with an Australian (Rhoades and Smart), and a U.S. author with Thai scholars (Fry, Bovonsiri, Uampuang). What we have gained through this collaborative effort is a book that integrates cross-cultural perspectives on higher education that each author could not manage individually. Through our collaboration, we make no attempt to provide a comprehensive worldwide coverage but focus instead upon case studies that illustrate the significance culture plays in defining specific facets of a nation's higher education system.

In our particularistic focus on specific nations, we have attempted to expose the underlying cultural effects that give meaning and definition to higher education. We rely, therefore, on the book as a collection of case studies that together offer a comparative analysis of the unique and individualistic effects culture has on a particular system. What links these chapters and the authors' collective perspectives together is the reliance on culture to explain the inherent and persistent differences between and among seemingly similar systems of higher education. Rather than assuming ideas and conceptions of higher education easily travel across national boundaries, the basic premise among the authors is that differing cultural contexts yield equally different structures, problems, and solutions for higher education.

By presenting a range of case studies, we illustrate a variety of cultural circumstances and their individualistic effects on higher education. These case studies are not meant to be representative of specific prototypes or geographic regions of higher education but, rather, demonstrate the cultural circumstances of each unique case. Similarly, other countries and other systems have their own unique circumstances that must be recognized if we are to truly understand the social role higher education plays in a particular country. For this reason we rely, as well, on the larger context of comparative work and on the reader's own cultural context to assist in bringing meaning to the individual investigations presented here.

We begin our survey of the cultural effects of higher education in chapter 2 with William Tierney's investigation of the academic profession. Tierney suggests that there are fundamental differences between what he calls the "traditional perspective" and the cultural view that is advanced here. He uses interviews from five Central

American universities as the scaffolding for analyzing the role that organizational and national cultures play in knowledge production. Tierney argues that we need to move away from traditionalist assumptions that suggest a metanarrative exists where international disciplines are the sole arbiters of what counts as knowledge. Instead he discusses national and regional roles in the advancement of science policy; he reasons that knowledge production is not simply a scientific process but one that has political and ideological implications as well.

Tierney's interpretation of knowledge production is followed by Kempner and Makino's assessment of how Japanese culture has shaped its system of higher education in chapter 3. Kempner and Makino question the relevance of the modernistic principles that guide contemporary higher education in Japan. In particular they address current reform efforts and consider the implications the modernistic structure has for the future development of Japan's higher education. The authors argue that because the current system of higher education provides more a rationing function than an educational one, higher education has not provided Japanese students with the "cognitive maps" they will need to guide themselves and the nation in the future.

After this consideration of the cultural effects on Japanese education, we turn in chapter 4 to how Thai culture influences its system. Varaporn Bovonsiri, Pornlerd Uampuang, and Gerald Fry provide a historical context for the study of contemporary cultural issues that continue to shape and influence higher education in Thailand. By drawing upon their collective experience in Thai higher education, the authors offer both historical and cultural examples to analyze the social function of higher education and how knowledge is constructed and transmitted in Thailand. In their analysis the authors use a "triangular model" that overcomes the tendency in studies of higher education to emphasize a Western approach and values. This model recognizes the importance of indigenous culture, the influences of Western culture, and their amalgamation into the creation of a unique Thai system of higher education distinct in its own way from the Japanese, Mexican, and Chilean systems considered in this volume.

In chapter 5 Rollin Kent situates how recent socioeconomic

changes in Mexico impacted on how public universities define their purpose, and what societal agencies such as the federal government see as the changing role of the university in the waning days of the twentieth century. Kent begins his analysis with an overview of the changes from elite to mass higher education and then outlines how the severe economic crises of the 1980s in Mexico redefined the culture and structure of the universities. In effect the universities' external environment—government policy, changing public perceptions, the international scientific community, and the consumers of higher education—has shaped the internal dynamics and structures of the universities.

Susan Twombly makes an exploration in chapter 6 of how academic and national cultures shape institutional roles that is consistent with Tierney's and Kent's chapters. However, Twombly analyzes the position of women at the University of Costa Rica. She asks why women have assumed a comparatively high percentage of leadership roles in a university in a society that many think of as *machista*. She locates her analysis by way of life history interviews of eighteen women in senior administrative positions and argues that individuals exist as subjects and objects within the organization. They are capable of creating change, yet they also must function within cultural webs that constrict and define options for change.

In chapter 7 Gary Rhoades and Don Smart turn our attention to the entrepreneurial aspect of higher education and the market for international students by comparing educational policy toward foreign students in Australia to the United States. Rhoades and Smart argue that although the United States is typically portrayed as the "exemplar" of entrepreneurial culture, the Australian higher education system eclipses U.S. higher education in its entrepreneurial policy toward foreign students. Whereas Australian federal policy encourages universities to actively recruit foreign students, Rhoades and Smart explain U.S. policy is based on considerations of "economic dependency, domestic human resources, and national security." From their analysis of primary documents at the national level and secondary sources at the state and institutional policy levels, the authors find that Australian policy characterizes international students as "products" in the global marketplace whereas the United States lacks a clear, identifiable policy. Through their analysis the authors contrast the cultural differences between these two Western countries that yield differing policies within their system of higher education. Rhoades and Smart's findings contradict the prevailing functionalist perspective in comparative higher education that presumes the United States is the most advanced and well-adapted global society.

Following the comparative assessment of student policy, in chapter 8 Claudio Figueroa and Marcos Valle offer a case study of the conflicting cultural and political definitions of "decentralization" in Chile. As Rhoades and Smart focus upon the cultural influences between the United States and Australia that yield differing policies regarding international students, Figueroa and Valle look at the effect political culture has on defining the meaning of decentalization in education. By contrasting the meaning and policy development of the same concept—decentralization—under the Allende and the Pinochet governments, the authors illustrate how the unique Chilean cultural context affected the social outcomes in education, similar to the distinct Thai and Japanese systems examined earlier in this volume. Figueroa and Valle not only consider the context of Chile in their analysis but also frame their investigation in the rapidly evolving cultural context of Latin America, similar to the educational and social changes Kent notes in Mexico.

Finally in chapter 9 Jussi Välimaa discusses the role of private and public intellectuals in Finland. As with Kent's and Figueroa and Valle's chapters, Välimaa points out how the changing social and economic climates of the country are creating dramatic alterations within the university. In particular he offers a historical analysis of the rise of Finnish universities and suggests that the definition of "intellectual" is a socially constructed term that depends on the social and cultural contexts in which the intellectuals reside. Similar to Twombly, he concludes that intellectuals have both shaped and are shaped by the larger societal forces. Intellectuals have played a crucial role in defining national identity, but they also increasingly see their roles defined by the external environment.

In what follows, we struggle to bring a comparative perspective to the theoretical notion of culture. Ironically culture is a term whose conceptual home is by definition comparative in nature—anthropology—and yet most work that has been done on culture in academe has been located primarily in the United States and the United Kingdom. This text is a first step in employing comparative rigor in order to enhance our understanding of the social and cultural contexts in which academe resides. As opposed to the more cookbook solutions that have recently populated academic journals that offer specific recipes, we develop here a way of thinking about, and hence acting in, the organizational world. In a dynamic environment such as now exists throughout the world, the academic citizenry is not well served with "how to's" about life in a static environment. Instead, our suggestions are more strategic than linear and lockstep. The analysis of culture in an international context enables us to conceive of new models about how to act as we move closer to the twenty–first century.

References

Altbach, P.G., C.H. Davis, T.O. Eisemon, S. Gopinathan, H.S. Hsieh, S. Lee, P.E. Fong, and J.S. Singh. 1986. *Scientific development and higher education: The case of newly industrializing nations.* New York: Praeger.

Fay, B. 1987. *Critical social science: Liberation and its limits.* Ithaca, N.Y.: Cornell University Press.

Giroux, H. 1992. *Border crossings: Cultural workers and the politics of education.* New York: Routledge.

Gouldner, A.W. 1954. Cosmopolitans and locals: Toward an analysis of latent social roles. *Administrative Science Quarterly* 11(3):281–306.

Kelly, G.P. and P.G. Altbach. 1986."Comparative education: Challenge and Response." In *New approaches to comparative education,* eds., P.G. Altbach and G.P. Kelly. Chicago: University of Chicago Press.

Noah, H. 1986. The use and abuse of comparative education. In *New approaches to comparative education,* eds., P.G. Altbach and G.P. Kelly. Chicago: University of Chicago.

Tierney, W.G. 1993. *Building communities of difference: Higher education in the 21st Century.* Westport, Conn.: Bergin and Garvey.

———. 1994. Cultural politics in a Latin American university. La Educacion 118 (II):265–284.

Valle, M. 1994. Discussant remarks, American Educational Research Association Annual Conference, New Orleans, April.

Chapter Two
The Academic Profession and the Culture of the Faculty
A Perspective on Latin American Universities

William G. Tierney

Investigations pertaining to knowledge policy often highlight the centrality of universities in the accomplishment of scientific research. From this perspective, faculty work and knowledge production have a natural interrelationship and symbiosis. Although much discussion currently exists about redefining the role of universities and rethinking the appropriate role for faculty, as Schwartzman observes, such analyses are "basically concerned with fine-tuning an otherwise sound and firmly entrenched research and educational establishment" (1985, 101). However, a curious assumption exists about the assumed role of the professoriat in the production of knowledge in this "firmly entrenched research establishment."

The assumption pertains to how knowledge gets defined as the accumulation of facts around a common intellectual discourse. The discourse becomes codified within the confines of a profession and discipline. As Burton Clark has written, "The disciplines can readily be seen as primary. . . . The disciplines rather than the institution tend to become the dominant force in the working lives of academics" (1983, 40). In this chapter I explore what I feel Clark and others (Lodahl and Gordon 1972; Beyer and Lodahl 1976) overlook when they generalize in this manner about knowledge and, of consequence, the role of faculty. In particular, I argue that knowledge is a social construct dependent upon institutional and national contexts, as well as the discipline and profession.

My point is not simply to suggest that an institution or nation is involved in the production of knowledge as intensively as a discipline. Instead I argue that knowledge is a discourse constantly reconstructed over time and place. Knowledge production needs to be reconceptualized so that it is thought of as tied to the contingencies and reconstructions of the manifold cultures and ideologies of social groups such as the faculty. How does such a definition affect institutional life and the work of the faculty? The answer to such a question pertains to what I will call a cultural perspective on knowledge production.

I highlight the argument by first contrasting a traditional view of academic work with what I define as an interpretive, or cultural, view of knowledge. I then elaborate on a cultural view of knowledge by way of an analysis of five Central American universities where I interviewed over 150 individuals during 1992 through 1993. I discuss the situations in which these institutions find themselves, and I consider some of the challenges that confront the Central American professoriat. I conclude with three implications of a culturally constructed view of knowledge for Latin American universities and their professoriat.

Interpretations of Knowledge Production
A Traditional Perspective

The advancement of knowledge is most often seen as a neutral investigation undertaken by objective scientists who form part of a particular discipline. The knowledge domain of individuals ties them together not by locality or subjective beliefs but by scientific interest. The community of scientists, then, is international in flavor and enables parochial or cultural differences to break down insofar as all researchers of a specific discipline "speak the same language"—that of science. As Burton Clark has observed, "It is the discipline mode of organization that has rendered higher education over time and space, basically meta-national and international" (1983, 29).

This view is premised on at least two core beliefs. First, a discipline's subject matter reflects neutral categories that have accumulated over time. Second, the advancement of knowledge is accretionary; one scientist learns one fact and adds it to the knowledge base so that the field advances. These beliefs enable individuals to generate generalized questions about the advancement of knowledge irrespective of nation or institution. "If an omniscient social engineer were to devise a comprehensive national knowledge policy," asks Roger Geiger, "what would be the optimal role for university research?" (1985, 54). Such a question assumes that the response one develops will be similar throughout the world in large part because scientists undertake basic research in a similar manner with similar needs and objectives. The extent to which a nation is unable to meet the "optimal role" would suggest that basic research should be undertaken in some countries and not in others; again, where such research takes place is relatively unimportant insofar as knowledge is impartial and shared by the community of scientists.

If we follow this line of thought, we see that how particular topics become important or why scientists investigate one topic and not another depends on two influences. On the one hand, substantive growth occurs when a discipline absorbs new ideas. A scientist works in a laboratory and achieves a breakthrough that enables other investigations and scientific questions to arise. On the other hand, the needs of society—defined as the international community—also cause scientists to turn their work toward a specific question. The depletion of the ozone layer, for example, or the desire of a cure for AIDS prompt scientists to search for solutions. Even when the stimulus for change comes from outside the discipline, the scientist retains control of the investigation and production of knowledge in large part because the investigator works in the rarefied atmosphere of a university where life is presumed to be nonpolitical.

The implications of this view for a university are vast. The department, school, or faculty, as the logical structure for a field of study, becomes the basic unit that directs intellectual thought. The work of the faculty, and of consequence the reward structure, is geared toward basic research. Those who are most capable of evaluating a scholar's work are like-minded scholars in similar fields at other universities. The relationship between the institution and society is tenuous. Society—in the form of a governmental authority, a funding agency, or the like—may suggest topics for study in one form or another, but it is the research faculty at the university who decide the parameters of the investigation. One of the chief functions of the university becomes the ability to train new researchers who will be able to conduct research. Hence, graduate education becomes important. The university's purpose is also to create the climate where research can be undertaken without the intrusion of the outside world.

The research function benefits the university because it enables the most current ideas to find their way into the undergraduate and graduate curriculum. Research is a dynamic activity that in turn creates a dynamic intellectual environment. As researchers, faculty are more involved with intellectual activities than political ones, which again makes the university less ideological and more scientific. As Geiger observes, "The inherent strengths of university research are in theory related to the intersection of discipline and institution. Scientists in their research roles are oriented more toward their peers in the scientific community, rather than their bureaucratic superiors in their institution" (1985, 67). Of consequence, argue Geiger and others, the objective nature of research rubs off on the university environment so that academic work and evaluation is more frank and critical than personal and political.

Such a view of knowledge production is one where lawlike generalizations are possible and desirable. Objectivity is the sine qua non of the professional undertaking. Professional associations, then, provide the necessary bonds of affiliation for scientists to have their work evaluated, rejected, or accepted.

Parenthetically, this sense of the academic profession differs somewhat from other occupational communities. The traditional definition of a profession is a group of people who engage in similar kinds of work, share common values and beliefs, and derive a similar sense of identity from their work (Tierney and Rhoads 1994). The profession of medicine, for example, regulates all of its members, for in one way or another everyone works in the health profession. In the academic profession, of course, there is no one set definition of a "professor." Obviously, a Latin American historian and a molecular biologist share the same professional title—professor— but they nonetheless share few of the requisites that would make them professional colleagues. Their work, values, beliefs, and identity differ, although they have broad affiliational ties to abstract concepts such as academic freedom and integrity. The specialty of a specific discipline, then, takes on importance in the professional lives of an academic. Thus from a traditional perspective, the discipline drives the work of the faculty and, to a large extent, the function and purpose of the university.

A Cultural Perspective
My point here is not to reject the idea that the disciplines have a role in the advancement of knowledge. It would be a mistake, not to

mention foolhardy, to suggest that disciplines do not form a crucial arena where scientists puzzle over a particular dilemma. However, I take exception to the portrayal of the advancement of knowledge as a neutral and natural undertaking that occurs within the parameters of different disciplines. To come to terms with how knowledge gets produced, we need to look not merely at disciplinary areas but also at a variety of other cultural agencies.

By using the term "culture," I am suggesting that individuals and groups are interpretive beings who are in a constant state of reconstruction of their worlds. The analysis of culture is an undertaking involved with understanding the manifold interpretations of the symbolic-expressive acts of individuals, groups, and organizations. Culture is not simply the functional or structural aspects of a particular group or organization as if those structures or functions exist in a codified reality. Rather, culture pertains to how particular groups and organizational participants make sense of their lives through the use of specific structures or functional vehicles. Individuals and organizations, then, are in a dynamic system that both frames and is framed by human interaction.

A cultural perspective assumes that knowledge is socially constructed. Individuals and groups define knowledge not merely through an objectively situated context such as a research project but also through the historical and social situations in which individuals find themselves. The point of course is not that knowledge advances whimsically but that discursive fields exist that play a powerful role in framing how individuals think about knowledge. Knowledge is not discovered; it is created. From this perspective, the great mysteries of the universe are not preformed and "out there" awaiting to be found. Instead, individuals are involved in the undertaking of the production of knowledge.

Again, I do not wish to overdraw the distinction or downplay the advancement of scientific thought. Obviously knowledge is to a certain extent accretionary; scientists do learn from others and build upon previous work. However, to assume that science advances in such an objective fashion offers a linear view of reality; a cultural view suggests that we eschew linearity and the idea that knowledge resides within a coherent disciplinary framework. Knowledge is a social product with political roots (Tierney 1991, 204). Knowledge policy has political consequences that shape the way individuals think about and act in the world. The question turns not only on how disciplines codify knowledge or on how governments and universities might create an environment conducive to knowledge production but on how knowledge gets constructed and employed in different contexts and situations.

Of consequence, a cultural view takes into account the production of knowledge from a localized viewpoint instead of from a "metanational" perspective. Knowledge production is neither neutral nor simply taxonomic. Specific interests are involved in the development of a comprehensive national knowledge policy, and they are investigated not as objective advocates but as subjective participants. To understand knowledge production and knowledge policy, one looks at the university as a contested terrain where different interests struggle over what counts for knowledge, instead of as a neutral site. And especially for the purpose of this text, the traditional view of knowledge is investigated with regard to whose national interests are advanced and whose are in jeopardy when one assumes research is objective and apolitical.

A cultural perspective, then, argues that knowledge production is a dynamic process that helps define and is defined by the worlds in which it is situated. The manner in which individuals define knowledge creates a particular way of seeing the world. Too, the way knowledge gets defined privileges certain discourses and organizational arrangements and silences others. Thus, to understand how knowledge gets produced, we need to investigate the many areas where knowledge is located rather than unproblematically assume that a university is a disinterested arena where objective scientists may pursue their work. Knowledge, then, from a cultural perspective, becomes an ideological construct that organizes beliefs, actions, and expectations. To expand on these ideas, I turn to a discussion of Latin American higher education. After portraying organizational life in Central American public universities, I then consider the ramifications of traditional and cultural perspectives.

The Culture of the Faculty in Central America

In many respects Central American universities and their professoriat mirror many of the aspects of institutions and faculty members throughout much of Latin America (Brunner 1992a, b). Some institutions, such as the University of San Carlos in Guatemala, have a centuries-old tradition of higher learning. Other institutions, such as the University of Panama and the University of Costa Rica, are about fifty years old. All of the institutions were initially planned for an elite group of students who would eventually assume positions of leadership in their respective countries. In a manner somewhat similar to Mexico (Kent 1986) during the 1960s and 1970s, the idea of mass education swept through Central America so that institutions such as the University of Panama went from 6,972 students in 1964 to over 52,000 students in 1990 (Gandásegui 1992, 546).

The faculty, and the expectations of their roles, also have changed. The traditional view of professorial life as a part-time teaching job filled by a handful of leading citizens has been transformed due to a variety of factors. The sheer number of students necessitated a dramatic increase in the number of faculty. Faculty who returned from postgraduate studies in Europe and the United States pushed for greater research efforts. In many countries, universities such as National University in Costa Rica also developed roles for faculty as change agents within local communities. As Winkler notes, the faculty now "play a critical role in producing both research and highly-skilled labor" (1990, 94). Consequently, by the 1990s the goals and desire for faculty in Central American universities in many respects mirrored the roles of faculty in the United States; Central American universities sought full-time faculty who engaged in teaching, service, and research.

Central American universities have tried to increase the number of full-time faculty and professionalize the academy by seeking to hire greater numbers of individuals with advanced degrees. Indeed, advanced training has become an indicator of organizational quality so that it is assumed that the more faculty who hold doctorates, the better the university will be. Nevertheless, current estimates are that not more than 10% of Latin American universities are actually "research universities" and only 15% of the faculty conduct research (Brunner 1992a, b).

The research function of the university has become one of the major areas of discussion with regard to the scope and purpose of many Central American universities. With the rise of private universities in Costa Rica, for example, one way the University of Costa Rica and National University differentiate themselves is with regard to their stated purpose to conduct research. For most countries, over half of all researchers are located in public universities (Winkler 1990, 94). Nevertheless, most individuals involved with Central American research activities agree with the assertion that "research has not reached a high level of development" (Orellana 1992, 276). Further, not much dialogue has been given to how one defines research; in the absence of such dialogue, three definitions have arisen. Research mirrors what occurs in developed countries; research is intended to be the "R and D" arm of the government; or researchers are concerned with praxis and the direct involvement in the struggles and lives of the citizens of the country.

Given the present situation, and these issues and problems, how might one think about the nature of research in Latin America? How does it fit within the traditional and cultural views of research? How might we define the problems and develop an action agenda? Evidence of the acceptance of the *traditional perspective* of knowledge production is manifold.

From a traditional perspective, at least three problems confront Central American universities if the faculty are to conduct research and the universities are to be thought of as research oriented. First, although the Universities of San Carlos and Costa Rica, for example, claim that approximately 60% of their faculty are full time, the category of "full-time" holds little meaning. Few people, if any, believe that 60% of the faculty are full-time employees of the university; one normally hears that individuals who work full time at a Central American university are no more than 20%. The difficulty of the universities to pay sufficient salaries and the ability of the private sector to offer better incomes has created a long-term manpower problem. If the professoriat is to carry out the manifold responsibilities of teaching, research, and service, then of necessity a greater cadre of full-time individuals will be needed to conduct the work.

Second, if the university needs individuals who are equipped with advanced training to conduct basic and applied research, then it must find the funding available to train individuals in graduate programs as well as acquire the requisite resources to keep the individuals at their institutions once they return from their studies. The

University of Costa Rica, for example, sends close to one hundred individuals a year abroad for doctoral level studies. Five years after their return, however, well over 50% of these individuals are not doing academic tasks for which they were trained. Surely, if the research policy of the country is to train individuals to become biochemists, engineers, and the like so that upon their return they will be able to undertake needed research in these areas, then it is a failure if these individuals five years after their return are involved in work that is tangentially, if at all, related to their respective fields.

Third, the climate within Central American universities in the closing days of the twentieth century is generally pessimistic. The overbureaucratization of the academy, where at the same time everyone and no one has authority to make decisions, has led many who otherwise might work in the university to look for employment outside the academy. To many individuals, private research institutes seem more adept and amenable to proposal writing and research activities than public universities where facilities are poor and the impetus for conducting research is viewed as low. Again, from a traditional perspective, if the university wants to increase research, the climate needs to change. And as Vessuri has argued, in order to compete in the new world economic order, the university must adapt (1993).

Analysis and Action from a Traditional Perspective

As noted, universities desire to improve, and discussions revolve around how to increase research activities. In order to have more research, the university needs more researchers and sends young scholars abroad to attain a doctorate or advanced degree. The assumption is that they will become knowledgeable in a specific area, and in doing so they will learn how to become scientists. They will take this knowledge back to their institutions and seek to create research centers.

Similarly, the advent of international telecommunication such as the Internet or e-mail is heralded in Central America because it will permit investigators "to communicate on a world level with other investigators and gives researchers access to international data bases" (Garita 1991, 53). Individuals who conduct research also are more likely to attend conferences on an international level than within their own countries or region; indeed, regional communication or coordination of activities across faculties and universities is rare in Central America. International journals are more commonly found in university libraries. Only in Costa Rica is there a significant number of scholarly journals, but again, these journals do not extend much beyond the confines of the country, and even within the country, there is not a great amount of scholarly cross-fertilization.

Participants generally have a two-tier response to how they think of institutional quality. They talk about how they meet the needs of the local citizenry—the teaching and service functions—and then they respond to how they fit within a regional and global framework—the research function. Although an organization's participants differ with regard to how they feel they are meeting the needs of its citizens, they inevitably comment that they fall short in a global arena.

Analysis and Action from a Cultural Perspective

A *cultural view* calls upon the same facts as the traditional view but offers a different interpretation. Since research is value oriented and socially constructed, one needs to begin with the struggle against a mind-set that knowledge is value neutral and objective. If we consider the political nature of knowledge production, then the road to improvement is neither necessarily through an increase in research nor through the definition of research that is commonly accepted by Western authorities. Advanced training in Western countries reinforces a specific definition of knowledge that researchers then return home to develop in their own institutions. At a minimum, one must question the manner in which research is done, the topics that are involved, and who is involved in doing it. Similarly, institutional structures that mirror internationalized forms of knowledge will be analyzed to see if different knowledge sets will be more applicable for institutions in Central America.

As much effort will be spent in trying to develop regional relationships as in developing ties with European countries and the United States. In this light, journals, conferences, and a host of communicative interchanges will be highlighted in Central America rather than trying to develop solely international exchanges. Quality will be determined not by the primacy given to international definitions of research but to the community's development of culturally specific criteria.

The point here is that as long as Central American institutions accept the traditional view of knowledge production, they will inevitably shortchange themselves, reward developed countries, and maintain traditional forms of power and privilege. From a cultural perspective, to assume that universities in Central America ought to strive for North American notions of research seems as shortsighted as assuming that research should not be conducted at all. Instead of buying into the notion that the road to academic quality is through Western notions of research, researchers in Central American universities might develop their own concepts of what counts for knowledge and concentrate on achieving quality within that framework.

Indeed a Central American concept of knowledge production may reorient faculty work yet again so that discussions about pedagogy and curricular formations take precedence rather than Western ideas of the development of basic research. Instead of sending individuals outside of the region, more emphasis might be placed on postgraduate studies within Central America. And if we accept that knowledge is socially constructed, then we need to question why the structure of academic life in Central America mirrors so closely those structures of the United States and Europe. Rather than assume that research is value neutral, one investigates the political nature of investigations to see how they relate to the larger social realities. The point, too, is not that the research and work of Western universities is value neutral and in Latin America it is political; in a cultural framework, all research is political, and the challenge is to discover and struggle over the political nature of knowledge.

As noted above, it is relatively clear what one must do if he or she subscribes to the traditional notion of knowledge production. Indeed most universities in Central America, some with greater success than others, are attempting to conform to the traditional notion. The problem from a cultural perspective is that the power relation of the areas will never change as long as participants in Central American universities accept a traditional definition of knowledge production. What are the implications for a university that desires to work from the cultural framework?

Steps to a Cultural Framework

If knowledge is socially constructed and the work of the faculty in large part pertains to knowledge production, then we need to consider the manifold cultures of the faculty that influence how they construct knowledge. Faculty exist in four cultures, that of the discipline, profession, institution, and nation. The argument of this text is that we have assumed faculty life to reside within the culture of the discipline at the expense of the other cultures. The point is surely not to deny the importance of the discipline, and in this light, the traditional concerns of faculty life expressed above remain as dilemmas. A larger cadre of full-time faculty are needed; those individuals trained in particular disciplines need the resources to conduct appropriate research within the university; and institutions need to clarify and streamline decision making.

Increasing the number of full-time faculty also alters the culture of the profession to a certain extent in the sense that larger groups of individuals affiliate to a specific concept called "professor" (Levy 1992, 4). At the same time, merely increasing numbers does not suggest what the work of an individual involves. Further, the traditional solutions also do not draw upon the specific cultures of the institution or nation. At least three strategies might be developed that speak specifically to institutional and national culture that in turn also affects how individuals conceptualize the professional cultural of the faculty.

Regionalization

If knowledge has roots in the social and cultural contexts in which it is located, then it makes sense for Central American universities to concentrate more fully on activities that foster knowledge production within a Central American context. The suggestion here is to move journals, conferences, and workshops toward greater interaction within the region, where individuals may concentrate more fully on the development and extension of Central American concepts of knowledge.

The implications of this view range from fostering faculty interchange and on-going discussions across countries to ensuring that funds exist for yearly conferences for individuals in specific disciplines. Journals and books published in Central America hold significant potential for communicative vehicles about problems that are of concern, for example, to the Costa Rican educator as well as the Guatemalan. The ability of governments to create alliances that allow scholarly books and journals to be published in the region so that they are not taxed in a manner that printed matter is taxed from outside the region offers the potential for a significant increase in regional scholarly interaction.

As noted, at present there is little more than a handful of individuals who have sustained conversation with colleagues across Central American universities. Communication is often easier with colleagues in the United States or Europe than it is with individuals a few hundred kilometers from one's campus. Yet rather than accept the situation as a given and continue dialogues on an international level, the suggestion here is to seek ways of enhancing dialogue and communication on a regional level with colleagues who conceivably have more in common with one another than with individuals in the United States. To create Internet links with campuses within the region, for example, is extremely achievable and of potentially greater utility for most faculty.

The purpose of such interchange, of course, is not simply dialogue for the sake of conversation. As with any scholarly conferences or materials, the goal is to foment thinking so that solutions to particular problems might be moved closer toward solution. The point is also not to eschew relationships with colleagues in the United States or Europe but to concentrate more fully on developing the often tenuous relationships that currently exist with colleagues within the region.

Advanced Training

If one agrees that different regions face problems specific to their context, then it seems prudent to develop advanced training that specializes in that particular problem. This suggestion is a logical extension of the idea of regionalization. Obviously problems in biology or public administration will differ between Panama and Honduras, but they will share greater similarities than do Honduras and the United States.

The development of graduate programs has been the clearest way for universities and nations to create traditions of research (Winkler 1990). It is also self-evident that graduate programs are more costly than undergraduate programs. Accordingly regional and institutional planners need to develop a coordinated series of doctoral and postgraduate degrees. To develop such degrees, international agencies might concentrate monies on scholarships and grants for individuals and programs within the region. Such transitions do not happen overnight, so that scholarships such as Fulbright/Laspau will still be needed; at the same time greater concentration on intrainstitutional arrangements enables fund sharing across institutions and countries and creates greater cohesiveness than currently exists.

Most importantly, the goal of localized knowledge production is put into place, and individuals will undoubtedly have greater understanding of a Central American perspective of research than if they attend institutions in Europe. Further, a logical principle of socialization is that individuals bond with those individuals with whom they attend graduate school. It stands to reason, then, that a Honduran and Salvadoran will have greater potential for sustained discussion after graduate school if they attended the same university and developed bonds of personal and scholarly fellowship.

Research and Pedagogy

A traditional perspective of research assumes that one either does research or does not and that one either does basic or applied research. A hierarchy also exists, so one assumes that to do research is better than not doing research and to do basic research is more important than to do applied. We need to extend our thinking with regard to what one means by research, and in doing so, we might conceivably transform how we think of teaching and learning. As Schwartzman has observed, "The value assumptions taken for granted in Western culture concerning the nature of education, research and organizational behavior are only a very limited subset of a much larger array of possibilities" (1985, 102). Nevertheless, the overwhelming strength of traditional notions of research have extended to Central American universities so that academic quality and research are inevitably defined within a context that for the most part exists exclusively in the developed world.

In essence, then, I am suggesting that Central American universities concentrate on expanding the "subset" of possibilities and consider alternative configurations of research and pedagogy that meet more fully the needs of the individuals with whom they are involved. At times such work will pertain to the international community of scientists, but at other times it will concentrate more fully on the students who attend the university, and at yet other times the work will extend into the local communities.

The ability to develop alternative configurations of what it means to do research or to create new relationships between pedagogy and knowledge is perhaps the greatest challenge that intellectuals face in general, and in particular for Central American faculty. To call for expanded notions of knowledge production, and of consequence, research, suggests moving beyond current paradigmatic thought. Such movement is by definition revolutionary in nature and substance. And yet, history has shown the truth of Schwartzman's comment. Research in Germany in the nineteenth century was a radically different configuration than what it is today in the United States. Such changes are not merely accretionary; they are epistemological and ontological as well. What I am suggesting is that similar changes can take place within Central America that will more fully meet the needs of the people in the twenty-first century.

Conclusion

A cultural view of knowledge has far-reaching implications for Central American universities and their faculty. I stress for a final time that a cultural view in some respects incorporates some aspects of a traditional perspective. Disciplines still play a critical role in the development of knowledge, and consequently international relationships will still be maintained. However, the overwhelming importance that disciplinary frames of thought have generated has resulted at the least in the shortchanging of cooperative arrangements with institutions within the region, and at the worst with the solidification of power arrangements between the developed and developing worlds.

To clarify the differences between the cultural and traditional models, I have resorted to institutional extremes. Obviously, universities in Central America to a certain extent have incorporated cultural perspectives with the traditional view. Regional confederations are examples of a cultural perspective. The recent creation of a regional group pertaining to liberal arts and the humanities is but one example of a cultural perspective at work. Yet as I have shown, in general, Central American institutions have placed their efforts in the more traditional contexts of the global community.

I have suggested that institutions utilize a cultural view of knowledge production to generate alternative institutional frameworks that are more localized, and call upon specific social and cultural arrangements. In doing so, individuals move away from the idea of "metanarratives" where knowledge is neutral and objective. The national and institutional culture of faculty take on as much importance as the cultures of the profession and discipline. In turn, definitions of institutional excellence and how we conceive of faculty work are transformed to more adequately meet the needs of society.

References

Beyer, J., and T. Lodahl. 1976. A comparative study of patterns of influence in United States and English universities. *Administrative Science Quarterly* 21:104–129.

Brunner, J. 1992a. *América Latina: cultura y modernidad.* Mexico: Consejo Nacional para la Cultura y las Artes.

———. 1992b. *Educacion superior, sociedad y estado en America Latina.* Santiago, Chile: Mimeo.

Clark, B. 1983. *The higher education system.* Los Angeles: University of California Press.

Gandásegui, M.A. 1992. Panama. In *The encyclopedia of higher education,* eds., B. Clark and G. Neave. New York: Pergamon.

Garita, L. 1991. *Informe del rector.* San Jose, Costa Rica: University of Costa Rica.

Geiger, R. 1985. The home of scientists: A perspective on university research. In *The university research system,* eds., B. Wittrock and A. Elzinga. London: Almquist and Wiksell.

Kent, R. 1986. *Modernización conservadora y crisis académica en la UNAM.* Mexico: Nueva Imagen.

Levy, D. 1992. The academic profession. Paper presented to the Latin American Studies Association. Los Angeles, California.

Lodahl, T., and G. Gordon. 1972. The structure of scientific fields and the functioning of university graduate departments. *American Sociological Review* 37:57–72.

Orellana, C.G. 1992. Guatemala. In *The encyclopedia of higher education,* eds., B. Clark and G. Neave. New York: Pergamon.

Schwartzman, S. 1985. The quest for university research: policies and research organization in Latin America. In *The university research system,* eds., B. Wittrock and A. Elzinga. London: Almquist and Wiksell.

Tierney, W.G. 1991. Academic work and institutional culture. *Review of Higher Education* 14(2):199–216.

Tierney, W.G., and R. Rhoads. 1994. *Beyond promotion and tenure.* Washington, DC: ASHE/ERIC.

Vessuri, H. 1993. The development gap: Implications for higher education and research in Latin America. *Higher Education Policy* 6(4):25–28.

Winkler, D. 1990. Higher education in Latin America: Issues of efficiency and equity. In *World Bank Discussion Papers,* 77. Washington, D.C.: World Bank.

Chapter Three
The Modernistic Traditions of Japanese Higher Education

Ken Kempner and Misao Makino

Similar to the 1950s when the United States became the leader of the free world, the Japanese are now learning how to assume their role as the global economic leader. With the burst of the "bubble economy," however, government, business, and educational leaders are reexamining what Japan's responsibilities should be as the foremost economic world power. The changing world order is causing the Japanese to consider how prepared their social, economic, and educational systems are to take the country into the next century. What role higher education, in particular, is to play in preparing Japan and its people for its future global, economic, and social responsibilities is not abundantly clear, however, nor is it well studied (Amano 1986).

In this chapter we consider, specifically, how Japanese culture has shaped the contemporary structure of higher education and the problems this structure poses for Japan's global leadership. We question, as well, how adequate the modernistic structure of Japan's higher education is to prepare its citizens for the future they will face in the coming century.

We begin our discussion, first, by addressing the theories of modernism and postmodernism and their relevance to understanding a nation's system of higher education. Next, we consider the modernist structure of Japanese higher education and the problems it poses for Japan's future development. In our assessment of Japanese education, we use the postmodern concept of "cognitive mapping" to help understand the role culture plays in defining the place of higher education in contemporary Japanese society. Third, we present a critical analysis of the current reform efforts in Japanese education, and offer some comparative perspectives on the future of

Japan's higher education. We conclude this chapter by considering the problems inherent in modernistic change and the implications for the future development of Japanese higher education.

Modern and Postmodern Theories

Traditionally, formal education in Japan served to educate either the ruling samurai or the common people. The samurai were educated in the *hanko* schools while the common people were schooled in the *terokoya*. This historical differentiation provided a functional distinction between those who would lead the country and those who would serve it.

This differentiation of education was certainly not limited to historic Japan, as most other feudal societies separated the education of the leaders and nobles from that of the common people. As more democratic societies emerged, however, education became a central component in the maintenance of a free and open society. Even in these democratic societies, education typically followed a functional and modernistic strategy where students were educated either to be competent citizens or trained to reproduce the existing workforce (Carnoy and Levin 1985). The modernistic premise of such education is based on the belief in rationality and reason and that science provides the solutions for all social, cultural, and economic problems. Advocates of this modernist perspective assume technological progress is advancing and inherently good.

Modernists are guided by the belief in rationality and the linear progress of science and technology. Because the modernist perception is that science offers neutral solutions to society's problems, Giroux (1992, 44) proposes that modernism is "synonymous with civilization itself." Modernists believe progress and beneficial social change are accomplished through science and technology and that national development is achieved, therefore, by becoming more modern. This concept of modern development, or "modernization" theory, is based on the principles of rationality and progress that the path to a nation's social and economic improvement is found through reliance on technological advancement and "modernization." Unfortunately, as Arnove, Kelly, and Altbach (1982, 5) explain, modernization theory "assumes, in part, that all societies follow the same path to development and the countries at different stages of development represent different points on the same continuum or trajectory."

The modernist premise assumes that becoming modern through technological progress is the path to economic and social development. Neither all people nor all countries share equally, however, in the benefits of modernization. Many rapidly industrializing countries, such as Brazil, have great discrepancies between those who benefit from modernization and those who continue to live in poverty. For another example, the rapid economic development in some Latin American countries since the 1960s has changed little the plight of the lower classes. These countries provided cheap export goods for consumers of the industrialized world at the neglect of their own underclasses. Rather than planting crops to feed the country, many of these colonized nations have historically used their precious land for nonfood crops such as sugar, coffee, or cotton.

While many industrializing countries jockey for places on the periphery of the world economy, the major industrialized countries continue to maintain their economic, social, and political dominance of developing countries (Altbach 1982). As Walters (1981, 95) explains: "all nations cannot develop equally since inequality is necessary to maintain the system." By not considering the deeper historical, cultural, and social circumstances of a country or the inequalities of colonization and development, modernization theory is incomplete in explaining why one nation succeeds economically and another fails.

The success or failure of a nation's development is more complex than simply the implementation of modernistic principles of science and technology. The global context of economic, political, social, and economic relations has grown so complicated since World War II that Jameson (1988, 359) concludes we are no longer in the era of modernism, "we are in something else." This "something else" Jameson proposes is "postmodernism," in part, because of the failure of modernism to account for the not always rational development and linear progress of global change.

Rather than accepting the singular, knowable reality of modernists, postmodernists question the order and construction of social reality. Postmodernists focus upon the role human beings and their cultures have in the construction of their social realities and the inherent complexity diverse cultures and human perceptions bring to the creation of these realities. The search for postmodernists is not for definable truths but for an understanding of the multiple voices defining separate realities. Latimer (1984, 120), for example, explains that the postmodernist "abjures the authoritarian and celebrates the people's will." Whereas modernism categorizes effects as linear and rational, postmodernism acknowledges multidimensionality. Latimer (1984, 121) suggests further that a modernist needed to know where one was, but a postmodernist no longer knows: "One must be stripped of coordinates." The unidimensional comfort that science and technology will lead to progress is absent in postmodern thought. There is no one path to the truth or to progress.

How then are we to understand and explain this postmodern world? Jameson offers "cognitive mapping" as one solution to understanding social reality that no longer offers the modernist's coordinates. Jameson's conception of cognitive mapping is derived from Kevin Lynch's (1960) study where he asked individuals to draw maps of their cities from memory. Lynch found that individuals carry around "maps" in their heads of the physical space in which they live and operate. Although these maps did not always represent the actual order of the city, individuals were typically able to draw maps that represented what was most important or functional for them in their cities. These mental maps differed from individual to individual, however, based on their use of the city and the guiding geographic or constructed markers (rivers, hills, monuments, distinctive buildings) that enabled people to negotiate their movement within the city. Jameson suggests that the mental maps of city space that Lynch explored are analogous to the mental maps of the social and cultural space we carry around in our heads.

The mental or "cognitive" maps we each possess, as Jameson proposes, provide individuals the directions and paths to negotiate their social world. An individual's cognitive map provides the behavioral and directional cues for interaction both with internal and external reality. Cognitive maps guide individuals in their daily actions at work, at home, and in the community by providing information on how to behave, talk, react, and think. The information that comprises an individual's cognitive map is determined by the culture within which the individual lives, the individual's personality, and the lifetime interaction of the individual with a variety of social realities. Because each person possesses a uniquely individual cognitive map Jameson proposes that these maps define and distinguish individual consciousness. Since "each consciousness is a closed world," as Jameson (1988, 350) notes, "a representation of the social totality now must take the (impossible) form of a coexistence of those sealed subjective worlds and their peculiar interaction."

From Jameson's postmodern perspective, we can understand cognitive maps as uniquely personal guides to the complex and bewildering array of social realities. "Social totality" for Jameson is determined, therefore, by the coexistence and interaction of all individual's subjective cognitive maps. Although postmodernism can offer no certain way to identify individual reality or chart an individual's cognitive map, postmodernism does account for the effect of culture on collective social interaction. Understanding and identifying this collective interaction is the cultural effect modernists are so deficient in recognizing. Postmodernists' recognition of multidimensionality enables a more in-depth understanding of how individual consciousness or cognitive maps collectively form culture and behavior. Rather than assuming there is an inherent or knowable truth, postmodernists recognize that knowledge and truth are social constructions. Postmodernists reject the modernist "illusion that disengagement and objectification are central to the construction of knowledge" (Belenky, Clinchy, Goldberger, and Tarule 1986, 18). The postmodern perspective understands that scientific knowledge is a social construction, "rather than simply a process of discovery of facts waiting for the cleverest scientists to find them" (Kempner 1992, 70).

Postmodern interpretations are helpful not only in identifying the process of knowledge construction but also in aiding our understanding of the nonlinear process of national development. Because each nation's development is dependent upon the larger global context, modernistic interpretations are insufficient to explain the role culture plays in such development. Rather than assuming change is linear and progressive, postmodernists look to culture, history, and individual human agency to explain developmental processes that are not necessarily rational.

In this chapter we are guided by postmodern criticisms in our search to understand the capacity of Japan's current system of higher education to serve its future social, economic, and educational needs. A postmodern perspective is particularly helpful for understanding the role higher education plays in a country's social and economic development because, as Giroux (1992, 56) observes, postmodernism "not only challenges the form and content of dominant models of knowledge, but it also produces new forms of knowledge . . . unrepresentable in the dominant discourses of the Western canon." Because higher education institutions in most democratic societies are the principal location where knowledge is constructed and disseminated, proponents of postmodernism take seriously the effects of culture, power, and politics on this construction of knowledge. Herein the concept of cognitive mapping is particularly helpful in identifying the role higher education and its faculty play in the intellectual development of students and in helping students locate their places within society.

The faculty of higher education institutions do not simply discover truth, however, and objectively pass it along to students. The postmodern perspective presumes that multiple truths emerge from individual human explanations of the natural and social phenomena observed. Scientific truth is constructed from the interaction of individual cognitive maps formed by unique cultural and social circumstances. As cognitive maps are "peculiar" to an individual, according to Jameson, so are the collection of cognitive maps "peculiar" to a society or culture. For example, an individual Japanese man possesses a very different cognitive map from a Japanese woman. They each locate themselves in distinct places within their own culture and society. Likewise, a Japanese man's cognitive map will be different from the cognitive map of an American man and very different from an American woman's map. Similarly, because the cognitive maps higher education faculty possess in the United States are different from the maps of Japanese faculty, these maps and the cultural circumstances that influence them help explain the equally differing role of higher education in each of these countries. Furthermore, how the different cognitive maps of faculty influence the formation of students' maps enables us to understand the place of higher education in the social circumstances of a country and the capacity of higher education to affect social and economic development.

In our investigation of the cultural influences on Japanese higher education we follow as well Carnoy and Samoff's (1990, 3) premise that: "Analyzing education . . . is an important way to understand larger economic and political change, or the lack of it." We believe that a cultural perspective is central to understanding the place of higher education in Japanese society and, consequentially, the effect higher education has on the development of students' cognitive maps and the social, economic, and scientific knowledge constructed in Japan. We believe, further, that modernization theory does not provide an effective model to understand and guide educational change because it supposes linear progress and offers a rationalistic perspective that is incapable of understanding the complexity and chaos of the larger cultural and global context. Furthermore, modernism fails to account for the cultural influences and individual circumstances of a nation's unique development. In the next section of this chapter, we focus specifically on these unique cultural circumstances of Japan's national development and how culture defines both the purpose and structure of Japan's institutions of higher education.

The Modernist Structure of Japanese Education

In order to understand the influences of culture on Japanese higher education, we begin with a brief overview of the historical foundations of education. Next, we consider the function contemporary elementary and secondary education have in preparing students for the well-known "examination hell" they face. We address, as well, the roles of the mother, the teacher, and the *juku* (cram school) during these formative education years. Following our brief overview of elementary and secondary education, we discuss higher education and both the sorting function it has in Japanese society and its function in placing students within business and government, or "Japan, Inc.," as it is often called. We conclude our discussion of the modernist structure by summarizing the major problems of contemporary Japanese education.

Historical Antecedents of Japanese Education

The foundational element of formal Japanese education, as we have noted, was a dual system for the samurai leadership and the common people. This distinction remained intact throughout the "Edo" period under the Tokugawa Shogunate until the Meiji Restoration in 1868. The Meiji era ushered in the opening of Japan to the Western or "modern" world in its social and commercial relations. The Meiji era also established the "First Educational Reform" that abolished the dual system of the *hanko* and *terakoya* schools (Tokutake 1988; Reischauer 1988). Although the dual structure was eliminated, the underlying distinction between the elite samurai and commoners remains an implicit part of the contemporary Japanese educational system.

The Meiji Restoration had a profound impact on the traditionally isolationist Japanese society. Japan, of course, eventually grew into a world military power that culminated in its defeat in World War II. Following Japan's surrender in 1945, the Allied Occupation forces set about restructuring the political, economic, and educational systems of Japan. Although the U.S. philosophy of equal educational opportunity was the basis for educational reform, this perspective has evolved within the mandates of contemporary Japanese culture. Whereas modernist interpretations of educational reform might assume Japan's system of education "modernized" by becoming Western, even the simplest analysis of contemporary Japanese education displays vast cultural differences between the system that evolved and the U.S. system it emulated.

Outwardly, Japanese education with its 6–3–3–4 structure (elementary, junior high, high school, and college, respectively) appears similar to the U.S. educational system. On further examination, however, the remnants of the dual system are evident in the strict hierarchy extending from preschool to the collegiate level. What is important to understand here is not simply that Japan adopted the U.S. model of education, but *how* Japanese culture affected this adoption to fit the historical, social, and cultural circumstances of Japan.

Whereas "education is one of the major factors that made it possible for Japan to found a modern state in such a short period of time" (Tokutake 1988, 11), this same system may not be so effective in moving Japan into the next century. What was functional and modern for the mid-twentieth century may not be modern enough for the new age of the twenty-first century. We question if Japan can afford to be only modern in its educational system. Does not the educational system need to be postmodern to foster the development of students who will be better prepared to face the economic and social changes now demanded of Japan as a new world leader?

Elementary and Secondary Education

Because detailed explanations of the size and structure of the Japanese system of education are widely available elsewhere, our focus here is on the underlying meaning of this contemporary system, not its specific demographic structure. Whereas the basic function of Japanese education is for the full development of the individual (Thomas and Postlethwaite 1983), we characterize contemporary education in Japan as highly functional. Although the distance from the top of Japanese civil society to the bottom is not as great as in many developing countries, or even a developed country such as the United States, Japanese society is still highly differentiated. If a child does not or cannot begin in the "right" preschool, access to the elite levels of higher education is not likely. In previous research (Kempner and Makino 1993), we related a story where a three-year-old child was denied entrance to a preschool because she did not have the appropriate references. Similarly, Beauchamp (1991) retells a story of Dore's (1976) where a preschool decided to test the mothers, since it could not devise an effective entrance examination for its two-year-old applicants.

Tracking begins at the onset of education for Japanese children where merit plays only a part in a child's access to the best employment in government or business. Although the emphasis on testing would seemingly assure a meritocratic system in Japan, the meritocracy begins *after* the student has gained entrance to the appropriate preschools and elementary schools. Without access to the finest schools, financial support to attend the best *jukus* (examination cram schools), and daily educational assistance at home from the mother, a student is not likely to succeed at the higher levels of education.

Perhaps one of the strongest cultural components of the Japanese educational system is the *kyoiku mama,* the "education mama." In Japanese households the mother assumes responsibility for tutoring and guiding the children in their daily studies. As students advance in school, the mother typically advances with them to assist with the actual homework and the management of daily assignments. A woman generally becomes well educated to serve her children, not necessarily for her own professional advancement.

In addition to the unique role the mother plays in Japanese education, the teacher too has a different status than in most other countries. Legislation in the 1980s placed teachers' salaries among the highest of all public employees in Japan (Tokutake 1988). Obedience to masters and teachers is a traditional cultural component of Japanese society. Zen philosophy expects "absolute subordination of a terribly hardworking student to a strict but ultimately loving teacher" (Frost 1991, 296). The Japanese use the title *sensei* to show respect for masters and teachers and to honor elders or individuals of high status. The reverence for teachers is no longer universal, however, as violence against teachers poses a significant problem in some schools. Nonetheless, teachers in Japan still hold a special status above their contemporaries in most other countries. For example, teachers in the better private schools receive quite substantial gifts from their students twice a year. Many parents allocate as much as $500 a year for gifts they are expected to give their child's teachers. Even non-Japanese language instructors at private schools receive expensive gifts from their employers. One U.S. instructor reported receiving a beautiful lacquered box containing a gift certificate worth over $1,000 at a fashionable department store.

The point, of course, is that teachers in Japan have status in accord with the importance placed on education in general. Again, education is attributed by many individuals as the reason Japan was able to rise so quickly to global dominance in the economic marketplace. Although Japan's educational system has been quite successful to the present, is it now capable of fulfilling Japan's social and economic needs for the coming century?

Higher Education

Whereas the infrastructure of the Japanese elementary and secondary systems is quite rigorous, the system of higher education serves a very different purpose in Japanese society (see Table 1 for an overview of the Japanese higher education system compared to the United States). Since the reformation of education after World War II, the Japanese have emphasized the role elementary and secondary education play in laying a firm foundation for children, but somewhat at the neglect of higher education. Although critics of Japanese education accuse it of being overly focused on rote learning and repetition and lacking in problem solving and creativity, much of this emphasis is due to the complexity of the written language. As opposed to Western students who only have to learn a twenty-six-letter alphabet, Japanese students must learn hundreds of characters each of their years of schooling. Because there is little other way than sheer memory to learn the Japanese characters *(kanji, katakana,* and *hiragana),* rote learning is a cultural necessity to becoming literate. With repetitive learning the core of educational literacy, it is not surprising to find this method of instruction permeating all of Japanese education.

Table 1 Comparison of Japanese and U.S. Higher Education

Type of Institution	Number of Institutions		Number of Students	
	Japan	U.S.	Japan	U.S.
National	98		563,596	
Public	39	599	66,694	6,318,000
Private	390	1,536	1,725,215	3,005,000
Total	527	2,135	2,355,505	9,323,000

Japanese data are from 1991 (Husén and Postlethwaite 1994). U.S. data are estimates from 1993 (U.S. Digest of Educational Statistics 1994).

Once Japanese students begin their formal education, which as we have noted often begins at two years of age, the goal becomes an obsessive quest for entrance into the most prestigious institutions of higher education. Entering one's school of choice is the single goal for most Japanese students. This quest for entrance translates into examination hell. The pressure leading up to notification of acceptance or rejection is so severe it ends in suicides for some of the most distraught students who did not get into the university of their choice.

As opposed to the broad base of excellent universities throughout the United States, elite education in Japan is centralized in Tokyo, where the finest universities train students for the most prestigious positions in government and business. Graduates of the University of Tokyo (Todai), for example, are rewarded with entrance into the highest levels of the federal bureaucracy and business. As Greenfeld (1994, 150) explains: "The Todai entrance exam determines who is destined for what passes for the good life in Japan." The key to success for Japanese youth, therefore, is not *what* they learn at the university but *where* they attend. A student Greenfeld (1994, 153) interviewed explained: "Once you get into Todai . . . you know everything will be easier, that everything will be okay, that you've made it. So what's the point of doing anything once you are at Todai if there is no longer anything to be gained?"

Because of its functional reliance on a seemingly meritocratic system and its emphasis on certification rather than education, we consider Japan's educational system to be merely "modern." From a postmodern perspective, Japanese higher education, in particular, is often form without substance. For Japanese students the most difficult part of higher education is getting into the "right" university where they can exchange their degree for a position in government or business. Education is simply a commodity to be bartered in the job market (Wexler 1987). What a student has learned is somewhat incidental to the name of the institution on the degree. Because of the role higher education plays in Japanese society, once inside the university, students typically are free to socialize and relax from the examination hell they endured to gain admittance.

The sorting function of college examinations is far more important than the academic content of higher education (Amano 1986). One student we interviewed characterized his prominent private institution as a "Disneyland" where his main purpose was to drink and socialize with his future business colleagues (Kempner and Makino 1993). Many such students form "gangs" where one individual attends class to take notes for the other group members. In a class of several hundred students, only a handful may actually attend because they are the designated member whose job it is to take notes. Moreover, it is quite easy for students to skip class because Japanese universities operate on a yearly term, administering only one or two examinations during the year. Because university students have already survived the examination hell, they are good test takers and do well on the usually objective tests. Most tests at the universities require only simple memorization of facts, many of which they have already learned in high school and *juku*—the "cram" schools that prepared them for the entrance examinations. As Reischauer (1988, xviii) has observed: "the squandering of four years at the college level on poor teaching and very little study seems an incredible waste of time for a nation so passionately devoted to efficiency."

Among the many criticisms of the functional nature of Japanese higher education, examination hell is the foremost concern. Whereas the need for advanced education has rapidly increased, the path to the "good life" is only through the examination hell that leads to Tokyo, the economic, cultural, governmental, and educational center of Japan. As one professor observed, to be "truly educated" an individual must be educated in Tokyo (Kempner and Makino 1993, 189). The competition for entrance into the University of Tokyo, a small number of private institutions (Keio, Waseda, and Meiji, for example), and the major national universities in Osaka and Kyoto is incredibly fierce because it is entrance to these few institutions that determines who will be assured economic and social success in Japanese life.

Although there is fierce competition for entrance into the elite United States universities, top quality institutions are found throughout the country that still offer students access to the excellent jobs. While United States students may be unhappy when they are not accepted to the university of their first choice, there is not the same pressure to go to one university in one city (Tokyo) as in Japan. Whereas good scores on the SAT examination assure United States students a place in a prestigious university, if a student is not accepted at Harvard, there is always Stanford, MIT, Princeton, Berkeley, Michigan, Wisconsin, or any number of world-renowned institutions. The peak is not quite so narrow in the United States, which assures increased opportunities for entrance to the "good life."

Training for Japan, Inc.

As the *hanko* schools before them, the national universities are responsible for training the nation's leaders, although these leaders are no longer the samuri. In contrast to many other developed countries where politicians hold the power of the government, in Japan it is the top-level federal bureaucrats, many educated at the University of Tokyo, who run the country—"Japan, Inc.," as it is often called.

For this reason the bureaucrats of the Ministry of Education, Science, and Culture (Monbusho) exert a powerful control on national policy both at the national and private levels of education. As one Todai professor noted (Kempner and Makino 1993, 188), the focus of the national universities is to "raise very able bureaucrats for governing the country."

The hierarchical nature of Japanese universities typically has a greater influence on a student's placement in the job market than the student's performance while at the institution. The most prestigious companies hire their employees from the elite universities, the less prestigious companies hire from the less elite institutions, and so on down the hierarchy. Private institutions even of minimal educational quality, however, may still place students in good Japanese companies. The personal contacts by the president, owner, or alumni of a private institution often have as much to do with placing students as the academic quality of the institution. For this reason, the main task of the president of a private university is to successfully place the institution's graduates so as to raise the prestige of the institution. The elite private universities, of course, have already secured their place in the hierarchy and are much freer to devote their interests to improving the academic quality of their institutions. The majority of private institutions, however, have no such luxury. The top administration and owners must devote themselves to courting businesses to hire their graduates to assure their schools a prominent place in the market for future students.

Because the peak of the public higher education system in Japan is so narrow, approximately 70% of the students attend private institutions. While some of the private universities are of exceptional quality, many private institutions merely serve as a consolation prize for students who could not get into a public university or one of the elite privates. Because the education a student actual gains is somewhat peripheral to the purpose of higher education, many students are presently well served by attending private institutions, even those of minimal quality. This modernistic and quite functional purpose of higher education in Japan is changing, however, as the business culture in Japan becomes more Westernized. Although Japanese companies used to hire a worker for life, this is no longer a certainty with the burst of the bubble economy and the increasing mobility of workers from one company to another. Furthermore, the managers and executives of Western companies in Japan are not as likely to hire college graduates only because they attended a particular private school (except for the very best, such as Keio or Waseda). Whereas the modernistic structure of Japanese higher education has served the nation well, the contemporary system is rapidly becoming an anachronism in the postmodern world.

How best to reform this current system of education is, therefore, a concern for many Japanese political and educational leaders. Although conservatives and liberals disagree on the root cause of the problems, we believe three basic issues encompass the majority of concerns regarding the educational system. *First,* the examination structure, culminating with admission into higher education, casts a dark shadow over the entire educational system. Because of the fierce competition for entrance into higher education, even two-year-olds, as we have noted, are not spared from the effects of examination hell. *Second,* the contemporary cultural environment in Japan has a great effect on the schools and the daily interaction of students, teachers, and parents. Violence against teachers and bullying, or *ijime,* of students against one another is the subject of considerable national concern. The changing nature of the Japanese family, disobedience to parents and elders, defiance of group norms, and lack of respect for public property by some youths are new behaviors in direct conflict with traditional Japanese culture. *Third,* the influence of the external environment is also responsible for changes both within the schools and the larger Japanese society. Japanese children are constantly exposed to the effects of Western culture through the media, music, fast food, and clothing. The influence of the external environment is not only cultural but economic and social. The global environment affects the value of the Japanese yen, the demand for products, and even what is important for the educational curriculum. English, for example, has become the international language taught in virtually every Japanese school.

With the growing economic global competition, however, policymakers and Japanese intellectuals are increasingly questioning the value of the modernistic training function of Japanese higher education. Whereas many Japanese credit education as responsible for Japan's rapid economic growth, higher education is often criticized as the impediment to the nation's continued development (Amano 1986). On the one hand, modernistic Japanese bureaucrats accuse higher education of simply being inefficient in contributing to the welfare of the corporate state. On the other hand, many intellectuals question the inadequate academic role higher education institutions play in Japanese social and national development (Kitamura 1991). This criticism of Japanese higher education we interpret as inadequately furnishing Japanese youths with cognitive maps appropriate for the needs of the postmodern world.

Although no one can be certain what cognitive maps will be needed for the future, it is our premise here that higher education should equip individuals with the ability to adapt to the changing social and economic circumstances life in the "new age" will require. Functional and modernistic approaches to higher education that merely certify existing knowledge or anoint graduates of the appropriate academic stream will ultimately jeopardize the collective's ability toward intellectual development. How well Japanese higher education helps its students form cognitive maps to guide them in the new age is of great consequence to the nation's future.

Many politicians, bureaucrats, and intellectuals recognize the need to transform the present educational system from its modernistic focus on certification to a more postmodern one that embraces the complexity and chaos of the external environment. Because of these pressures both from the internal and external environments, a number of reform efforts have been attempted. We review next some of these reform efforts and consider the effectiveness of these changes.

Educational Reform Efforts

The Japanese Fundamental Education Law of 1947 proposes, among other concepts, that education should "aim" at developing individuals "imbued with an independent spirit as builders of a peaceful state and society" (quoted in Thomas and Postlethwaite 1983, 57.) How well the present educational system achieves this goal is under considerable examination and has been the subject of numerous commissions and reports over the past ten years. Many individuals express concerns over how well the education system meets the needs of contemporary Japanese and global society. For example, as one professor explained, he believes the purpose of the national universities has become simply to provide "people useful for running Japan, Inc." (Kempner and Makino 1993, 188). This focus on training, even at the most prestigious universities, is alarming for many Japanese intellectuals who see this functional purpose of education as providing a narrow vision of the role higher education should have in society. Expressing concerns over education, but focusing primarily on violence and delinquency in the schools as the problem, former Prime Minister Nakasone commissioned the Provisional Council on Educational Reform (PCER) in 1984.

The PCER deliberated for three years and ultimately was quite critical of the present educational system. The PCER reported Japanese education was excessively rigid and was failing to respond to the changing circumstances of students' lives. Furthermore, the council found the educational system to place little importance on individual development or the need for lifelong learning (Tokutake 1988; Monbusho 1992). The PCER additionally proposed three themes for educational reform: "an open mind, a sound body and a wealth of creativity"; "freedom and self-determination, and a sense of public spiritedness"; and "Japanese and the world order," or internationalization (Tokutake 1988, 52).

In a series of four reports, the PCER provided recommendations and specific proposals for remediating what it found wrong with the national educational system. In summary, its recommendations considered the need for improving moral education, teacher training, reducing uniformity in the curriculum and in the examination system, improving choice among public schools, internationalizing the schools, and decentralizing school administration. The actual implementation of these reform efforts has ultimately been rather modest. Perhaps most disappointing for higher education in particular was the failure to accomplish significant changes in the examination system for entrance into universities.

The exclusive reliance on examinations for gaining entrance to higher education creates, in Tokutake's (1988) terms, a "distorted" educational system. The Japanese educational system is a pyramid with a broad base that culminates in a narrow peak that only a few can reach. Unfortunately, with everyone trying to reach the top, all but a few individuals will fail in their attempt. Drucker (1964) noted that the pyramid structure in the U.S. labor market creates an inherently dissatisfied workforce because not everyone can be a top executive. Similarly, although most Japanese compete vigorously for the relatively few openings at the top universities (e.g., Tokyo, Waseda, and Keio), many are distraught at failing to gain entrance to the school of their choice. In fact, many students who fail at their first attempt, or *ronin* as they are known, will spend a year or more studying to take the examinations again.

While this pyramid structure of Japanese education appears dysfunctional for the mental health and ultimate education of the majority of students, it serves as an effective "rationing device" for higher education (Evans 1991, 214). Because higher education in Japan is principally a commodity (see Wexler 1987) to be bartered for a job, the actual learning a student receives is of minor importance to where this learning occurs. Unfortunately, by its definition, elite higher education cannot be universal and must be rationed. This reality of rationing conflicts, however, with the strong norms in Japanese culture toward uniformity and group cohesiveness. The dilemma, as Vogel (1979) suggests and as elaborated by Frost (1991), is how to differentiate students into separate levels or tracks when everything in the culture and classroom aims toward group unity. The solution appears to be the intensive screening experience or examination hell where students are given one chance to succeed in this single-elimination tournament (see Temple and Polk 1984).

Because of the group-oriented culture, there are relatively few ways to screen students on the basis of individual work throughout the school year. Therefore, as a rationing device, the examination system does effectively screen students at several critical times in their education. Rather than consider the cumulative success of students throughout their educational career, the Japanese system employs the single-elimination tournament model. Students have one chance, typically on one day, to regurgitate all the information they possess. Because knowledge is not the issue, students spend hours upon hours memorizing facts and figures to prepare for the one chance they will have to demonstrate their proficiency at accumulating knowledge. Freire (1970) terms this process the "banking concept" of education where teachers make deposits into students' heads and then recall these deposits later in an examination of the knowledge they have retained in their accounts. Little if any concern is given to thought process, problem solving, or any of the other integral components to the student's intellectual development when this banking concept of education is followed.

As Frost (1991) suggests, there are other interpretations of the reasons for maintaining the current banking system of education in Japan that culminates in the examination hell. The present system continues to operate, in part, because a number of parties have so much invested in it. *Jukus* exist for the sole purpose of examination preparation and publishers of examination guides benefit greatly from the current system. Entrance examinations are also one of the principal sources of revenue for many private institutions. Institutions prepare and grade their own exams and charge the equivalent of over $400 to each student. Because a student will often take examinations at four or five institutions, giving examinations is a lucrative business for many universities and colleges. While there is constant concern over how the examination system affects all of Japanese education, few fundamental changes have actually been instituted in the examination system. Some general reform efforts have been accomplished, however, as the Japanese reassess the effectiveness of the current education system.

Among the rhetoric and actual changes taking place in reforming Japanese education, the recognition of the need for lifelong learning is notable:

If our nation is to foster a society which is rich and dynamic enough to face the challenges of the 21st century, people must be provided with opportunities for participating in learning throughout their lives. (Monbusho 1992, 100–101)

As an alternative to the existing tournament model of education, where once individuals fail or leave, there is no return, the Central Council of Education submitted a report in 1990, "The Development of an Infrastructure for Lifelong Learning." This report was followed in 1991 with "Reforms of Various Educational Systems for Relevance in a New Age" (Monbusho 1992). To foster lifelong learning, the reports encouraged cooperation of the family, school, and industry "toward building a lifelong learning society" (Monbusho 1992, 101). This cooperation is to be accomplished through the implementation of lifelong-learning fairs, a five-day school week, a university transfer-credit system, alternative ways of accessing higher education, moral education, and improvement in test questions. While each of these issues has the potential for stimulating change, reform for the entire system is unlikely without fundamental modifications at the peak of the pyramid, elite higher education.

The University Council of Monbusho has also recommended a number of changes to "promote the reform of higher education" (Monbusho 1992). Among the changes the University Council advocated was encouraging diversification of higher education institutions by simplifying and making more flexible the procedures for establishing universities. The logic for this proposed change is to stimulate the development of distinctive institutions that will serve the differential academic needs of students and research interests of the nation.

The council also proposed strengthening higher education through the development of "world class standards of education and research." These standards, the council suggests, are to be attained by improving faculty skills and upgrading graduate education by doubling the total number of graduate students by the year 2000. The council specified, as well, the need for increased funding to promote scientific research and the development of programs for young scholars and scientists.

In addition to improving existing institutions and research facilities, the council encouraged further improvement in entrance examinations. One significant change that has been made in the examinations procedure has been the implementation of the "joint first-stage achievement test," or screening examination. Prompted by the need for national universities to limit the number of students taking their examinations, this first-stage test is given early in the calendar year as a way to screen students who will be allowed to take the specific institutional and subject examinations later in the spring. While the national universities have embraced the first-stage test, since they do not benefit directly from charging students, most private institutions do not wish to lose the money they receive from having large numbers of students take their examinations. Although the first-stage test serves an early screening function, it has done little to change anything substantive about the role examinations play for student's chances for entering higher education. Realistically, the first-stage test is simply a screening device for the examination hell most students will endure later in the year anyway.

In its proposed changes for higher education, the council also acknowledged the need for increased scholarship programs both for Japanese students and foreign students wishing to study in Japan. Relative to the United States, however, scholarships or financial aid for Japanese students are quite modest. While the council expects further expansion of such programs, the details on how this is to occur have not been specified.

Although we have characterized Japanese education as primarily modernistic, Monbusho (1992, 137) likewise recognizes the need for an educational system to meet the demands of the coming age: "When we consider the role of formal education in the context of internationalization, the most important issue is how to develop Japanese citizens who are trusted in the international community." How the educational system can best equip Japanese students with cognitive maps that insure this trust and guide their future in the postmodern world should be, we believe, the essential question underlying educational reform and future social and economic development.

Conclusion

Innovative "production and organization concepts" in business and management, according to Best (1990, 2), are responsible for Japan's economic success. This new competition, Best argues, is the reason as well for the economic decline of the United States. Deterioration of U.S. industrial competitiveness, Best explains, is due to problems of organization, not of productivity, as is commonly argued:

. . . *defining America's industrial decline in terms of slow rates of productivity growth is consistent with an image of an organizationally sound economy in need of minor adjustment. It implies that industry can be revived by a set of government and managerial policies that do not require deep-seated organization changes. (1990, 3)*

Similar to the need for reform in the U.S. economy to meet the new competition, we believe Japanese education, particularly at the collegiate level, is in need of accomplishing the same "deep-seated organization changes" facing the U.S. economy. We agree with

Kitamura (1991, 318) that: "The days of simply emphasizing the traditional screening function are over for Japanese higher education." If higher education is to serve Japan's future economic, social, and educational needs, it must meet the "new competition" posed by educational systems in other countries.

As we have reviewed in this chapter, although the contemporary system of Japanese education has been quite functional thus far for the cultural needs of business and government, we question the ability of this present system to effectively serve "Japan, Inc.'s" future role as a global leader. Our interpretation is a postmodern one, wherein we believe the cognitive maps students develop in the present system of education will be inadequate to guide them successfully into the future. Because it is impossible to know what students should possess in their cognitive maps, the task of an educational system should be to prepare students with the capacity to understand and adapt to the changing needs of the future. Unfortunately, as we have noted, contemporary Japanese higher education is modernistic in its structure; it serves more to ration education, bank knowledge, and dispense information than to fully educate students. The true educational function has traditionally been the responsibility of the employers who knew, to a certain extent, that they were hiring a student effectively socialized to the culture of Japanese government or business. Changes in Japanese society and the economy, however, are altering not only the schools and the family, as we have noted, but also the expectation of permanent employment with the same company. Whereas businesses could afford to train employees, knowing it would be a lifelong investment, the risk is growing that employees may actually leave the company or have to be laid off. In the United States, this problem of training was solved, somewhat, by students receiving a better education at the collegiate level, although many employees still undergo some initial training after college.

The current economic and social changes Japan is now facing are already causing declines in the college population and rising costs of preparing for and attending college. Because such a high proportion of universities are private and tuition driven, it is not likely that all institutions will survive this changing demographic and economic climate. Kitamura (1991, 311) suggests that "Japanese higher education will face a period of 'institutional self-selection' in which a number of higher educational institutions could be closed or severely cut back." The United States faced a similar survival period for higher education with the decline in the college-aged population in the late 1970s and 1980s and drastic reductions in funding in the 1990s *(Chronicle of Higher Education* 1993).

While the survival of the major Japanese national universities is secure, adequate funding for these institutions is of great concern to the faculty, as reported by the Survey and Study Committee for the Financial Base of National Universities (1991), presented in Kempner and Makino (1993). Nevertheless, as the college-aged population declines in Japan and as costs increase, state bureaucrats continue to question "those aspects of higher education that do not directly and substantially contribute to the national goals of Japan, as defined in economic terms" (Kempner and Makino 1993, 191). The problem with this modernistic definition of education, however, is that now as a world leader, Japan has obligations beyond only economic ones. Japan can no longer afford an education system that operates only on modernistic principles. This present system leaves Japanese students with cognitive maps unsuitable to guide them in the new age. Rather than postmodern maps that embrace complexity and a multicultural awareness for the evolving internal and external cultural environments, Japanese students possess maps whose main purpose is to guide them to the right college.

As Japan continues to internationalize, the economy, government, and universities become even more dependent upon the global marketplace of products, ideas, and, politics. The increasingly multinational nature of business requires employees, especially executives, to be equally multicultural in their outlook, understanding, and education. While the traditional educational system may effectively create the "salary man" for Japan Inc., this practice may not be as functional for international businesses that wish to hire Japanese employees (Beauchamp 1991). When hiring Japanese college graduates, either in Japan or globally, multinational companies will expect these individuals to be well educated, not merely well selected. This selection process, which has seemingly been so functional for Japan, has much less value for multinational corporations or agencies that expect college graduates to be knowledgeable, not merely socialized. This cross-cultural difference in the expectations of higher education is quite apparent for the unknowing Japanese student who enters a prestigious U.S. university and is shocked at the rigor and demands required. It is not the "Disneyland" experience some expect.

Because increasing numbers of Japanese students will be employed by multinational companies in Japan and because more students will fill positions with Japanese companies in other countries, the modernistic nature of the "salary man" is transforming. Although the economic and educational climates are changing, the Japanese educational system is only slowly responding, despite the encouraging rhetoric of some agencies and intellectuals. Monbusho (1992, 138), for example, recognizes well the need to internationalize Japanese education, not only for economic purposes: "It is expected that Japan should actively take an international role in the field of culture as well."

The modernistic nature of Japanese higher education is beginning to give way to the new ways and influences of the larger global culture. Japanese education is being internationalized, whether the institutions want it or not. As Monbusho (1992, 143) notes, the number of Japanese living overseas for extended periods of time is rapidly increasing. In 1992, for example, approximately 51,000 Japanese school-aged children were living abroad. Monbusho reports as well that during the 1990–1991 school year, approximately 13,000 elementary- and secondary-aged students returned to Japan to be reintegrated into Japanese schools.

Japanese children who live in another country carry the seeds of internationalization and possess cognitive maps much different from their peers who have stayed at home. Not surprisingly, the different needs and perspectives of these children and their reintegration into the modernistic educational system has become an "important task for the Government" (Monbusho 1992, 143). Just as the United States faces the new economic competition from Japan's industries, Japan now faces a new educational competition to more adequately prepare its children for the needs of the postmodern age. Similar to the problems the United States confronts with the adaptation of new organizational practices to the mandates of U.S. culture, Japan should consider how its educational system can be reformed in culturally appropriate ways. While each country's educational and economic system offers valuable approaches for adaptation, neither system can be imported without considerable cultural accommodation.

As the new world economic leader, Japan should prepare to assume its role in the cultural and social aspects of global leadership. Because education is so critical in insuring this international leadership, we have questioned in this chapter how well the present Japanese educational system is preparing its children and future leaders with cognitive maps appropriate for the new age. By comparison, even though the United States now faces increasing economic and educational difficulties at home and in the world marketplace, it continues to exert a pervasive influence through the exporting of culture, knowledge, technology, and ideas. This influence, to a large extent, is attributable to the role the U.S. education and economic systems play in fostering and rewarding creativity and individual initiative in the production of knowledge. An indication of the control the United States continues to exert in the production and dissemination of knowledge is reported by the Japanese National Institute of Science and Technology Policy (Niwa et al. 1991), which shows the United States accounting for over 50% of the scientific papers published in the world compared to approximately 7% for Japan.

While the United States may face stiff competition for its manufactured products, its control of knowledge production continues to dominate in the fields of science, computers, technology, communications, transportation, space, military, and, not inconsequential, entertainment. Whereas the Japanese education and economic systems have been quite modern and functional until the present, the burst of the bubble economy and the rapid industrialization of the Asian Tigers (e.g., Taiwan, South Korea, and Thailand) have created a new, postmodern competition for the future. How well Japan is able to adapt its educational system to the needs of the coming information age will affect not only its economic prominence but its importance as a global leader. In particular we question how capable the modern structure of Japanese higher education is to provide students with the cognitive maps they will need to find their way in a postmodern future.

References

Altbach, P.G. 1982. Servitude of the mind? Education, dependency and neocolonialism. In *Comparative education*, eds., R.F. Arnove, G.P. Kelly, and P.G. Altbach. New York: Macmillan.

Amano, I. 1986. Educational crisis in Japan. In *Educational policies in crisis: Japanese and American perspectives,* eds., W.K. Cummings et al. New York: Praeger.

Arnove, R.F., G.P. Kelly, and P.G. Altbach. 1982. Approaches and perspectives. In *Comparative education,* eds., R.F. Arnove, G.P. Kelly, and P.G. Altbach. New York: Macmillan.

Beauchamp, E.R. 1991. The development of Japanese educational policy, 1945–1985. In *Windows on Japanese education,* ed., E.R. Beauchamp. Westport, Conn.: Greenwood Press.

Belenky, M.F., B.M. Clinchy, N.R. Goldberger, and J.M. Tarule. 1986. *Women's ways of knowing: The development of self, voice, and mind.* New York: Basic Books.

Best, M.H. 1990. *The new competition: Institutions of industrial restructuring.* Cambridge: Harvard University Press.

Carnoy, M., and H.M. Levin. 1985. *Schooling and work in the democratic state. The Chronicle of Higher Education,* October 27, 1993, p. A29–34. Stanford: Stanford University Press.

Carnoy, M. and J. Samoff with M.A. Burris, A. Johnston, and C.A. Torres. 1990. *Education and social transition in the third world.* Princeton: Princeton Press.

Dore, R.P. 1976. *The diploma disease: Education, qualification, and development.* Berkeley: University of California.

Drucker, P.F. 1964. *The concept of the corporation.* New York: New American Library.

Evans, R. Jr. 1991. The contribution of education to Japan's economic growth. In *Windows on Japanese education,* ed., E.R. Beauchamp. Westport, Conn.: Greenwood Press.

Freire, P. 1970. *Pedagogy of the oppressed.* New York: Continuum.

Frost, P. 1991. Examination hell. In *Windows on Japanese education,* ed., E.R. Beauchamp. Westport, Conn.: Greenwood Press.

Giroux, H. 1992. *Border crossings: Cultural workers and the politics of education.* New York: Routledge.

Greenfeld, K.T. 1994. *Speed tribes: Days and nights with Japan's next generation.* New York: HarperCollins.

Husén, T., and N. Postlethwaite, editors. 1994. *International encyclopedia of education (2nd ed.).* New York: Pergamon.

Jameson, F. 1988. Cognitive mapping. In *Marxism and the interpretation of culture,* eds., C. Nelson and L. Grossberg. Urbana: University of Illinois Press.

Keifer, C. 1974. The psychological interdependence of family, school and bureaucracy in Japan. In *Japanese culture and behavior,* eds., T.S. Lebra and W. Lebra. Honolulu: University of Hawaii Press.

Kempner, K. 1992. Wolves in sheep's clothing: Positivists masquerading as phenomenologists. *Educational Foundations,* 6:67–80.

Kempner, K., and M. Makino. 1993. Cultural perspectives on Japanese higher education. *Comparative Education* 29:185–199.

Kitamura, K. 1991. The future of Japanese higher education. In *Windows on Japanese education,* ed., E.R. Beauchamp. New York: Greenwood Press.

Latimer, D. 1984. Jameson and post-modernism. *New Left Review* 148:116–127.

Lynch, K. 1960. *The image of the city.* Cambridge: MIT & Harvard Press.

Monbusho (Ministry of Education, Science and Culture). 1992. Japanese government policies in education, science and culture 1992. MESC 4–9207. Tokyo: Monbusho.

National Center for Educational Statistics. 1994. *Digest of Educational Statistics, 1993.* Washington, D.C.: U.S. Department of Education.

Niwa, F., H. F. Tomizawa, F. Hirahara, O. Kakizaki, and O. Camargo. 1991. The Japanese science and technology indicator system: Analysis of science and technology activities. NISTEP Report #19. Tokyo: National Institute of Science and Technology Policy.

Reischauer, E.O. 1988. *The Japanese today: Change and continuity.* Tokyo: Tuttle.

Survey and Study Committee for the Financial Base of National Universities. 1991.

Interim status report: National university scholars now face the fund problem of education and research. Unpublished document. Tokyo: University of Tokyo.

Temple, M., and K. Polk. 1984. "A dynamic analysis of educational attainment." *Sociology of Education*, 59:79–84.

Thomas, R.M., and N.T. Postlethwaite. 1983. *Schooling in east Asia: Forces of change.* New York: Pergamon Press.

Tokutake, Y. 1988. Education in Japan, Series #8. Tokyo: Japan Foreign Press Center.

Vogel, E. 1979. *Japan as number one.* Cambridge, Mass.: Harvard University Press.

Walters, P.B. 1981. Educational change and national economic development, *Harvard Educational Review* 51:94–106.

Wexler, P. 1987. *Social analysis of education: After the new sociology of education.* New York: Routledge Kegan, Paul.

Chapter Four
Cultural Influences on Higher Education in Thailand

Varaporn Bovonsiri,
Pornlerd Uampuang,
and Gerald Fry

Introduction and Methodology

In order to thoroughly understand the significant and fascinating cultural influences on Thailand's institutions of higher education, we use a highly eclectic methodology for our study of this issue. The use of multiple research methods provides an opportunity to gain an in-depth understanding of the complex relationship between culture and higher education. Therefore, in this study we attempt to perform what Denzin (1978) refers to as "triangulation." Furthermore, social science research often tends to be ahistorical, which limits researchers' understanding of many social phenomena. We, however, hold that it is critically important to provide a historical context for the study of contemporary issues. To this end we provide an overview of the historical evolution of Thai higher education.

Within Thailand's tradition of Buddhist epistemology, there exists a strong emphasis on one's own direct experience as the optimal way of knowing. In this study we draw extensively on the authors' direct experiences in Thai higher education. We have not only taught at many of Thailand's major universities, but our collective experience also spans four decades, making participant-observation one of our major methods. Furthermore, in support of relying on similar methods, Argyris (1980), in a strong critique of conventional social science research, calls on social scientists to immerse themselves in real organizational settings as a potentially fruitful way of knowing and learning.

We also draw upon the case study approach that has been emphasized by Yin (1989) and others. One of the authors taught at Kasetsart University and lived on the campus as a means to develop insight into the authentic campus culture of a major Thai university during the first three months of 1994 (Kasetsart University 1992). Though this author had taught at many Thai universities before, this period represented his first opportunity to become an integral part of campus life, living on the campus grounds and interacting with both students and faculty daily.

In studies of higher education in developing countries, there has been a tendency to emphasize a Western approach and values. In this study we attempt to correct this bias by implementing a triangular model that recognizes not only the importance of indigenous culture and Western cultural influences but also their amalgamation into something distinctly Thai (see Figure 1).

Figure 1
A triangle model for viewing Thai culture

An Amalgam of Thai and Western Values/Perspectives

Thai Values/Perspectives   Western Values/Perspectives

Our basic objective in this chapter is to analyze the social function of higher education and how knowledge is constructed and transmitted in Thailand. Drawing on a critical postmodern perspective, we frame our study of Thai higher education within a cultural perspective, using the multiple research methods just described to assess how both indigenous Thai culture and Western external influences have shaped the modern form of Thai higher education. A major question we intend to examine is whether Thai higher education has included or excluded "the other" (other people's and minorities' voices) and what effect it has had on social mobility and related socioeconomic equity and equality.

Traditional Modes of Knowledge Production and Dissemination

During Thailand's earlier empires of the Sukhothai period (early thirteenth to fourteenth centuries), Ayudhya period (middle fourteenth to eighteenth centuries), and early Bangkok period (late eighteenth to middle nineteenth century), Thai society in general was rather closed, with an emphasis on subsistence agriculture, making the Thai way of life and work quite simple. As Buddhist temples and monks were at the center of social activities, temples with monks as teachers became the locus for learning where students (males) could receive their basic education: chiefly reading, writing, and moral education. With respect to job-related education, such knowledge was mainly transmitted within the family context where women learned skills such as cooking, weaving, and farming.

During all three of those earlier periods, Thai society was highly stratified (Akin 1969). Consequently, as advanced education became available, it was offered in the palace primarily to royal families and those of high social class. In contrast, those within lower social classes learned by becoming Buddhist priests and studying such fields as theology, ethics, philosophy, and Buddhism, or by receiving informal training in their households in arts and crafts.

Such implications of social classes and their varying abilities to access higher levels of education persist to this very day. The Ministry of University Affairs maintains detailed data on the social background of those passing the difficult entrance examinations to selective universities (Ministry of University Affairs 1994). Few students from farming or working class families have the abilities to succeed in such examinations. In the 1987 examination, for example, of those successful, only 5.1% came from farming families, even though such families represented approximately 75% of the population (Ministry of University Affairs 1993a). Opportunities for females from the remote Northeast provinces such as Sisaket, Surin, and Buriram are also particularly limited. For example, from these three provinces, all of which are large demographically, only 109 female students out of a total of 87,358 candidates were able to pass the university entrance examination in 1987 (Ministry of University Affairs 1993a).

The middle and latter part of the nineteenth century marked a turning point in the history of Thai education, particularly during the period of dynamic leadership (1868–1910) under King Chulalongkorn (Rama V). During the forty-two years of his leadership, King Rama V implemented major political, economic, administrative, and educational reforms to promote the modernization of Thailand (Wyatt 1969). As a result, the social structure of Thai society grew more fluid with greater opportunities for business-oriented people, resulting in the rise of a middle class. Moreover, under the leadership of both King Mongkut (Rama IV) and King Chulalongkorn (Rama V), Thailand became more receptive to Western culture, ideas, and influences. For example, the first medical college was founded in 1889; a law school within the Ministry of Justice was established in 1897; followed by the Royal Pages School, which later became the Civil Service College in 1902; and finally the Engineering School at Hor Wang was founded in 1913. All of these institutions arose with the primary intention to train and prepare students to work in the newly reformed government (Ministry of University Affairs 1993b).

Training for Elite Roles in the Thai Bureaucracy

On March 28, 1917, the first university in Thailand was established under the Ministry of Education and was named Chulalongkorn University after King Rama V. It consisted of the amalgamation of the following above-mentioned institutions: the Civil Service College, the Medical College, and the Engineering School. The philosophy underlying the establishment of Chulalongkorn University was to train highly skilled and knowledgeable personnel to work for government agencies in order to meet Thailand's urgent needs as a country undergoing the process of modernization. The establishment of this new national university reflected both Western influences of university education coupled with the need to provide higher levels of knowledge to Thai students. Chulalongkorn offered training in four fields: medicine, public administration, engineering, and arts and sciences. Initially only males were allowed entrance, and it was not until 1927 that Chulalongkorn opened its doors to female students for the first time (Vanida n.d., 1).[1] From that point on, university-level education began to include increasing numbers of female students.

The second university established in Thailand arose in 1933, named the University of Moral and Political Sciences, and later renamed Thammasat University in 1952. This institution began one year after the revolution of 1932, the military coup that transformed Thailand from an absolute to a constitutional monarchy. The goal of this new second university was to provide the public with an advanced knowledge and understanding of politics and administration responsive to Thailand's new, more democratic regime. Thammasat University had an open system of admissions without compulsory class attendance. Only in 1960 did Thammasat University shift to the system of admission by incorporating a competitive entrance examination as part of the Thai national system. Highly influential in founding and directing Thammasat University in its early years was Pridi Banomyong (1957), the politician and political philosopher. Particularly in terms of political philosophy and reflecting the strong influence of Pridi, Thammasat has been known for its progressivism and radical political orientation.

In 1943 three additional universities were established: Kasetart University under the Ministry of Agriculture, Silpakorn University under the Ministry of Education, and Mahidol University under the Ministry of Health. Kasetsart University offered courses in the area of agriculture, Silpakorn in the area of culture and fine arts, and Mahidol in the area of medicine and dentistry (the former Faculty of Medicine of Chulalongkorn University).

Providing Social Mobility to the Children of Rural Thais

Though varied in objectives and formats, all the universities described above are located within the capital of Bangkok. Moreover, those individuals passing the competitive university entrance examination generally come from Bangkok or neighboring provinces. One partial explanation for this phenomenon is that secondary schools located in the Bangkok area tend to have superior facilities and offer higher quality education than most schools in provincial or rural areas. In response, a policy was adopted to expand university education to the regions to better serve students from the provinces and remote areas.

Towards this end, Chiang Mai University in the north was established in 1960 as a comprehensive university. Subsequently in 1962 Khon Kaen University was established in the northeast region, and the Prince of Songkla University was established in the south in 1965.

To implement their more inclusive admissions programs, these three regional universities were allowed to adopt a quota system to guarantee a fixed number of admissions for students from the respective regions. In some instances, the number of students admitted under the quota system may be as high as 50% of admissions. Such policies have increased the opportunities for students from provincial, rural, and remote areas to have access to higher education. This policy also contributes to the national goal of decentralizing development outside Bangkok and encouraging more even development among Thailand's various regions.

Graduates of Thai universities, particularly the elite and highly selective institutions described above, generally have the ability to secure prestigious jobs with increasingly attractive salaries. Such university degrees are associated with occupational and career success (Fry 1980, 21–34). Traditionally, Thai higher education has provided social mobility to bright and ambitious Thai children from rural areas. The Thai government has allocated scholarships for talented students from the rural areas and remote regions to study in elite public institutions. Numerous high-ranking individuals, primarily in the governmental and educational sectors, have attained social mobility through such mechanisms. Some of these individuals actually lived in Buddhist temples (where they have free room and board) while going to college. In exchange for staying at the temple, they assisted the monks in various ways.

Socializing Thai Elites for European Liberalism and Indigenous Political Values

Following the establishment of Thailand's first university, Chulalongkorn, in 1917, the majority of the faculty of Thai universities have received advanced training at the master's and doctoral level from Western countries such as the United States, England, Australia, and France. The Thai government has had a policy to provide special scholarships for such study at all levels: bachelor's, master's, and doctoral. Thai faculty have also had opportunities periodically for short-term in-service training both in Western countries and other Asian countries such as Japan, Singapore, and the Philippines. As a result, faculty educated abroad naturally bring back Western ideas related to philosophy of life, teaching methods, and political values within the framework of what might be termed European liberalism. Moreover, these Western values and knowledge among faculty are inevitably transmitted to students.

Despite these Western influences and values, Thai society and culture have their distinctive patterns of living and thinking that tend to be rather conservative and traditional. Thus Thai higher education faces the challenge of helping students to integrate both Western and local values and knowledge into a distinctive political culture, including a mix of European liberalism and indigenous values.

In the current era of globalization and internationalization fostered by the powerful forces of modern telecommunications, outside influences are inevitable. A major challenge to Thai institutions of higher education is to encourage an appreciation of indigenous culture while at the same time giving students the capacity to critically assess and selectively choose external values from the West, Japan, and elsewhere.

The Impact of Traditional Thai Culture on Higher Education

There is an extensive literature on Thai culture, comprised primarily of the writings of Western and Thai anthropologists. In terms of basic Thai culture, the work of Phya Anuman Rajadhon (1961) is particularly noteworthy. In terms of Western volumes on Thai culture, Klausner's (1987) *Reflections on Thai Culture* is especially informative. Among the major Western anthropologists (many of these individuals trained at Cornell) who have written significant works on Thai culture are Lauriston Sharp, Lucien Hanks, G. William Skinner, Herbert Phillips, Charles Keyes, A. Thomas Kirsch, and Robert Textor (see Sharp and Hanks 1978). Currently, the well-known Thai anthropologist Suthep Soonthornpasuch is doing a comprehensive study of these Western anthropologists and their work on Thai culture. Other Asian scholars from areas such as Japan and Sri Lanka have also contributed to the literature on Thai cultures. Among such individuals are Yoneo Ishii and Stanley Tambiah (1978).

One major problem in the study of "Thai culture" is the ethnic diversity of contemporary Thailand. For example, over seventy distinct languages are spoken in Thailand. Major differences also exist between central Thai language and culture and northeast Thai (Isaan) language and culture. There are also numerous Sino-Thai cultures present such as Teochiew, Hakka, Hainan, Hokkien, and Cantonese. Among other prominent minority cultures present in Thailand are the Mons, Khmers, Vietnamese, Indians, Malay Muslims, and many hill peoples such as the Hmong, Akha, Karen, and Lahu.

Among Thais writing about culture, there has been some impressive work linking culture and other areas of Thai society such as politics. Professor Saneh Chamarik (1993), for example, has recently published an impressive study, *Democracy and Development: A Cultural Perspective*, which considers Thai politics from a cultural perspective. The prominent politician and intellectual Pridi Banomyong (1957) has also published an unusual volume analyzing the links between Buddhism and Marxism (see also Morell and Morell 1972).

From this extensive literature, several key elements emerge as central to Thai culture. First, there is persisting influence of wet rice cooperative culture. From a strong tradition of growing rice as a group effort, the Thais have developed an elaborate form of collaborative and affiliative culture (Hanks 1972). The extended-family phenomenon also is a reflection of the communal culture norm along with temple-centered festivals and other group activities. While this cooperative culture has elements in common with others in Asia, such as the Japanese and Korean, it has its own distinct features. Although the group is critically important in Thai culture, there is still considerable flexibility, allowing individual deviations and personal liberties in the Thai context.

A second feature of Thai culture is the persisting characteristic of patron-client relations. Loyalty to a potential patron is an important part of Thai culture and plays a significant role in Thai politics, at both the national and local levels (Riggs 1966). Loyalty to individuals often takes precedence over loyalty to a particular organization.

A third feature of Thai culture relates to the extensive debate on whether Thai culture is "loosely structured" (Skinner and Kirsch 1975). Though this long-lasting discussion may never be definitely concluded, it seems clear that Thai society provides for a rather impressive degree of tolerance and related personal freedoms. Even the word "Thai" itself means free. Thai society is much less rigid than many other Asian societies, particularly Japan and Singapore, which display tight social structures.

A fourth important feature of Thai culture is reflected in the extensive *jaj* words in the Thai language. There are over 200 words in the Thai language that have *jaj,* meaning heart, as part of the compound. These words reflect the extreme importance and subtleties of personal feelings and emotions in the Thai context, as the Thais place considerable emphasis on smooth and harmonious social relations.

The eminent scholar of Pacific studies Ron Crocombe has raised the question of whether traditional cultures are iron or clay pots. This same question can be posed most aptly in the Thai context as well. Have Western influences, particularly in the form of higher education, shattered traditional Thai culture, or does the traditional culture persist despite the powerful influences of higher education and modernization and the development that it promotes (Jacobs 1971)?

Thai Culture and Contemporary Higher Education

Perhaps the most concrete visible influence of Thai culture on contemporary campus life is the prominence of students studying in groups. It is rare to find students studying alone and individually. Also, especially at residential universities such as Kasetsart, students participate in a wide range of group activities such as sports, parties, fairs, and field trips. Thus, one of the major advantages for Thais of doing their undergraduate work in Thailand is the large number of lasting personal contacts made during student days. In a culture such as Thailand's that emphasizes affiliative values, personal networking is of great significance. Thais remain highly loyal to old friends and classmates and will do much for them in later employment or occupational contexts.

Another result of Thailand's emphasis on group activities is that the average Thai student typically has far more personal friends than is common in a typical U.S. university where most students are preoccupied with their individual situations. Such personal networking in Thailand is an extremely important part of student life, which contributes directly to elite career opportunities. With such a strong emphasis on group work, we might question how this group-oriented culture affects opportunities for individual creativity and the development of a lifelong love for learning of a type that is individual in nature such as reading and writing.

Another element of Thai culture that is clearly visible on Thai campuses is an atmosphere of *sanuk,* literally meaning enjoyment. Thais often use the criterion of *sanuk* to judge a wide variety of activities such as a class, a seminar, a conference, a field trip, and their general university experience. In activities the stress is on group relationships, enjoyment, pleasure, or *sanuk.* The Thai people are taught not to be too serious. In instructing and learning in college classrooms, teachers seek to avoid boredom by giving examples that are fun or enjoyable. Even Buddhist monks, such as the popular Phra Payom, use a great deal of *sanuk* and humor in their sermons to stimulate interest and attention. The Thai ideal is that work and pleasure *(sanuk)* should go together. In fact the Thai word for work, *ngan,* is identical to the word for party.

As in Japan, Thai undergraduates certainly apply this sense of *sanuk* to enjoy themselves. Somewhat similar to Japan, Thai society significantly pressures students to gain admission to selective, prestigious universities. Once admitted to such institutions, students are on the fast track to an elite job and career. Contributing to the *sanuk* atmosphere is the low level of anxiety among students. Few Thai students at prestigious selective universities have to work because such students generally are of elite status. Thai public universities are highly subsidized, keeping costs extremely low to the students. This situation actually represents a highly inequitable system from a political and economic perspective. The poor are literally paying for the rich. Thus, most Thai students at elite institutions do not have to balance the complex time demands of full-time study and work. Overall, Thai college students, particularly those in elite institutions, are probably among the most happy in the world since they experience little loneliness or alienation on Thai elite college campuses.

Integral to Thai culture is the tradition of paying great respect to teachers, elders, and individuals of high status. Extreme politeness is an important Thai cultural norm. In this regard, a Thai classroom would be exceedingly different from one in Chile or the United States. For example, one major Thai university canceled a special program for students from abroad because they showed inadequate respect to the Thai lecturers recruited for the program. While this tradition contributes to an atmosphere of social solidarity and lack of disciplinary problems, it may adversely affect the learning environment in that students may feel reluctant to challenge professors in intellectual matters. Students tend to accept the professors' ideas without questioning them.

Another fascinating manifestation of the culture of higher education is dress. Unlike Lao female university students who wear the traditional *sin* that covers their legs, or Brunei female college students who cover their heads, women in Thai universities wear standard uniforms of dark skirts and white blouses.[2] For Thai men, the dress is dark trousers and white shirts. The students also may wear pins showing their university designation. Graduate students, however, are free to dress individually without such "uniforms." Thai students only wear traditional dress at special ceremonies or occasions. This Thai dress code is rather serious, and students whose skirts are too short may be reprimanded. The use of a uniform dress code, however, socializes students for the world of work in Thailand, which also has fairly rigid dress codes, often, rather ironically, unsuited for a tropical country.

The "hidden" curriculum of elite, Thai higher education is the powerful socialization for assuming elite roles after leaving the university. Proper socialization is a key element for success in Thai culture and society. The Thai university setting actively cultivates values and behaviors that are critical to success in Thailand's corporate and bureaucratic world. This is particularly pertinent for Thais of Chinese ethnic background whose parents may lack the social graces demanded in elite Thai society. Among such values and behaviors, the following are particularly prominent:

Respect and deference to superiors
Knowledge of etiquette for interacting with royalty and those of highly elite status
Ability to maintain and foster social harmony
Development of high levels of politeness and related polite Thai language forms
Knowledge of foreign languages and cultures to facilitate interaction with international residents and visitors to Thailand
Ability to work well in cooperative group situations

The Impact of Western Culture on Thai Higher Education

As mentioned earlier, Thailand's quest for modernization began with the reforms introduced by King Chulalongkorn in the latter part of the nineteenth century. The schools and colleges established at that time were inadequate both in terms of number and quality to meet the need for trained personnel. The nobility and wealthy people, therefore, considered sending their children to study in European countries such as England and France to prepare them for jobs in the civil service upon their return to Thailand. The king himself set an example by sending many of his sons to study in Europe in a variety of fields related to government service. Those finishing their education in Europe returned to Thailand and often assumed high-level positions. Such a phenomenon even manifests itself in the Thai language in the term *chub dua,* which means to acquire prestige by studying abroad. Consistent with this value, there also exists a popular conception that those educated abroad are more competent than those trained locally. Consequently, individuals with overseas degrees are more likely to have better and higher paying jobs. These phenomena have contributed to a strong tradition of studying abroad for Thai society. Currently, there are thousands of Thais studying in the United States, Australia, Japan, Canada, many European countries, and other Asian countries as well.

This phenomenon of studying abroad and its impact on status in a prestige-conscious society is an important dimension of the influence of Western education on Thailand. Initially, only the king and the nobility could afford to send their children to study abroad. These individuals became part of a small, highly elite group with top administrative positions within the bureaucracy and their lifestyles differed significantly from those of the ordinary people. Over time, the size of this elite group increased as a wealthy business class emerged who could also afford to send their children abroad to study. Furthermore, the Thai government established scholarships for study abroad, and bright individuals from humble backgrounds were on occasion able to win such scholarships.

Western culture has influenced not only Thai patterns of education and values related to education but the Thai way of life as well. Generally, the traditional Thai way of life is associated with an agricultural society. Despite Thailand's rapid industrialization, even today 75% of the Thai population remains rural. Theravada Buddhism continues to permeate traditional rural Thai life, and nearly every village has a Buddhist temple. As a result, social values and patterns of social interaction are rooted in the Buddhist philosophy. This philosophy is based on the Eight-Fold Path leading to the reduction of desires, which includes: right understanding, right purpose, right speech, right action, right livelihood, right effort, truthfulness, and meditation (Watson 1980, 24–25). Such a social pattern emphasizes *contentment* and a simple way of life in which money and material things are not considered the most important things.

The reforms introduced by King Chulalongkorn to modernize Thailand have resulted in the dramatic influx of Western cultural influences that have changed traditional social values in Thailand. As the social critic Sulak Sivaraksa indicates, the Western development pattern has brought not only new technologies to Thailand but also materialism promoted by advertising and the media (Sulak 1985, 31). New social values are replacing the old with increased respect for power and money rather than the goodness of others. Rich people are often respected without regard to the way in which they acquired their assets. Wealthy individuals, including the influential and powerful military, have tried to control society to protect and enhance their own economic interests. It is widely recognized that corruption is fairly pervasive, particularly in the areas related to government-financed construction and issuance of permits, licenses, concessions, etc.

The extent to which Western influences on Thai higher education have contributed to Thailand becoming a consumer and "having society" cannot be answered definitively. The emphasis on individual grades as extrinsic rewards for learning certainly reflects, however, the Western influence on education as a commodity. Thai university students now have access to a remarkable diversity of magazines, many of which promote materialistic values and the acquisition of modern material status symbols. Huge modern shopping complexes now stand near many major Thai universities such as Chulalongkorn and Ramkhamhaeng where students spend significant amounts of leisure time. Currently, in a highly pragmatic university system with an emphasis on degrees such as the MBA, there appears to be relatively little questioning of the consumer society. Instead, the emphasis seems to illustrate what should be learned to land the best paying, most prestigious private-sector jobs that will enable young people to join the consumer society.

This emergence of materialism and the related prestige society has resulted in social and political frustration, as only a small group of individuals can gain access to high levels of wealth. The political turmoil resulting in the student revolution of October 1973 reflected such social and political frustrations; a revolution that succeeded in overthrowing Thailand's military dictatorship. Two major factors contributed to the student uprising. First, many students had employment expectations that could not be met by the limited Thai modern industrial and service sector. Second, a corrupt and authoritarian military government abused its power and limited the freedom of the Thai people. Kanya (1990, 32) and Watson (1980, 28) similarly argue that the 1973 student revolution reflected "essentially an education and economy born out of frustration." Because of the repressive military coup in October 1976, the 1973 student "revolution" was short lived, and its impact on the Thai political order was limited. However, the 1973 revolution did make possible a number of important policy reforms, including a major educational reform movement.

The involvement of the Thai military in politics has been pervasive since 1932. Though there have been numerous civilian governments during the past fifteen years, there is always the shadow of military power in the background. Since the violent confrontations between the military and students in 1973 and 1976 and a similar clash involving Thais from many other levels of Thai society in May 1992, the military has been trying to change its image by helping the government solve national problems. The military, for example, was active in the five-year Greening of the Northeast Project, launched in 1988. The Thai military has included both an active Young Turks movement and a group called Democratic Soldiers. The former were involved in several unsuccessful coup attempts in the 1980s because of their dissatisfaction with the government's inability to solve pressing problems such as uneven development and corruption. The latter consider themselves to be highly professional soldiers committed to a democratic process and opposed to the military's intervention in politics.

Given the weight of the military in Thai politics, it is important to consider the nature of Thai military education, a type of education that is largely segregated from the national education system. An elite military preparatory school (grades 11–12) prepares students for entry into one of the four special colleges to train military and police officers, namely the Royal Army Academy, the Royal Air Force Academy, the Royal Naval Academy, and the Royal Police Academy. The public perception (and indeed a correct one) is that these are elite institutions that train Thailand's top military and police leaders. Furthermore, many Thai military leaders have received specialized training at various military bases in the United States under a special joint program of the U.S. and Thai military.

Another important Western influence on Thai education was the introduction of two open universities, a concept pioneered in the United Kingdom with influences from the many open universities and community college systems in the United States.

In contrast to the four elite military/police institutions, the two open universities do not require entrance examinations. These institutions provide for the equality of opportunity for higher education and access to the thousands of high school graduates who cannot pass the national university examination for the prestigious, selective public universities such as Chulalongkorn and Thammasat. In 1987, 79% of high school students taking this examination failed (Ministry of University Affairs 1993a). In more recent years, the competition has become even tougher as increasing numbers attempt the examination. The establishment of the two open universities, which have hundreds of thousands of students, has been crucial in helping to meet the dramatic growth in the social demand for higher education. This decision was a stroke of political genius because it helped defuse a potential "political time bomb"; that is, huge numbers of frustrated students with high and rising expectations encountering no access to higher education.

There is, however, a controversy concerning these two universities and their real impact on equality of opportunity. These universities emphasize the fields of social sciences, humanities, and education, where employment opportunities are limited. Some view these open universities as merely postponing potential employment problems. With regard to these employment issues, one of the two open universities, Sukhothaithammatirat, stresses upgrading skills of those already employed. The other open university, Ramkhamhaeng, has established relatively tough standards, and a proportionally small percentage of incoming students actually graduate in four or five years. Consequently, the public perception is that Ramkhamhaeng graduates have great perseverance, since study in an open university requires much more self-motivation and discipline. Employers generally have also responded favorably to Ramkhamhaeng graduates. The students who do not graduate, however, tend to blame themselves because technically they were given an opportunity to complete a bachelor's degree.

Knowledge Production in Thai Universities

As in Western universities, Thai professors are expected to spend time researching and writing. Actual teaching loads at Thailand's elite universities are quite light, and potentially faculty have time to engage actively in research. Also, some institutions provide special financial incentives to encourage such research. At most research universities there are special institutes whose staff are able to devote their full-time efforts to research.

Thai universities have an identical ranking system to that in the United States related primarily to research accomplishments, though the percentage of full professors is much lower in Thai universities than in the United States. A major difference in evaluation standards is that Thai professors are encouraged and rewarded for producing textbooks in Thai. Considerable debates occur as to whether this type of writing is knowledge production. In numerous cases, such texts are primarily translations of existing Western volumes that often contain considerable cultural baggage irrelevant to contemporary Thailand.

Unlike the United States, Thailand does not have a "publish or perish" system. Thai professors are civil servants, and after completion of an initial six-month probationary period are given permanent tenure. Thai professors do not face the same pressures to publish as junior U.S. faculty, although they must publish to be promoted to the ranks of associate and full professor.

The biggest obstacle to knowledge production in Thai universities relates to the economics of academia. Thai professors in the

Bangkok area often have considerable off-campus opportunities to gain additional income by lecturing, for example, at other universities or coaching schools, or doing consulting for private business. Such income is often needed to supplement relatively low government salaries. Faculty actively engaged in such outside teaching and consulting have little time for research and knowledge production. Because of the lack of such incentives, Professor Kraisith Tantasirin of Mahidol University argues that few young scientists are interested in scientific research for the reason of accumulating knowledge (Varaporn 1994). Reflecting on this situation, Professor Pornchai Matangkhasombat, dean of the Faculty of Science at Mahidol University states:

Our learning process in the past followed this pattern. We sent students to study abroad and made them lecturers in universities when they came back. These lecturers were mere "learned persons" and not researchers. It was only about thirty years ago that scientific research work has found its place in Thai academic circles. (Varaporn 1994, C1)

Despite such economic obstacles, there has been a dramatic growth in the past decades, particularly the 1980s and 1990s, in the production and distribution of research by Thai scholars both in Thai and English. With significant improvements in Thai education stemming from major reforms in the 1970s, the market for books, journals, and magazines has increased dramatically in recent decades, providing an enhanced incentive for Thai professors to produce academic work for publication. Although Thai television and radio have controls, the print media are quite open.

In actuality, Buddhist epistemology is highly consistent with both science and research. In the well-known Kalama Sutta, the Buddha states:

Yes, you may well doubt, you may well be uncertain . . . Do not accept anything because it is the authoritative tradition, because it is often said, because of rumors or hearsay, because it is found in the scriptures, because it agrees with a theory of which one is already convinced, because of the reputation of an individual, or because the teacher said it is thus and thus. . . . But experience it for yourself. (Khantipalo 1975)

Such a philosophy is highly conducive to critical thinking, critical theory, and the modern scientific method. Despite such Buddhist ideals, the norm in most Thai universities for students is quite different. Students tend to be "cups to be filled with knowledge and information" rather than "candles to be lit" to produce creatively new knowledge.[3]

The major form of knowledge production among Thai students is the master's or doctoral thesis. Thai universities now have a number of doctoral programs, and the thesis is normally a requirement of Thai master's degree programs. In regular coursework at both the undergraduate and graduate level, term papers and research papers are not so common for the following reasons:

> The mode of learning emphasizes lectures and related note taking to prepare for examinations rather than for writing.
> There are no real incentives for professors to spend extensive time reading and commenting on such papers.
> Library hours are inadequate, especially in the evenings and on weekends.

Despite a bureaucratic system that does not particularly reward knowledge production and research, there has been a significant increase in Thai research and knowledge production in recent decades. Unfortunately not enough of this research is in the area of science or technology. In the decades ahead, Thailand faces important challenges to remain internationally competitive. With significant increases in Thai wages and anticipated labor shortages, Thailand must improve its productivity through applied science and technology to compete with countries such as Singapore, Malaysia, Hong Kong, China, Taiwan, and Korea. A number of critics of Thailand's academic milieu argue that Thailand's lack of homegrown technology and scientific knowledge could be its undoing (Varaporn 1994). In 1993, Thai scientists produced less than a tenth of the scientific papers of Taiwanese scientists (Suthas Yoksan cited in Varaporn 1994). Given such pressures, the Thai government is presently reconsidering its university structure. For example, the government recently established a new science and technology university in Korat Province in the northeast, which is free from the normal rules and regulations of Thai public universities. It will be fascinating to witness the impact of this new university structure on research and related knowledge production.

Conclusion and Summary: A Critical Cultural and Political Perspective

Prior to 1973, Thai higher education's primary role was to facilitate modernization by providing a workforce for Thailand's traditional bureaucracy and emerging modern industrial sector. As indicated earlier, the system also allowed for a certain degree of social mobility as a way to incorporate and co-opt those from nonelite backgrounds into an elite system. Thailand imported many models for various Thai institutions of higher education from the West. Chulalongkorn University was oriented toward the British system, Thammasat drew upon French influences, and Kasestart University was based largely on the U.S. land-grant university. Despite these different arrangements, the Thais adopted in nearly all cases the rather narrow model of individual disciplines and early specialization.

The unexpected "student revolution" of October 14, 1973, resulted in a serious shock to this modernity-oriented system of higher education, as students became much more demanding and outspoken. Written materials from virtually all perspectives became available, including Marxist thought, representing a new postmodern ambiance in which the voice of the "other" and nonconventional discourse became increasingly common, challenging conventional and traditional views. Thai radical thinkers such as Pridi Banomyong, Chit Phumisak, Sulak Sivaraksa, and Boonsanong Punyodyana became popular among young people and students, clearly representing a period of "let a thousand flowers bloom."

For the first time, newer thoughts and people from an extremely wide variety of influences challenged the conventional model of Thai development with its serious problems of inequality and injustice. Radical university lecturers called on college students to go into the countryside and into the factories to raise the political consciousness of the farmers and workers. Other more moderate intellectuals urged students to engage in community development work in the villages and to learn firsthand about conditions in remote rural Thailand, particularly the drought-plagued northeast. These changes ush-

ered in by the student revolution of October, 1973, which over-
threw the military dictatorship of Thanom Kittajakorn, became a
serious threat to the Thai elite, especially when 1975 witnessed successful Communist revolutions in neighboring Cambodia, Vietnam,
and Laos.

A harsh military coup in October 1976 brought an abrupt end,
however, to Thailand's postmodern experiment with populist democracy and installed perhaps the most repressive political regime
in modern Thai political history. Many radical books and materials
were confiscated and, in some instances, burned. This extreme political polarization represented a fundamental shift in basic Thai
cultural values that stress the middle way and nonconfrontation.

In the 1980s, Thai politics under the able and moderate leadership of Prime Minister Prem Tinasulanondha returned to what some
have termed "half-leaf democracy." During the past decade and a
half, universities have resumed their primary role in Thailand of
providing opportunities for individuals to gain access to elite mod-
ern-sector jobs. The rapid economic development that Thailand experienced in the 1980s and 1990s resulted in a dramatic expansion
of well-paid private-sector jobs. Currently the MBA is without question the most popular degree in Thailand, reflecting the new dominant value of modern materialism. Also indicative of the pervasive
nature of materialistic values in a "having" consumer society, many
Thais now encounter the popular norm that the ideal modern man
should have the eight Cs; car, club membership, condo, computer,
cellular handheld phone, credit cards, canned drinks and food, and
condoms.

Despite the resumption of the modernist pattern, Thai universities have become much more pluralistic. Environmentally oriented
students, for example, played a significant role a number of years
ago in opposing a major dam in Kanchanaburi Province that would
have destroyed huge areas of tropical forest and habitat. The late
1980s and early 1990s experienced a dramatic growth in Thai Nongovernmental Organizations (NGOs) and Private Voluntary Organizations (PVOs) often deeply concerned about the high social, cultural, and environmental costs of overly rapid, uneven development
in Thailand. The leadership for these organizations comes primarily
from idealistic, recent university graduates who have developed criti-

cal perspectives. Also, in the university environment, students gain exposure to an *alternative other literature* that is highly critical of the materialistic values of contemporary Thai prestige society. Among major critics of this type are the prolific Sulak Sivaraksa and the late Buddhadas Bhikku (Sulak 1992). The success of Thailand's people power in the May 1992 confrontation with the military reflects the strength of pluralism in Thai society to which Thai higher education has certainly contributed significantly.[4]

It is impossible for us to predict future changes in the relations between culture and higher education in Thailand. At this point it may be useful to return to the important metaphor of clay versus iron pots. Despite the dramatic evidences of modern materialistic culture to which higher education has certainly contributed, fundamental Thai values persist, ironically, also fostered by higher education. In this sense the Thai may be much like the Japanese in their ability to mix Western and indigenous patterns of thought and values. Therefore, Thai culture is neither a clay nor an iron pot but instead perhaps a bamboo pot that can easily adapt to external changes.

The upcoming twenty-first century will present an amazing array of challenges to the Thai. The critical question is whether the current system of higher education is capable of preparing the Thai for these challenges and opportunities. Given Thailand's history of successfully dealing with crises, such as the threat of colonialism, World War II, and the Communist expansion in mainland southeast Asia, it seems reasonable to conclude that the Thai people will develop their own distinctive system of development and higher education that is neither modern nor postmodern but uniquely Thai.

Notes

A note of thanks to Matthew Newland for assistance in editing.

1. Following the cultural convention, all Thai authors are cited by first name in the references.

2. The *sin* is a long woven skirt that is an elegant expression of Lao culture. The lower part often has exquisite artistic patterns. It is considered the Lao national dress and is worn in the classrooms, factories, fields, and offices (Mayoury 1993; "To veil or not to veil" 1994).

3. See the excellent BBC video, a part of the New Pacific Series, "Jugs to be filled or candles to be lit."

4. "People power" refers to the recent phenomenon of political and social confrontations and protest movements involving increasingly more Thai people from varied occupations and social levels. For example, though the protests of 1973

and 1976 at the Democracy Monument and Thammasat University, respectively, mainly included students, the most recent political protests in May of 1992 included not only students but participants of many ages and from of different occupations from the new broad Thai middle class as well as other people.

References

Akin, R. 1969. *The organization of Thai society in the early Bangkok period, 1782–1873*. Data Paper #74, Southeast Asia Program. Ithaca: Cornell University Press.

Argyris, C. 1980. *The inner contradictions of rigorous research*. San Diego: Academic Press.

Ayal, E. (ed.) 1979. The study of Thailand: Analysis of knowledge. Papers in International Studies: Southeast Asia Series No. 54. Athens: Ohio University Press.

Denzin, N.K. 1978. *Sociological methods: A sourcebook*. New York: McGraw-Hill.

Fry, G. 1980. Education and success: A case study of the Thai public service. *Comparative Education Review* 24(1):21–34.

Hanks, L.M. 1972. *Rice and man: Agricultural ecology in Southeast Asia*. Chicago: Aldine Atherton.

Ishii, Y., and S.Tambiah, (eds.) 1978. *A rice-growing society*. Kyoto: Center for Southeast Asian Studies.

Jacobs, N. 1971. *Modernization without development: Thailand as an Asian case study*. New York: Praeger.

Kanya Worawichawong. 1990. Higher education and political development: A case study of open universities in Thailand. Unpublished master's thesis. University of Oregon.

Kasetsart University. 1992. *Kasetsart University: Concise information, academic year, 1992*. Bangkok: Foreign Relations Office, Kasetsart University.

Keyes, C.F. 1987. *Thailand: Buddhist kingdom as modern nation state*. Boulder: Westview Press.

Khantipalo Bhikku, (trans.) 1975. *Kalama Sutra, Lord Buddha's discourse to the Kalama people*. Bangkok: Mahamakut Rajavidyalaya Press.

Klausner, W. 1987. *Reflections on Thai culture*. Bangkok: Siam Society.

Mayoury Ngaosyvathn. 1993. *Lao women: Yesterday and today*. Vientiane: The Ministry of Culture, Lao PDR.

Ministry of University Affairs. 1993a. *Report on the joint higher education examination: Academic year 1987*. Bangkok: Ministry of University Affairs.

———. 1993b. *Universities in profile*. Bangkok: Chulalongkorn University Printing House.

———. 1994. *Song Todsawat Tabuang Mahawitalai* [Two decades of the Ministry of University Affairs]. Bangkok: Chulalongkorn University Printing House.

Morell D., and S. Morell. 1972. The impermanence of society: Marxism, Buddhism and the political philosophy of Thailand's Pridi Banomyong. *Southeast Asia: An International Quarterly* 2 (4): 397–424.

Phillips, H. 1992. *The integrative art of modern Thailand*. Berkeley: Lowe Museum of Anthropology.

Phya Anuman Rajadhon. 1961. *Life and ritual in Old Siam: Three studies of Thai life and customs*. Trans. and ed. W.J. Gedney. New Haven: HRAF Press.

Pridi Banomyong. 1957. *Kwampenannicang khong sangkhom* [The impermanence of society]. Bangkok: Kwien Tong Publishing Company.

Riggs, F.W. 1966. *Thailand: the modernization of a bureaucratic polity*. Honolulu: East West Center.

Saneh Chamarik. 1993. *Democracy and development: A cultural perspective*. Bangkok: Local Development Institute.

Sharp, L., and L. Hanks. 1978. *Bang Chan: Social history of a rural community in Thailand*. Ithaca: Cornell University Press.

Sippanondha Ketudat with R.B. Textor. 1991. *The middle path for the future of Thai-*

land: Technology in harmony with culture and environment. Honolulu: East-West Center.

Skinner, G.W. 1957. *Chinese society in Thailand: An analytical history.* Ithaca: Cornell University Press.

Skinner, G.W., and A. T. Kirsch. 1975. *Change and persistence in Thai society.* Ithaca: Cornell University Press.

Sulak Sivaraksa. 1985. *Lawk krab sangkhom Thai pua anakhot* [Peeling Thai society for the future]. Bangkok: Nangsue Thai.

———. 1992. Seeds of peace: *A Buddhist vision for renewing society.* Berkeley: Parallax Press.

Thak Chaloemtiarana. 1979. *Thailand: The politics of despotic paternalism.* Bangkok: Social Science Association of Thailand.

To veil or not to veil: Malaysian Muslims debate how women should dress. 1994. *Asiaweek* 20 (33), August 17; 32–33.

Vanida Poonsiriwong. No date. A summary on the status of Thai-women university graduates during the last three decades. Mimeo. Bangkok: Department of Foundation of Education, Chulalongkorn University.

Varaporn Chamsanit. 1994. A certain type of suicide: Thailand's lack of home-grown technology and scientific knowledge could be its undoing. *The Nation,* August 23, 1994, C1.

Watson, K. 1980. *Educational development in Thailand.* Hong Kong: Heinemann Asia.

Wyatt, D. 1969. *The politics of reform in Thailand: Education in the reign of King Chulalongkorn.* New Haven: Yale University Press.

Yin, R.K. 1989. *Case study research: Design and methods.* 2nd ed. Vol. 5, Applied Social Research Methods. Newbury Park, California: Sage.

Chapter Five
Modernity on the Periphery
Expansion and Cultural Change in Mexican Public Universities

Rollin Kent

This chapter will examine how universities and socioeconomic change in Mexico have, over the past three decades, been intertwined in a tense, sometimes arduous, and increasingly complex process of creation and dissolution of cultural identities. Rather than rationally planned *modernization,* this lopsided and accelerated experience of *modernity* has proven to be a creative yet conflictive display of disparate rationalities and values that defy one–dimensional definitions (Brunner 1992). I will ponder the most visible traits of the multifarious experience of rapid expansion, politicization, and institutional diversification in public universities before attempting to provide an interpretation of some of the meanings it has had for institutions and for academics, central and yet often passive participants. Lastly, I shall reflect on some of the broader cultural consequences of the manner in which higher education in Mexico has evolved.

From Elite to Mass Higher Education in Two Generations

In the 1940s Mexico made a push for industrialization and urbanization that, coupled with mass education, transformed the country over two generations. Until the 1960s, the relatively small public universities founded in the decades after the 1910–1917 Revolution accompanied and supported this process, although this was also a period of conflict over the definition of autonomy. The national university (UNAM) and a small number of state universities produced doctors, lawyers, and engineers out of middle- and upper-class males through a specialized undergraduate curriculum. Graduates went on to business, politics, or the professions. Those who became politicians had previously made themselves visible as student activists, as long as they operated within the rules of the establishment game and did not move toward open antagonism against the government. As a matter of fact, student activism in this context seemed to have been an integral part of the *hidden curriculum,* providing a first taste of politics for the bureaucratically ambitious and opening lines of recruitment to the government, a one-party, semiauthoritarian system that operated through personalist clientele networks rather than open party politics.

Since the graduate level and research organization were virtually unknown, universities were mainly teaching institutions geared to reproducing elite knowledge and status. Except for some isolated enclaves, the academic profession as such did not truly exist before the 1970s. Professors were middle- and upper-class males, usually practicing professionals who taught part time. The only full-time professors were in the humanities and the budding social sciences. A very small number of academics were full-time researchers, mostly in the natural sciences.

This system of cultural and political reproduction seemed to have functioned properly on its own terms for a generation after the onset of industrialization in the 1940s. It was viable so long as only 3 or 4% of the relevant age group attended higher education and so long as a closed economy placed few demands on higher education for high-level expertise or technological development. The first circumstance changed in the 1960s, and the second one was transformed twenty years later.

By the late 1960s, the public universities were faced with the onslaught of a new wave of students leaving upper-secondary school. The offspring of the first drive for economic development and urbanization arrived in large numbers and changed the face of higher education. These young men and women came from the new service and industrial sectors who had benefited from the rapid expansion of educational opportunities at the primary and secondary levels in previous years. Since their parents or grandparents had been public-sector workers, industrial laborers, and to a lesser extent farmers, their occupational future was crucially dependent on obtaining higher educational credentials. National enrollment grew from about 250,000 in 1970 to over 1 million students in the mid-1980s, reaching 15% of the college-age population. Over very few years, universities lost their elite makeup, and male predominance gave way to the new middle- and upper-class female population in search of professional degrees in the health sciences, education, psychology, and administration.

Accelerated growth forced institutions to hire professors and ancillary personnel at an exhausting pace: whereas in 1970 there were about 25,000 professors, in 1985 this figure had surpassed 100,000. That is, every year for a decade and a half about 5,000 young people were hired to work as university teachers. The lack of developed postgraduate institutions and the tradition of regarding the *licenciatura* (first degree) as sufficient training for a university instructor meant that most of these new academics were in a position to, at most, replicate the existing state of knowledge through instruction but hardly to produce new scholarship through research. Additionally, this new academic workforce brought unionism with it, thus facing the universities with higher costs and unforeseen types of conflict and negotiation over hiring and promotion rules. The new academic profession was composed, then, of thousands of young people who returned to teach at the same universities from which they had only recently graduated without having experienced graduate school, research, or further socialization in philosophically or educationally diverse settings (Gil, Gediaga, Pérez Franco, et al. 1994).

The oil-exporting economy of the 1970s and increasing foreign indebtedness allowed the government to finance this surge in a way that few other Latin American countries had been able to do. Federal funds payed for salaries and for the growing number of institutions: in 1970 there were 54 public institutions (both universities and technological institutes), but by 1980 there were 105, and in 1990 they had grown to more than 140 institutions. The private sector also began to grow significantly, pushing the number of institutions from 34 to 103 in the 1980s (doubling again by 1990). Institutions proliferated in the provinces, allowing access to young people in regions that had historically been excluded from higher education and attenuating the centralization of resources in the capital city that has historically characterized Mexican society (Kent 1992).

Although educational planning became a key term of official discourse in the 1970s, in fact the government developed an atti-

tude of *benign endorsement* and accomodation with the new ideological and political realities through negotiation with unions and
increasingly activist universities governed by the left. The *expansion-
ist coalition*—the implicit but very real pact between government
and the emerging middle strata—was one of the political realities
underlying such rapid growth (Fuentes 1989; Brunner 1990; Kent
1993). Funding followed growing student demand, and no effective
quality control was put into effect.

This mode of unregulated expansion was seen by government
as a necessary response both to growth and to the intense political
struggles that took place within public universities. Throughout the
1970s, the government's benevolent relationship to public universities was also a means of washing away the stigma of 1968, when a
massive student movement that had mobilized against government
intervention in universities and police repression was violently put
down by the army. The movement and its bloody conclusion had
prolonged repercussions for the government's image and represented
an important turning point in contemporary Mexican politics as
the one-party system stumbled over the following years toward a
more democratic form of government. Throughout the succeeding
decade, the government's relationship with public universities was
heavily tinged by the 1968 movement: universities were suspicious
of the government, and the latter stepped about gingerly in this political minefield, trying to avoid accusations of interventionism in
university autonomy.

Since the 1920s, autonomy has been a central value in Mexican
(and many Latin American) universities. It was a decisive aspect of
the struggle between authoritarian political systems that needed
trained but politically docile expertise and the emerging middle-
class intellectual communities seeking to establish culturally free zones
in a cramped political and intellectual space. Additional to its cultural content, university autonomy has also had a political meaning
since the public university—although it is mainly funded by government—has been a vehicle for criticism and opposition (Levy
1980).

In consequence, university leadership was left to embark on the
courses of action chosen by the disparate local coalitions that governed their institutions. The unwritten rule of the game was a *politi-*

cal pact to the effect that government refrained from interfering in decisions of institutional policy as long as activism did not surpass certain limits of state power. Thus, universities learned to turn political pressure into the main instrument for obtaining funds.

But as this was occurring, a less boisterous but crucial shift was taking place in the relationships between higher education and society. Long the cultural bastion of the elite, public universities were being abandoned by the children of industralists, financiers, functionaries, and professionals. The 1970s and 1980s were also years of significant growth in private institutions, both new and old. Daniel Levy has depicted this process as elite flight from the perceived failures of the public universities, for reasons of religious attachments, social distinctiveness, or inability to provide occupationally relevant training (Levy 1986). *Reconversion strategies in search of new bases of distinction* (Bourdieu 1988) were initially deployed by elite sectors, some of whose children also started going to the United States for undergraduate and postgraduate training. But increasingly the emerging middle strata also moved away from public universities and seemed willing to pay for diplomas even in newly created private institutions with little to offer in the way of academic quality, those portrayed by Levy as *demand-absorbing* institutions. In 1993 almost 240,000 students—more than 20% of the total—were enrolled in 258 private institutions of the most varied types and qualities, ranging from firmly established universities—both religious and secular—to small educational businesses offering diplomas in the administrative professions, education, and computing.

The *diploma explosion,* fed by demographic growth as well as by the political pacts between government and public universities, took place mostly in the public universities, which absorbed about 70% of all newcomers to higher education over the past twenty years. Nonetheless, processes of institutional diversification and changing public perceptions opened a crack in public-sector monopoly. The economic crisis of the 1980s would widen the fissure even further.

The Economic Crisis of the 1980's, Globalization; and New Challenges for Higher Education

When increasing interest rates coincided with lowered oil prices in the early 1980s, the premises of Mexico's closed economy crumbled.

Inability to meet payments on the massive foreign debt that had accumulated during the previous decade reached a crisis point in 1982. For the following seven years, high inflation, unemployment, low production, and capital flight shook Mexican society, to the extent that the 1980s have been called the *lost decade*. Initially, the government's hands were tied with the economic emergency: servicing the national debt, reducing the public deficit, and controlling inflation. This led eventually to a profound shift in economic strategy, which since then has been based on privatizing public-sector firms, restructuring the tax system, lowering commercial barriers, and reorganizing industry toward the world market. Crisis and economic restructuring are two faces of the crucial departure from the statist, closed economy that had accounted for the first period of industrialization but had outlasted its effectiveness.

The consequences of this shift have been significant for politics, education, and culture in Mexico. Public spending for education and other social services came under severe restrictions. Between 1982 and 1989, government funding for higher education fell by 40% in real terms. Since a large proportion of funding went to salaries (about 85%), this drop had drastic effects on teachers' incomes (Fuentes 1992). Its attention being concentrated on economic affairs, government developed a nonpolicy of *benign neglect* toward education (Fuentes 1991).

This sharp change occurred alongside another shift. By the mid-1980s yearly growth rates of first-year enrollment in higher education dwindled to roughly 1%, and it became clear that student demand had lost its impetus. Thus two of the crucial determinants of expansion in the previous decade had been transformed: benevolent incremental funding became a thing of the past, and population growth tapered off, thus stabilizing the numbers of upper-secondary-school leavers. The high drop-out rate at the elementary school level (about 40%) also took its toll on the growth of higher education. Additionally, it would seem that growing unemployment and the diploma explosion undercut the occupational value of a higher-education certificate (Fuentes 1991). The economy has not been creating enough jobs in the professions for the 150,000 young people who have graduated every year from higher education since the mid-1980s.

University morale deteriorated as institutions either laid low or entered into struggles among constituent groups over dwindling resources. The political role of various large public universities was also put into question, and activism entered a phase of abatement. Political parties, unions, and student organizations—so conspicuous in universities during the 1970s—lost their capacity to influence events. The academic profession not only suffered a lowering of income but also a sharp loss of public prestige. It grew clear that the limit of unregulated expansion had been reached, and respected intellectuals became increasingly vocal in their criticism of public universities (Paz 1987; Zaid 1988).

By contrast, certain private institutions gained in prestige as it became known that more and more high government officials—especially economists and administrators—had attended private universities in Mexico and institutions in the United States. The latter seemed to have become the preferred model of the utilitarian calculus made by the middle and upper segments of the population who were attracted to the aura of economic relevance that surrounded certain private universities at home and abroad. Whereas the public sector in higher education stopped growing in the 1980s, the private sector continued to expand even into the 1990s.

Once positive economic growth rates returned in the early 1990s, government regained its activism toward higher education. During the Salinas administration (1989–1994), quality and relevance have been constantly reiterated in public discourse. Funding has increased, now following a more selective approach than previously. Evaluation has been introduced at different levels, although the degree to which it has been consummated is in doubt (Kent and De Vries 1994). Public universities have been abandoning their traditional open-door policies toward students, and entrance examinations are becoming the rule in many public institutions. Moreover, since the government has insisted that publicly funded universities increase their own sources of income, student fees have increased. Public universities in the early 1990s began to charge between $300 and $800 U.S. dollars yearly (as opposed to about $150 or $200 previously) (ANUIES 1992). On the other hand, the larger private universities currently charge between $11,000 and $26,000 U.S. dollars annually (Ayala and Ramo 1994).[1]

Increased support for scientific research under competitive bidding procedures is a notable feature of these policy trends (Kent, in press). Leaders in the scientific community have emerged as important and relatively differentiated players in definition of policy, and they have made a strong push for formal recognition of scientific merit based on international productivity standards. Policy discussion among government officials, scientists, and businessmen has opened up to the international currents of opinion, especially as Mexico has entered the North American Free Trade Agreement (NAFTA), the Organization for Economic Cooperation and Development, and the Asia Pacific Economic Council.

Now Mexican higher education is caught up in currents of change that originate not from within institutions but elsewhere: in government policy, in changing public perceptions, in the scientific community, and in the changing educational marketplace. Both government and business have expressed expectations in the supposed contributions of higher education to modernization. There is currently a sense of urgency in the public's attitudes toward higher education that has contributed to legitimize recent government policies. How will institutions and academics adapt and respond to these recent changes?

Social Engulfment and Hasty Bureaucratization

Taking leave of this overview of global trends in Mexican higher education, I will proceed to portray some of the specifically cultural dimensions of these turbulent episodes. I will refer to two levels of the cultural process. On the one hand, I will focus on the role of universities in the context of changing ideologies and forms of class identification. On the other hand, I will consider Burton Clark's (1983) internalist view of the changing roles and identities of teachers, researchers, and institutional leadership. The question I will seek to explore is: how did the various forms of self-perception developed by higher education establishments and their main actors—principally professors—adapt to a context of hasty expansion and major ideological transformation in the broader society? As will soon become evident, the specific traits of academic culture in Mexican higher education institutions differ widely from those portrayed by Clark in his study of universities in developed societies.

The wave of expansion and politicization I have described above took place in a period of cultural and political conflict. After the repression of the 1968 student movement, the political system was for the first time in decades faced with frank rejection by many social groups. Young people felt repulsed by the stringencies of dominant cultural patterns characterized by authoritarian, provincial, and patriarchal values. The political system and the cultural elites were no doubt surprised by the rapid emergence during the 1970s of a growing range of cultural and political expressions: socialist and revolutionary parties, unions, agrarian mobilizations, and movements of ethnic identity as well as feminist and gay activism. New expressions in the visual arts, music, and literature appeared. Writers and critics openly disparaged the one-party political system and the reigning cultural apparatus.

As Mexican society placed increasing demands of democratization and cultural pluralism upon a closed political system, the opening up of universities came to be seen as an expression of democracy. The public university model—a free, nonselective, autonomous, and, in some cases, massive educational institution—was perceived as a bulwark of democracy and social equity. Students from the emerging middle strata, unions, and popular movements identified the public university as a site of cultural convergence, political militancy, and even protection from repression. Various state universities became vehicles of open (and sometimes bloody) confrontation with local power groups, and throughout the 1970s urban Mexico and its universities became the home of many political exiles from South American dictatorships.

During a short period, Mexico made a shift to an urbanized society and the mass culture that comes with it (Brunner 1990). The very idea of *culture* was changing, moving away from the hegemonic notion of a unitary national culture that had, in official discourse, emerged from the 1910–1917 Revolution and had been crystallized in the nationalistic movements in art and literature in the 1920s and 1930s and later in the national history and civics textbooks for primary education. The nationalistic synthesis of popular and *high* culture, as expressed in a discourse of national identity and promoted for decades by officialdom through speeches and public rituals, seemed to lose its footing. By the 1970s, the production, transmission, and consumption of cultural goods and messages had become more diversified and competitive, as the mass media and emergent youth cultures combined and conflicted in new ways with the educational structure and official image of Mexican nationalism.

How did this process affect the traditional, clanlike institutions of higher education? In reacting and accommodating to the growing numbers and differing types of professors, students, resources, conflicts, and values, they seemed to stumble through the changes wrought by expansion. They were pushed forward and sometimes torn apart. Others were unable to resist when political conflict led to increased control by local political elites. Their institutional fabric was subjected to a hot process of profound sociocultural shift, not a cold procedure of rational planning. Institutional cultures, practices, and rules had to be continually renegotiated, the limits of negotiation being constantly expanded as new actors and interests were incorporated. They seem to have been *engulfed* from the outside.

In organizational theory, the idea of engulfment invokes others, such as forfeiture of institutional identity, the dissolution of traditional internal hierarchies, and the loss of control over institutional boundaries. According to Scott (1986), organizations in a turbulent or rapidly changing environment face a strategic question: "how to recruit participants and harness their roles and resources in the service of organizational goals, while avoiding or minimizing the danger of becoming captive to participants' external interests or personal agendas" (Scott 1986, 186). In such circumstances, organizations may move toward *debureaucratization* or toward *overbureaucratization*. The former occurs in the extreme when the organization virtually ceases to exist, that is, when "it does not maintain a delimited network of social relations to which a distinctive normative order is applicable" (Scott 1986, 186). Overbureaucratization occurs when an organization attempts to control all internal movements by strict regulations and controls. In the first instance, the extreme case would be a *socially engulfed institution* verging on dispersion, and an extreme example of the second type would be a *total institution*.

Both phenomena occurred in varying degrees in one or another public university. In some institutions, the old rules of the traditional academic setting were dissolved, and new ones emerged under the influence of social and political agents, not academic or disciplinary ones. Various public universities came to be governed by political parties on the left, and their institutional structures sometimes became indistinguishable from the rules of the political game that the left was intent on establishing at the national level: democratic election of rectors and directors, assemblies changing curricula, and academics hired through party cronyism or union pressure. Thus, from semiautonomous, socially elite, professional *clans* holding control over institutional borders, some universities were transformed into *networks,* porous locales through which transited the varied interests, practices, and identities of the emerging middle strata and the left opposition.[2]

Sometimes the opposite tendency triumphed. The public technological institutes, nonuniversity institutions that are managed centrally by the federal government, did not experience such massive growth as the universities, but bureaucratic regulation has been a notable trait of their institutional fabric. And in very large and diverse institutions, both tendencies developed, such as in the national university, UNAM, with its 250,000 students and 20,000 academics (Kent 1990).

The Fragility of Academic Culture

Being an institutional milieu where the academic ethos had scarcely taken root prior to the period of expansion (Schwartzman 1993), the traditional university model was rapidly dissipated. Existing conventions on curricular matters, promotion rules, and internal financial allocations were dissolved, and few long-lasting or academically cogent innovations took their place. Academic tasks and merits were homogenized, and meritocracy was either attacked as being oppressive or brought under bureaucratic regulation. Fuentes makes a radical critique of the extreme to which this type situation sometimes led:

Differentiation [of merits] became taboo . . . In an atmosphere of false egalitarianism, differential rights and responsibilities were dissolved in an amorphous collectivity, which tended to lower standards of academic work. Hence, there emerged a game of simulations, populist manipulation, escapism from individual responsibility, and parasitic attitudes to-

ward attempts to restore the virtues of intellectual discipline, rigor and
achievement, which became suspect as forms of elitist authoritarianism.
(Fuentes 1990, 208; translation by Kent)

Upon entering academic work, a typical university instructor lacked graduate training and research experience and was hired not for his or her academic competence but through union pressure or network contacts for a part-time contract (sometimes in more than one institution, public and private).[3] Instructors might have done some postgraduate study since being hired, but most likely their academic development followed the specific demands of the courses they taught, rather than the global trends of their discipline. Therefore there was little participation in national or international academic meetings, and publishing was mostly done in local newspapers or journals of limited circulation (not until recently was publishing a criterion for advancement). Exclusivity of teaching was not the rule, and individuals probably held several part-time positions in order to make ends meet. By working in various part-time jobs, an instructor was in effect *deprofessionalized.* This harsh but not exaggerated portrayal seems to have been the lot of large numbers of teachers who were on the margins of the academic profession. Other members of the profession (mostly full-time professors and researchers) have indeed been through a very different experience, however, leading to higher degrees of competence in teaching and research.

What changes came about in teaching, the main activity of Mexican universities? The new professoriat in the 1970s learned how to teach by replicating the way they were taught during their own primary and secondary schooling. Universities did little to support or improve teaching, except through programs of educational technology promoted by the government, with scarce effectiveness. Universities did not seriously modify their teaching organization in the face of new student populations. The old academic forms remained in place: instructors basically gave lectures, library services were scarce, and course programs and evaluation procedures resulted from the dispersed efforts and perceptions of individual teachers, without recourse to collegial discussion or institutional criteria. Instructors also had to learn on their own to administer massive and often politicized academic systems. Interaction between teachers and students was more often than not perfunctory or formalistic.

For many students, learning in this setting was an unstructured affair at best. A student's access to knowledge was spontaneous, erratic, precarious. Students arrived in great numbers because of open-access policies. But they were in effect selected through *academic attrition* (Moreno 1991). Those who made it through to graduation (no more than 50% on the average) probably depended more on their previous cultural capital than on the *value added* by the educational experience: the student as survivor (Kent 1994). Thus expansion served to reproduce and certify the cultural capital of young people from the middle and upper strata and to formalize exclusion of students from less-advantaged backgrounds. The fact that this problem was never an important issue in policy discussions is a revealing component of the accepted values in public debate on education.

All this no doubt expelled many of the more talented professors from the intellectually unstimulating teaching sphere to the relatively more challenging political and bureaucratic spheres of the university and beyond. Those with genuine intellectual interests did their best to develop some research on their own or to emigrate to greener academic pastures in research centers and institutes. Traditionally established in institutes separated from the teaching faculties, research has always been a specialized activity, a relatively protected niche within the larger universities. Since the 1970s, research has been promoted by the government through a grant scheme that circumvented direct subsidies for universities, allowing groups of scientists to take root in some institutions, where academic leaders were able to promote the interests of science. However, it is a striking fact that most scientific research is still carried out by the large institutions in the capital and three major industrial cities. The rest of the university system has only recently been able to develop significant research efforts.

In terms of consequences for academic quality, I cannot be sanguine about these changes. Nevertheless, I must counter this critical portrayal by pointing out that the *hot* process of expansion set the scene for the formation of strong identities within universities, especially those that had been influenced by movements on the left. It is the case that many students and professors of the 1970s and early

1980s look back on their university experience as one of intense meaning, of identification with social and cultural movements that have had great impact on Mexican society. Thus it is unfair to forget the broader educational value of this experience that resided in the formation of a new generation of active and critical citizens.

The fragility of this identification between the university experience and the emerging social movements became evident, however, in the mid-1980s when the financial crisis hit universities, and social movements retreated with confusion amidst the intense restructuring of the economy and the sudden collapse of socialist goals and Marxist thought. As funds grew scarce and ideological identifications dissolved, some of the larger public universities experienced gusts of internal conflict over lessening resources. In the public eye, the stature of private institutions grew in contrast to the confusion reigning in the public model. Dill's observation on the significance of academic cultures for surviving a turbulent environment are pertinent here:

The strength of academic culture is particularly important when academic institutions face declining resources. During these periods the social fabric of the community is under great strain. If the common academic culture has not been carefully nurtured during periods of prosperity, the result can be destructive conflicts between faculties, loss of professional morale, and personal alienation. (Dill 1982, 304)

As the dust settled, institutional cultures whose strength had lain in intense identification with social progressivism drifted toward anomie. Universities came to realize that they had rarely been able to generate solid academic leadership. In some cases they had lost their best academic talents to emigration abroad, to established research institutes, to government or business. Because of their fragile development, disciplinary cultures had been unable to provide academic forms of coordination in the weaker or previously more politicized institutions. In contrast to Burton Clark's ideal type of the university as a bottom-heavy organization based in active disciplinary groups (Clark 1983), some public universities seem to be rather like *bureaucratically top-heavy* institutions with a frail disciplinary footing.

Other institutions—especially in the capital and the larger cities—had, however, effectively moved toward the formation of sturdy academic groups, both in teaching and research. Additionally, during the same period, a new generation of Mexican scientists had formed both at home and at doctoral programs abroad. The stronger academic institutions—both public and private—and the new groups of scientific researchers became mainstays of an important change in government policy in the 1990s, when public spending began to recover and the words *excellence* and *quality* began to appear in all public pronouncements on education.

A New Environment, New Actors, and New Segmentations

Economic recovery and the internationalization of the economy in the 1990s has once more placed education high on the list of priorities for public policy. Funding has grown substantially, and new themes have been introduced: evaluation, competitive funding for research, modern institutional management, university links with local business, entrepreneurialism, entrance examinations, and international academic collaboration. Modernization is the key word.

Ten years earlier, this set of policies would have encountered strong opposition by universities. But their tarnished public image and their internal infirmity allowed the government to move forward rapidly in establishing policies that have represented a signficant departure from the old political accommodations. Led on by financial inducements, universities are groping to establish new rules in management, planning, and funding. The growing number of academics who have developed research interests in recent years provide legitimacy for a discourse of *academic excellence* emanating from funding agencies and scientific leaders close to government policymakers.

It is interesting to see how university rectors and academics have adopted the language of modernization. At a more visible level, these discursive accommodations are sometimes accompanied by curious changes in behavior. Rectors are making difficult transitions from the role of coalition chieftains to institutional managers, where attempts at modern forms of resource and personnel management are interspersed with the clannish modus operandi of yore. One sees professors who had made names for themselves as radical critics of government now posing as academic entrepreneurs eager to sell their wares as political consultants. Erstwhile leaders of ideological tribes apply their hard earned political wiles in lobbying for government funds.

However, for better or for worse, shifts are occurring in institutional practice at a more substantive level as well. In some cases, egalitarian forms of institutional governance are being displaced by more hierarchical forms in uneasy combination with collegiality and entrepreneurialism. Research has become an important goal in institutions that had been able to accumulate academic strengths. Public institutions have been subjected to greater social and governmental scrutiny, thus losing part of their inward-looking, ghettolike traditions. Union negotiations over hiring and promotion have in some cases been replaced by more academic procedures, although these often become bureaucratic power games given the scarce experience of many institutions with the development of such procedures.

Throughout the period covered in this essay, higher education as a whole has experienced great changes in institutional and academic roles, and more recently new forms of segmentation are appearing. Brunner puts it this way for Latin-American countries in general:

Higher education has gone through an intense and abrupt process of differentiation, giving rise to a growing system heterogeneity, which is characteristic of the way cultural modernization has developed in Latin America. Thus, one finds that a great variety of institutions coexist: old and new establishments, universities and non-university institutions, public and private, catholic and secular, elite and massive, single mission and demand-absorbing institutions, research-oriented and teaching establishments. All this has occurred in an apparently disorderly fashion, in the absence of coherent forms of regulation. (Brunner 1990, 111, translation by Kent)

The increasingly varied modes of cultural production and transmission have left institutions to find specific *niches*, rather than announcing themselves as *the* institutions of higher culture. Students and professors are making increasingly varied cultural uses of the university. It is certainly the case that public universities have lost their traditional monopoly of the production and transmission of knowledge. Thus one important cleavage is the public/private difference: alongside numerous *diploma mills* that have cropped up everywhere basking in the absence of government regulation, certain private universities attract students from middle- and upper-class families who go on to the higher posts in business and government. The privatization of the educational paths of the social and economic elites is one of the more notable changes that have occurred over the past two decades (Kent, in press).

Within some institutions and academic groups, there are new types of struggle to regain academic identity based on diverse sets of values. Some academics (especially in the social sciences) have abandoned their old role as ideologues and have become journalists, political advisors, and technocrats outside the university as well as researchers within it. Others in the natural sciences and the engineering professions have gained ground additionally as *experts*. The emergence of a professional scientific community is also evident. Here is where disciplinary identity is strongest, in the sense proposed by Becher (1987), and incidentally where academic expertise may be increasingly linked to political influence.

But there is also the *lower clergy*, the mass marginals. Numerous instructors hired on a part-time basis make up an important part of the total academic workforce (about 60%). They teach at the undergraduate level, sometimes in various institutions. They do not do research, and participate minimally in institutional decisions. The lower clergy operates at the margins of the discourse of excellence and modernization.

How far can current knowledge on academic cultures take us in explaining such processes that seem so distant from the relatively more homogeneous cultural context of developed nations where this knowledge has arisen?

Conclusions: All That Is Solid Melts into Air

The fact that in the past fifteen years 1.3 million people have gone to a higher-education institution is an important ingredient in the rapidly changing bases of citizenship, political participation, gender relationships, and cultural consumption in Mexico. The growth of higher education has produced a generation of Mexicans who are enormously more literate, politically active, culturally demanding, and probably more sceptical than their parents. They will also, in all likelihood, express demands on the quality standards and on the diversity that the educational system offers their own children.

But what is educational quality for a highly inegalitarian society that has experienced intense yet erratic modernization? The difficulty in defining educational values derives from the hybrid intertwining of identities and cultural attachments that delineate modernity in Mexican society (García Canclini 1989). Despite recent recovery, the economy is not creating enough jobs for the million people who reach the age of eighteen every year, of whom about 15% are enrolled in higher education. The enormous expansion of higher education was sufficient to extend coverage for the middle and partly the lower-middle strata, but growth reached the limits imposed by severe social selection at the primary school level, where about 30% of the children enrolled drop out before reaching sixth grade. Of the country's 90 million inhabitants, 35 million live in poverty and 6 million adults are illiterate. The modernized industrial areas in the center and north are increasingly integrated into the North American economy, in contrast to the poor south with an economy based on subsistence agriculture and a numerous and ethnically diverse indigenous population that has been historically excluded from economic and social development.

The contest for the definition of a *good education* is taking place in an open market whose rules seem rather like a game of images without substance. Now that status, wealth, and power are clearly associated with the possession of the *right* educational credentials, individuals are struggling to find value in a socially segmented educational market. There is confusion as to educational values among students, academics, policymakers, and political groups. I might simplistically make a caricature of three different stances that stand out in current debates: the neoconservative nostalgia for the orderly transmission of cultural tradition, the uncritical adoption of modernistic educational policies sometimes linked to technological messianism, and currents of resistance that express fear of the destruction of historically ingrained popular forms of sociability by intense modernization. Higher education institutions are enveloped by the tensions among these and other cultural forms.

The disorderly dialectic of expansion and differentiation subjected the higher education system to extreme tensions that proliferated and transformed academic and institutional identities. The dispute over the educational legitimacy of increasingly diverse forms of academic organization has been, and will surely continue to be, a crucial component of the cultural and policy shifts in higher education, as Mexico is faced with the double task of providing good basic education for everyone and simultaneously developing a sophisticated system of higher education that is needed to support international economic competitiveness and cultural integration.

Notes

1. One wonders whether these tuition rates will make U.S. institutions even more attractive to some of these students.

2. Certain groups on the left talked of fusing the university with the people, which usually meant political alliances with social movements. What resulted in many cases were corporatist arrangements between university unions and university leadership. Actually this intimacy between universities and organized political groups preceded the arrival of the left on the scene. It is a relatively stable component of the relationships between higher education institutions and the political system in general.

3. Out of approximately 115,000 academic posts in higher education nationally, slightly more than 30% are full-time contracts (Gil, Franco, et al. 1994).

References

ANUIES (National Association of Higher Education Institutions) 1992. *Cuotas por servicios en instituciones de educación superior, 1991–1992*. Mexico.

Ayala, D., and M. Ramo. 1994. ¿Cuánto por estudiar en escuela privada? *Reforma* (daily newspaper), July 1, Mexico D.F.

Becher, T. 1987. The disciplinary shaping of the profession. In *The academic profession: National, disciplinary and institutional settings,* ed., B. Clark, 271–303. Berkeley: University of California Press.

Bourdieu, P. 1988. *La distinción: criterio y bases sociales del gusto*. Madrid: Taurus Ediciones.

Brunner, J.J. 1989. *Universidad y sociedad en América Latina*. Mexico, Universidad Autónoma Metropolitana–Azcapotzalco.

———. 1990. *Educación superior en América Latina: Cambios y desafíos*. Santiago de Chile: Fondo de Cultura Económica.

———. 1992. *América Latina: Cultura y modernidad*. Mexico: CONACULTA/Grijalbo.

Clark, B.R. 1983. *The higher education system: Across national perspective of academic systems.* Berkeley: University of California Press [Spanish trans. *El sistema de educación superior: una visión comparativa internacional*. Mexico: Ed. Nueva Imagen, 1990].

Dill, D. 1982. The management of academic culture: Notes on the management of meaning and integration. *Higher Education* 11(3):303–320.

Fuentes, O. 1989. La educación superior en México y los escenarios de su desarrollo futuro. *Universidad Futura,* Autónoma Metropolitana–Azcapotzalco, 1(3).

———. 1990. La mirada hacia la izquierda. In *Universidad nacional y cultura,* ed., A. Azuela. Mexico: UNAM, 186.

———. 1991. Las cuestiones críticas de las políticas de educación superior en la década de los 90, *Universidad Futura* 3:8–9.

———.1992. El estado y la educación pública en los años ochenta. In *El nuevo estado Mexicano: Estado y sociedad,* eds., J. Alonso, A. Aziz, and J. Tamayo. Nueva Imagen.

García Canclini, N. 1989. *Culturas híbridas: Estrategias para entrar y salir de la modernidad.* Mexico: Grijalbo/CONACULTA.

Gil, G., P. Franco, et al. 1994. *Los rasgos de la diversidad: Un estudio sobre los académicos Mexicanos.* Mexico: Universidad Autónoma Metropolitana–Azcapotzalco.

Kent, R. 1990. *Modernización conservadora y crisis académica en la UNAM.* Mexico: Nueva Imagen.

———. 1992. Expansión y diferenciación del sistem de educación superior en México: 1960 a 1990. Mexico; Cuadernos de Investigación Educativa, Departamento de Investigaciones Educativas, Centro de Investigación y Estudios Avanzados.

———. 1993. Higher education in Mexico: From unregulated expansion to evaluation. *Higher Education* 25(1):68–78.

———. 1994. ¿Cómo le hacen para estudiar en las universidades? *Huaxyácac,* Oaxaca, Mexico, No. 2.

———. In press. What is changing in Mexican public universities in the face of recent policies for higher education? *Higher Education Policy.* Paris: AIU.

Kent, R., and W. De Vries. 1994. Evaluación y financiamiento de la educación superior, *Universidad Futura,* Mexico, Universidad Autónoma Metropolitana, 5(15).

Levy, D.C. 1980. *University and government in Mexico: Autonomy in an authoritarian system.* New York: Praeger.

———. 1986. *Higher education and the state in Latin America: Private challenges to public distinctiveness,* University of Chicago Press.

Moreno B.R. 1991. La política hacia los estudiantes. *Universidad Futura* 3(8–9):15–18.

Paz, O. 1987. *México en la obra de Octavio Paz: El peregrino en su patria.* Mexico: Fondo de Cultura Económica.

Schwartzman, S. 1993. Políticas de educación superior en América Latina: El contexto. In *Políticas Comparadas de Educación Superior en América Latina,* ed., H. Courard. Santiago de Chile: FLACSO.

Scott, W.R. 1986. *Organizations: Rational, natural, open systems.* 2nd ed. Englewood Cliffs, N.J.: Prentice Hall.

Zaid, G. 1988. *De los libros al poder.* Mexico: Grijalbo.

Chapter Six
Culture and the Role of Women in a Latin American University
The Case of the University of Costa Rica

Susan B. Twombly

In 1993 the University of Costa Rica (UCR), one of the premier Central American public universities, had what seemed like an extraordinary number of women in positions of authority. Most of these women were directors of their respective *escuelas,* or departments; four were deans; and three occupied positions in the highest ranks of the university. That four deanships should be held by women—including the dean of the School of Engineering—was surprising. That each of these women had to survive a potentially politically charged electoral process made the numbers seem almost unimaginable. In several cases these were not the first women to have held deanships of their respective schools. The School of Education has had a long history of prominent women deans.

From my perspective as a female North American academic, the number of women administrators holding prominent positions was a surprise for two reasons. First, in my own U.S. university there are few women in such high positions. Although women are increasingly gaining department chair positions, only the third female dean in the university, the first ever in the School of Education, assumed the position on July 1, 1994. My university is hardly unique. Women students outnumber men in North American colleges and universities, and yet women's struggle to gain faculty and administrative positions, and thus access to sites of influence, in these culturally powerful institutions has been less than totally successful (see for example, Aisenberg and Harrington 1988; Tack and Patitu 1992).

Second, North American writers tend to view Latin American countries as machista and Latin American women as leading constrained lives while portraying themselves to be more advanced (Behar 1993). Perhaps this is because the majority of research on Latin

American women has focused on lower-class women. (Stromquist 1992 is an exception.) We know much less about the potentially powerful class of professional women in these countries: how the larger society and institutional culture shape their professional choices and lives and how they, through their work, seek to maintain or make changes in those cultures. This chapter explores how culture shapes roles and possibilities for academic women in one university.

As major sites where knowledge is produced, culture mediated, and future generations of professionals trained, universities are sites of power. They have their own cultures that reinforce certain norms, attitudes, and behaviors, including how power is exercised and who has access to positions of influence (Kuh and Whitt 1988; Tierney and Rhoads 1994). Participants not only contribute to the development of institutional culture; their activity within the organization is shaped by that culture. If we accept the proposition that access to the professions is critical to improvement of women's status, it is important to examine how the university, as gatekeeper to professions, shapes women's roles. In this case we are concerned with how a particular group of people—women in positions of influence—participated in the life of a major university; how they perceived their roles to be defined by the culture and how they, in turn, shaped the culture. During the spring of 1993, there were approximately twenty-five women in positions of authority at UCR. How did the university culture shape the possibilities for women? What factors helped them and hindered them in their professional development? Did these women perceive they had equal power to men within the university? How did they view the role and status of women in the university and society and their role in either maintaining or changing that status? In the process of answering these questions, a picture of the university culture and how it did or did not create possibilities for women emerges.

In an attempt to answer these questions, I interviewed eighteen of the approximately twenty-five women who held elected positions of authority in April 1993. My Costa Rican colleagues helped me develop the interview protocol. All interviews were conducted in Spanish. The reader is reminded that in most cases these women were speaking from relatively elite positions; however, they also tried to speak for women more generally.

Women in Costa Rica: A Brief Overview

Girls and women fare relatively well in this small country the size of West Virginia in which the extremes of wealth and poverty so characteristic of much of Latin America are unfamiliar. In 1991, women comprised 49.5% of the total population of approximately 3,100,000 persons *(Market Data* 1992). Two of the factors that work in favor of women are a low birthrate and a relatively high level of education (García and Gomáriz 1989). Between 1960 and 1988, the percentage of women in the workforce increased from 17% to 28% (excluding domestic labor) (García and Gomáriz 1989).

It is the area of education that distinguishes Costa Rica most from its neighbors. In 1990 Costa Rica had one of the lowest illiteracy rates in Latin America, the second lowest illiteracy rate among rural women, and, with Argentina, the lowest gap between illiteracy rates of men and women (Stromquist 1992, 26). Only 6.9% of the female population was classified as illiterate in 1984 (García and Gomáriz 1989). Furthermore, in Costa Rica, women comprise 50% or more of the students at every level of education except that of higher education, in which their participation lags behind that of men by only 1% point or less (Blanco, Delgadillo, and Méndez 1989; García and Gomáriz 1989). In 1990, 37% of the the University of Costa Rica faculty were women (Universidad de Costa Rica 1992). The university has a dynamic gender studies program. A virtual alphabet soup of activist women's organizations exists in the country; and Margarita Penón, former "Primera Dama" of the country and a credible presidential precandidate in Costa Rica's recent national election, worked openly for women's rights while first lady. Married professional women seldom use their husbands' last names, and other very visible symbols of women's rights activities such as posters and marches are common.

Some reservation is warranted, however. Educational equality does not necessarily mean social equality, and Costa Rican women face many obstacles. (See Bonder 1992 and Mendiola 1992 for related discussions.) In fact, despite this picture of relative equality, the women interviewed described the society in which they live as machista and traditional, in which women face a number of problems, especially violence. They were optimistic that traditional gender role expectations were changing in the younger generation.

Social Class and Education

These women had grown up in a culture of social mobility in which it was possible for women to enter university and even to attain advanced degrees. Among this group of women, some clearly grew up in wealthy and/or socially prestigious families. For example, "I come from a family with a long academic tradition," said the dean of letters. "My grandfather, uncle, and father were all academics." They had been influential leaders in the founding and subsequent reform of the university. The vice rector for academic affairs had completed all of her higher education (bachelor's through doctorate) in the United States. However, some of the women came from poor homes. The director of the University Council described her family as "very poor." One dean used the term "culturally limited" to describe the fact that her parents had little formal education. Finding themselves forced to work due to illness or death of a family member, several dropped out of school for a period or changed career plans. By far the majority described themselves as middle class.

With few exceptions, families placed a premium on education, even for women. "There wasn't any exclusion," said the director of the Department of Sociology and Anthropology. "The perspective of our parents was to study and keep studying." The dean of education said that her good grades "motivated my parents because they had plans that all of us were going to study and today we are all professionals." She confirmed what several others said: "We all studied and found that education was the mechanism to mobility. This stimulated us further." Regardless, then, of social class origins, the majority of these women received much support to study. And study they did. Six of these women held doctorates, ten master's degrees, and only two the licenciatura. Some of the younger women will earn doctoral degrees. They ranged in age from late twenties to midfifties. The majority were in their forties.

University Culture and the Role of Women
University Organizational Structure

The present University of Costa Rica was founded in 1940 and enrolls 30,000 students in five faculties. The university is governed by the University Assembly (consisting of all tenured faculty); the University Council, a representative group elected to make policy; the rector (president); and five appointed *vicerrectores*: academic affairs, research, community outreach, administrative affairs, and student affairs. The institution is divided into *facultades* (colleges), *escuelas* (departments), sections, agricultural stations, research centers, and institutes and has four regional centers located throughout the country.

Each school is headed by an elected dean and a college assembly; each department, by an elected director. Terms for all elected positions are four years with the possibility of reelection for one additional term. In schools divided into departments, directors or department chairpersons hold more direct power than deans. See Table 1 for a listing of areas, schools, and departments.

Because all deans and director positions, excepting the vice rector positions, are elected positions, aspirations for careers in academic administration are constrained by the electoral process and, more generally, by the boundaries of the university. Most of the women in this study said that they ran for their current position because colleagues asked them to and because they believed they could make a difference. Most said they planned to return to full-time teaching after their four-year term ended; however, several clearly aspired to other administrative postions.

Women in the University of Costa Rica: A Statistical Picture

The official list of university administrators issued in January 1992, modified to bring it up to date, included the following women: vice rector of academic affairs, vice rector of community outreach, director of the University Council, a member of the University Council, the dean of engineering, dean of education, dean of fine arts, dean of letters, and five vice deans including the graduate division. Ten women held positions as directors of schools (departments) out of forty-one departments while eleven served as subdirectors. Two women directed interdisciplinary careers (majors) and women directed the law and education research institutes (two out of ten total). Assistant directors of three of these were women. Out of seventeen research centers, four were headed by women: history, hemoglobin research, electron microscopy, and training and research in public administration (*La Gaceta* 1992).

The data on the representation of women faculty reported in

Table 1 Women Faculty by Academic Unit, July 1990

Academic Unit	Percent	Number	Academic Unit	Percent	Number
Total	*36.5*	*854*	Faculty of Education	61.3	98
General Studies	*45.5*	*45*	Administration	27.3	6
Area of Arts and Letters	*48.4*	*104*	Teacher Education	67.2	41
Faculty of Fine Arts	32.6	30	Counseling and Spec. Ed.	80.0	32
Theater	33.3	4	Physical Education	41.7	10
Music	34.0	17	Library Science	75.0	9
Art	31.0	9	Faculty of Law	14.1	11
Faculty of Letters	60.2	74	*Area of Engineering and Architecture*	*14.5*	*42*
Philology/Linguistics	60.7	17	Faculty of Agriculture	13.0	10
Philosophy	33.3	8	Ag. Economics	14.3	2
Modern Languages	68.6	48	Fitotechnology	9.1	3
			Animal Science	14.3	4
Area of Basic Sciences	*24.1*	*49*	Food Technology		
Faculty of Sciences	24.1	49	Faculty of Engineering	15.1	32
Biology	50.0	14	Agricultural Engineering	18.2	2
Physics	16.3	8	Civil Engineering		
Geology	10.0	2	Electrical		
Mathematics	22.1	17	Industrial	20.7	6
Chemistry	28.6	8	Mechanical	9.5	2

Academic Unit	Percent	Number	Academic Unit	Percent	Number
Area of Social Sciences	*43.2*	*260*	Faculty of Engineering *(cont.)*	15.1	32
Faculty of Economics	26.1	42	Chemical	15.8	3
Business Administration	18.5	12	Architecture	26.7	4
Public Administration	44.0	11	Topography	9.55	2
Economics	20.5	9	Computer Science	38.2	13
Statistics	37.0	10	*Area of Health*	*33.3*	*154*
Faculty of Social Sciences	52.6	120	Faculty of Pharmacy	52.4	11
Anthropology and Sociology	49.2	29	Faculty of Medicine	32.8	107
Communication	39.3	11	Nursing	96.2	50
Political Science	40.0	4	Medicine	17.4	39
History and Geography	42.4	25	Faculty of Microbiology	44.0	22
Psychology	63.3	31	Faculty of Dentistry	21.2	14
Social Work	87.0	20			

Source: UCR, Oficina de Planificación Universitaria, Perfil del Funcionario Docente, 1992.

Table 1 indicate that women were more highly represented in some areas and departments than in others. Overall, women tended to be concentrated in the areas of arts and letters, social sciences, and health. Each area, however, represents a wide range of academic schools and departments, and women's participation must be analyzed carefully. From a comparative perspective, the most interesting figures are those in the sciences. Even within the area of engineering and architecture, where the percentage of women was low, 21% of the faculty in industrial engineering, 27% in architecture, and 38% in computer science were women. Women were also well represented in the schools of pharmacy and microbiology and the Department of Nursing.

Obtaining a faculty position is one thing, but promotion to the highest academic ranks is quite another. An individual who is hired for a position *propiedad* (with tenure) moves through a series of ranks beginning with instructor, adjunct, and associate, to the highest rank of *catedrático*. At the time of this study, there was no time limit for moving from one rank to another. Criteria for promotion from one rank to the next highest included publications, teaching experience, degrees attained, and mastery of foreign languages.

Available data revealed that women were more highly represented in the lower ranks (Blanco, Delgadillo, and Méndez 1989). In 1987, 47% of women faculty were at the rank of instructor compared to 40% of the men. At the other end of the spectrum, 26% of the men held the rank of associate and 21% that of *catedrático* compared to 24.3% and 11.9% of the women, respectively. However, 11.9% is approximately double the percentage of women holding full professorships in major U.S. research universities in the same time period (Moore and Sagaria 1993). These last percentages are important because one must hold at least the rank of associate to stand for election to positions of authority. Although the percentage of women who held the rank of *catedrático* had increased since 1982, from 6.2% to 11.9%, it still lagged behind that of men. Therefore, women were not as well represented in the rank that has the most influence within the university (González, personal communication 1993).

The Role of Women

How does the university culture define, facilitate, or constrain the role of women within it? This section will focus around three central aspects of women's role in the university: (a) their location, (b) factors that helped or hindered their success, and (c) their perceptions of their own power and influence. The interviewees described a larger societal culture that disadvantages women and a university culture that is more or less favorable to them. But their words also revealed many ambiguities.

Location in the University

With several notable exceptions, the women in positions of power in the University of Costa Rica were in departments or schools in which women constituted the majority or near majority. This was true in fact as well as in perception. "In the university the majority of women are in positions identified especially for women. There are a few exceptions, and in these cases, women have achieved the positions with a base of support," said the director of the University Council. She went on to say:

Although in UCR there are many women in positions of power, there are certain careers which are considered women's fields. . . . Engineering and medicine are masculine. The culture of the country is masculine. If we talk of women in positions of power in this Univeristy, we are talking about women who are luchadoras, very strong women with a very strong trajectory of struggle, and they are outstanding from an academic point of view.

The vice rector for academic affairs explained further, "The educational system is discriminatory at the level of training of students. . . . When students select majors, self-discriminating factors enter, perhaps cultural and universal factors. Women tend to choose certain types of careers."

The university system facilitates women's access to positions of authority in fields in which there are more women to vote. A department director explained: "The assembly in the School of Medicine is 80% men. Men are going to win any election for this reason." However, it did not always follow, said some, that women would win elections just because there were more women in a school or department. The system of electing administrators did seem to have facilitated women's chances of attaining positions in certain areas.

This apparent success was qualified by one dean:

We are women deans in school divided in departments. Why? Because the power in these schools is held by the departments. The dean is more or less a coordinator. Some would say a figurehead, but I don't agree with that. Deanships in schools not divided in departments, such as law and pharmacy, do not have women deans. [A woman had recently held the deanship of the School of Law.] Who are the deans then: in Letters—school divided in departments, in Engineering—also divided in departments. She is very important. There should not be a woman dean in Engineering.

The dean of letters provided additional insight into why there were more women in some fields than in others:

We have always said that Letters is one of the most matriarchial of the schools in the entire university. Traditionally, teaching has been viewed as women's work. Here, above all, primary, and later secondary education, was in hands of women. It was supposed that women were mothers and therefore good teachers. Above all, primary education was seen as an extension of the home, and education was directed by women. The School of Letters was a school that primarily trained for teaching. However, this has changed some recently. There has been greater specialization, and now we have postgraduate studies and emphasis on research has increased. But fortunately this happened when we already had the territory clearly controlled [she laughed]. The concern in the School of Letters has been that the department of philosophy had been very patriarchial as a result of the stereotypical idea that thinking is masculine and feeling feminine. Recently women have begun to invade this territory [she chuckled],demonstrating that philosophy is not just men's territory. When there is a male dean, he comes from philosophy.

At the time the interviews were conducted, the School of Education was also dominated by women with only the Department of Educational Administration headed by a man. The only other male in the assembly was the student representative.

Several of the women noted that the position of vice rector for academic affairs was also a position for women. "The vice rectorship of academic affairs is always in women's hands, because of its relationship to teaching. This is also a stereotype, but there have been extraordinary women in this position," said one woman. Another woman suggested that this was only compensation for the rector always being a man.

Factors that Enhanced or Inhibited Success
When asked how success was defined in the university, these women provided a broad answer of which promotion in academic rank was only part. They included factors such as recognition as a good teacher and as an expert in one's field. Election to positions of authority was one indication of this recognition.

With few exceptions, these women believed that it was more difficult for them than their male colleagues to achieve success. "I can't speak of equality," said the director of the University Council. "We have to be two times better to succeed in the university. If one is equal in qualifications, the man has more opportunities; but if one stands out and excels, she can achieve success more easily than a man. . . . For the Consejo, one has to be an outstanding woman in order to win. Men get points just for being men."

In commenting on success in the university, one dean laughed as she said,

Success? Officially or unofficially? Officially by ability, curriculum vitae and academic area. Unofficially, to be male carries more weight. . . . In practice one observes very subtle obstacles. For example, stereotypes function as rationality for men. . . . Recognition of scientific publications is very easy. However, recognition of literary works is much more complicated, and art is even more difficult. One has to demonstrate doubly that literary work and art have value because traditionally women are associated with emotion and men with science.

"Stereotypes still put women in subordinate positions. We aren't good administrators. We are good secretaries," said one woman. Moreover, "it costs women more to hold an administrative position." This was largely due to family responsiblities. All but four of the women interviewed were married or divorced. Only these four and two of the younger, recently married women did not have children. The three women in the highest positions were single, as predicted by one of the department directors. The status of being "single, never married" is still somewhat uncommon in Costa Rica. Although these women were viewed as being able to take on top positions because they did not have husbands and children, they were clearly exceptions.

Most agreed with the dean who said: "The university system does not disadvantage the woman. It is the real time available that limits one." She asked, "Does the woman have time to write? time for professional development? time to learn another language? Can she make the decision to go to another country to study if her husband is not an academic? These are the limitations." The system of academic ranks was described as being sex blind and nondiscriminatory. "Success doesn't have anything to do with sex," added one department director. "It is a matter of will, intention, ability, and free time."

However, one director's description of her efforts to produce scholarship shows how their time was limited. "In spite of a good family situation, it is hard to do research. One has to achieve a balance between family and work. One can't dedicate much more time to one area or the other. I am a housewife, nurse, wife, mother. This affects my ability and time to commit myself to research, thinking, and conceptualizing." For those who had children, it was clear that their primary responsibility was to the children, especially when they were young.

Although the university was quite flexible in allowing women with full-time appointments to work part time when necessary, there were no time limits for promotions; and one could teach in *interino* (instructor) status for as long as one wished, these advantages had potentially negative consequences for women as a young, recently married department director explained:

Five of us entered university careers in the same year. We all have the same number of years working in the univeristy and we are all at different ranks. One has a child. She is low on the scale. One does not do research. The third has children also, but now they are older. I am an associate and am preparing my papers for the catedrática. *I don't have any children. For me this is a factor which has weighed heavily on the women in this school: their condition as mothers and women, women who do not want to neglect their role as mother.*

It was true that some of these women had full-time housekeepers to care for the children; however, full-time help was too expensive for some. One of the deans remarked that even though she did have help in her home, she still bore the majority of the responsibility for transporting the children, helping them with their homework, and managing the home. She described her day:

Yesterday I worked here [at the university] until two in the afternoon. I went home [about fifteen miles from the university]. I worked at home with the children a little. I left them at school and returned to a meeting of the Consejo Superior of the School of Education. In the meantime I ran to buy some things for the children. On the way home I went to buy some groceries and returned to my house at 7:30. Then, for the next two hours I helped the children. . . . We have something that most North American families don't have: domestic help. However, the maid is more likely to attend to the man of the house. I can arrive very late and very tired, but she never asks me if I would like a cup of tea or if she can help me with anything. She shines my husband's shoes, puts out his clothes, asks him if he wants tea, etc. This is the structure I would change.

Women frequently complained about the lack of quality day care centers.

When asked specifically about the role of the family, the women generally agreed that societal expectations of women were the single most important limitation for women in general even if not for themselves. Even so, few labeled family as an obstacle. One woman who worked in a highly technical, typically masculine field in which men were suspicious of her competence made the following comment:

It is difficult to obtain positions of responsibility. Independent of whether there is open discrimination or not, of whether there are children or empleadas, *the woman has to do the housework. It is an unequal situation, very bothersome. One supposes also that if the woman accepts work outside of the home, she is a bad mother. People are going to ask why you aren't attending to your children. All my life I have been called a bad mother, even by some of my colleagues. The former director of my department used to ask me what I was doing at the university, why wasn't I home with the children? It is a catch-22 [her word].*

*There is no way to come out well because if you are a mother, you can't
be a good worker.*

Postgraduate degrees and knowledge of foreign languages are
important criteria for moving through the ranks (although not necessary to obtain positions). Until recently, the only option for men
and women to earn doctoral degrees was to travel outside the country. The interviewees described how this affected women:

*When I applied for a scholarship to study in Canada, a federal scholar-
ship, in an absolutely competitive situation, I didn't feel any limitations.
I had to pass through many filters. I did this with the benefit of having
many women in positions of leadership, including ————, the Vice
Rector for Academic Affairs. . . . There was never a question that my
being a mother or woman affected my getting the scholarship.*

The catch is that women are less likely than men to apply for scholarships. While several women told about husbands who took leaves
from their positions to accompany them abroad, most agreed with
the woman who said: "The opportunities are greater for men to
leave to get a graduate degree than for women because of their commitment as mothers." This woman also offered the opinion that
people still believed that education for a man was a better investment than for a woman. In addition, embassy sexism and the
university's narrow family reimbursement policy were cited as factors that discourage women from seeking study opportunities outside of the country. In general, these women believed that they lived
in a place and time in which, in the words of one, "Men can rise in
the ranks more easily because it is easier for them to travel outside of
the country."

Not all agreed the university presented more obstacles for women
than for men. Several women echoed the sentiments of one research
center director: "The obstacles are not very great. . . . They are sur-
mountable. . . . It costs to assimilate. . . . It depends in part on personality. There are men too who have been affected because their
personality is weak. It almost doesn't matter whether one is male or
female, but rather the personality counts more and what one wants
in life." Another woman noted that she had

personally not experienced any difficulty. It is a cultural problem, the limitations that one faces. It is also a problem of defining priorities. . . . For me, at a certain time my first priority was to be a mother, second was a professor, and third was to be a researcher. The limitation that one has is to define priorities. Obstacles one defines oneself.

"I haven't faced any obstacles," said the vice rector. "At the level of society, that is where women face obstacles.

While societal and cultural factors were identified as inhibiting women, they largely credited themselves for their success. The director of the University Council is an example:

I had to excel not only in my studies for the licenciatura but in the studies for the doctorate in Belgium also. . . . I worked harder than men. . . . My case is a special case. I am a very tenacious woman. If one has equal professional qualifications to a man, the man has more opportunities. If a woman stands out and excels she can achieve success more easily than a man.

A director of a scientific research institute attributed her success to her character: "I have never been one to stay behind." One department director became pregnant out of wedlock before having finished her education. She made the very difficult decision not to marry the father:

If I had married, I would not have worked, would not have earned my master's degree. . . . I would have run into a wall. The father of the child had told me that I could not work. Because I had my undergraduate degree and an established job, I couldn't become the housewife he wanted me to be.

This decision required an extreme amount of courage and foresight on this woman's part. She later left the child with her parents for two years in order to earn a master's degree in Chile.

"To be the only woman in a major had certain advantages," said another. "While I felt alone, it gave me pleasure to belong to this elite." It's all "personal attitude," said one dean. "I speak the language without losing my femininity. They respect me and I have always played within the men's rules even though they represent a handicap for me."

These academic women cited other factors that helped them. God was credited with having given one woman ability and forcefulness. "Because where did I get this strength?" she asked. "From my husband? No. He always has been against my working. Until now. Now I am attending to *my* needs." This woman, who had raised five children before entering the university herself, told the story of how she finally gained confidence in herself. She was teaching a course in special education:

There were thirty students from rural areas. . . . One of the students had serious health problems and couldn't attend classes. He had to have kidney dialysis. But he worked very hard. He was poor and shy. . . . One day he came to my office and told me that he needed a new kidney but there was no donor. . . . The story is that I gave him my kidney. This marked a very important situation for me. It was a tremendously important decision. My husband did not even want me to give blood. When I had the courage to tell him that I was going to donate my kidney, I did not even ask him. I told him and waited for what was going to happen. It was the most important decision that I have made in my life, and it has made a great difference in my whole life. From then on I lost the fear of making decisions.

It was clear that on a personal level, these women had worked hard to succeed, by their own accounts at least twice as hard as their male colleagues, and their ability to do so was a result of personal characteristics and having survived many battles.

However, the university was also described as being a good place for women to work—better than private industry. Two aspects of the university were particularly helpful to women: its flexibility and its growth during the 1970s and 1980s when most of these women began their careers. In the words of one director:

The advantages of UCR facilitate the entrance of women. . . . In one sense machismo favors this. The norm has been to enter the university as an interino *[nontenure, part-time faculty] and stay in this level for a while. Because women are married, it is not their responsibility to guar-*

antee work stability. I can be interino *and if they need me, fine; and if they do not, I don't have the same pressure that men have. Above all, the university woman does not have to maintain the family economically. The university also permits us to work part time when we have to. In a private company, one can't work part time.*

These particular women also benefitted from being in the right place at the right time. They began their careers during a period in which the university was growing rapidly and needed faculty. However, one department director noted that this boom period was now over and that it was not as easy to obtain a tenured position. The effect this will have on the number and percentage of women in the university is not known.

Several of the younger women credited their helpful husbands for making their ability to hold these positions possible. What was missing was any reference to mentors. While one or two women noted the importance of role models to their professional development, such as former deans, ministers of education, and a woman who had run for rector recently, mentors were apparently not a factor. Even when asked specifically, women did not indentify influential mentors.

Elections, Power, and Administrative Work

There were mixed opinions about whether women faced more obstacles than men in the election process or had equal power. A very prominent woman had run for, and narrowly lost, the election for rector in the late 1980s. She, and others, described the nature of the campaign rhetoric surrounding that election as being very personal. However, only a few described having experienced such "personal" campaign politics. "Women have to be purer than men," observed one woman. The recently elected member of the University Council explained how the election process worked against her:

All of the other candidates from my area were men, men who had followed traditional university careers. I had been coordinator of the master's program in the School of Education. The men had held ministry positions. There is also a political career. There were very subtle things. In one round table discussion they wanted me to speak first. I said "No señores," because it is a disadvantage to go first, and we drew straws.

There is a tendency to attack one's personal life. There is more interest in elections for high positions, and more weapons are used. In the case of the married woman, they invent a lover. If one has one, it becomes public. If one doesn't have a lover, they invent one. It isn't the same for a man. In my case they attacked me on, let's say, a professional issue.

A number of women reinforced the fact that a double standard operates with respect to personal life. Women, they said, are expected to be more perfect. In two cases, the candidates' husbands were also a member of the same unit. These women had to convince their units that the husbands were not really going to run things. As one woman said, "No one has ever asked any of the previous directors about the influence their spouses had over them." Perhaps because most women held positions in areas where women were well represented, they did not generally feel that the election process worked unduly against them. The stakes were higher for positions of higher rank, and elections potentially more volatile.

The interviewees disagreed about whether women and men in equivalent positions had equal power and how their status as women affected administrative work. Men and women have ". . . completely equal power. Here in the unversity there is no difference," said one woman director. This sentiment was shared by another director: "There is much sexual harrassment and more discrimination in the administrative area among the secretaries; however, in the higher level positions, there are fewer problems." Yet another woman added, "In the university in general, there is no difference, but some schools, such as medicine, are exceptions." Some women firmly believed that women's participation and power were significantly different in units in which women were the majority and those in which they were the minority.

One of the institute directors believed she had gained power: "When they elected me, they might not have had any confidence. That's why I said before that it is indespensable to demonstrate that one can act and that one knows how to make decisions."

These women generally considered themselves to be more dedicated, equally able to solve problems, and in some cases more effective at certain types of activities than men and therefore they had equal power: "Women are more dedicated to the university. Because men have to maintain a house and family, many have to work out-side the university. When women sign to do full time, they do it." This was true in part because in a machista society, men are ex-pected to support the family economically, thus forcing many aca-demic men to hold more than one job to earn a sufficient living. Women, on the other hand, when not the main economic support for a family, can survive on the university's salary and not have to take on additional jobs.

Once again these women attributed their equal power to them-selves as well as to policies. "Women have equal capacity to resolve problems [therefore equal power]," said one woman. Another added, "Women have more ability to visualize solutions to problems." "Women are more organized despite the fact that they are not in decision-making positions. If women had more access to positions of power, these countries would be better organized," offered an-other.

When a difference in power was noted, it was largely attributed to the fact that "power is determined by number of votes." Accord-ing to this theory, the larger areas and larger departments and schools have more power. "If one controls size, it doesn't matter if it is men's or women's field," argued one director. Another observed that "In general terms, when resources are distributed, the School of Social Sciences is the school that receives fewer resources, for example, materials and building, compared to the others. It is not because of gender," she said. However, it was also true that overall the social sciences had high numbers of women and students compared to medicine and engineering. One of the deans reported that the one woman director in her school had more power than male directors because she had more resources, including an entire building under her responsibility; but her success was totally up to her, said the dean.

There were others who provided a somewhat different picture. "By law, yes. Within the position, yes [men and women have equal power], but when it comes to work, the vice rector of administration (a man), for example, can work with other men—*majae*—the old boys' network. Women don't understand the informal language. . . . Women have to fight like men." Moreover, if a woman makes a deci-sion, "[she is] a loudmouth, a castrating woman," reported one. "If

I'm not forceful, I am incapable of making decisions. They don't want to recognize my technical knowledge," added another. One of the research institute directors spoke of a meeting she had just come from in which several male administrators had tried to convince her to give up her space and build a new building with less than sufficient resources:

Today I realized that the assistant to the rector thought I was a mere imbecile, an idiot who did not understand what was going on and that they could easily get what they wanted by pressuring me with the university administration and leave us with little. They pressured me in meetings with all sorts of important people sitting around a table. . . . One person by herself is not as strong as two. I brought the dean. They thought they were going to impress me with important surnames and all that. . . . These games are not professional. . . . I realized that most women are naive in this sense and we do not play these games. They had to listen when both of us came to the meeting.

Not more than ten to fifteen minutes later, this same director said emphatically "No, women do not face obstacles in the university."

One of the deans in a largely female-dominated school offered the opinion that the number of women in positions indicated that sexism and discrimination within the university had been conquered. "We haven't had a rector yet. We have had very good vice rectors in the last few years. I don't know how many. For more than ten years the major vice rector has been a woman." This woman went on to say, "The university system doesn't disadvantage women at all. It is the free time women don't have that limits them. . . . But from a legal point of view, we have real equality."

Conclusion

How, then, did the university culture shape women's participation, and how, in turn, did these women who held significant administrative positions support or subvert this culture?

For many of these women, the university was perceived to be an oasis in an otherwise machista society, and university culture itself, they believed, did not limit their participation. In fact the presence

of a relatively high percentage of women was itself an artifact, suggesting that women's participation in the university is acceptable.
Rather, they shared the belief that larger societal values regarding
women's role were responsible for difficulties faced by academic
women. Time and time again women said that the university was a
good place to work. Laws and university policy, they believed, established a more or less equal situation for men and women, while
societal expectations and stereotypes inhibited women's ability to
achieve by restricting the time they had to devote to activities such
as publishing, their ability to study abroad, and the way women
were viewed. In this respect, the university itself played the role of a
subculture that countered values of the larger society at least for
women in positions of power. Although some women talked specifically about discrimination, about having to work twice as hard and
be twice as competent as men, the old boys' network, and other
ways in which they were disadvantaged, they largely described the
rules as gender blind. The exact reasons for UCR's seeming receptiv-
ity to women are unclear but may be related to a variety of factors,
such as the coincidence of UCR's growth with the availability of
women to assume positions, relatively low professorial salaries, the
university's emphasis during critical formative years on preparing
secondary teachers, and the belief that this was an acceptable role
for women.

In other ways the university reproduced societal views of women.
The most overt way in which the university limited women faculty
and administrators was by "restricting" their participation to predominantly women's fields—areas that may have less influence within
the university. Even so there were several exceptional women included in this study, namely the dean of engineering and the director of the University Council, who did not conform to the pattern.
Women revealed ambivalent attitudes toward gender segmentation
in the university. They expressed concern about ghettos of power-
lessness and agreed that women should be able to pursue any field of
study, but many also spoke very positively about why they were in a
"woman's field." One dean even spoke defiantly about women having her area under control.

There are several ways to think about women being "restricted"
to women's fields. On the one hand, women working in traditional

women's fields such as nutrition, education, and health have an opportunity to affect services essential to the well-being of women and of a developing society. From a comparative perspective, although women historically dominated some fields such as home economics and nursing, women have not dominated such traditionally "women's fields" as education or social welfare in U.S. universities. Moreover, some social science fields that were considered "women's fields" in Costa Rica are not so in the United States. So even though women attained powerful positions in women's fields, at least they gained positions of power in these fields. However, while these traditionally female professions may have influence over individuals, they have not had as much political influence as medicine and law. In fact, statistics reveal relatively high percentages of women students in the schools of law, medicine, and dentistry (Blanco, Delgadillo, and Méndez 1989). Whether these women graduate and actually practice their chosen profession and if not, why not, are significant questions that should be addressed.

The important question is whether and, if so, how women academics in positions of influence used their power to bring about changes in the culture for women. Two questions about the definition of feminism and necessary changes in the university provided insight into how these women viewed their own situation and whether they worked to maintain the status quo or for change.

These women fell into three groups with respect to activism on behalf of women: The traditionalists essentially said that women experienced no problems except those imposed by society and identified nothing within the university in need of change. Reluctant activists, clearly recognizing obstacles, spoke in a more feminist way about their own lives, even while rejecting the term feminist as a self-descriptor. These women did not believe much change was necessary in the university and did little to change it. The quiet subversives recognized inequalities in the university and engaged in activities to change the status quo, but often in very subtle ways. These activities included gender inclusive language, and their recommendations for changes in the university included paying attention to how committees were constituted, hiring more women, and electing a woman rector.

Academic women in Costa Rica did not embrace the term "feminist" as typically defined from a Western perspective (see Perreault 1993 for a discussion of such definitions). Although most defined the term as equality between the sexes, most agreed that to adopt the label would make change more difficult for women because of the hostility it engenders. "I am not a militant feminist," said the member of the Consejo Universitario, "but I fight very hard." Others prided themselves on the same behavior—practicing gender equality, even being very proactive in their own lives and for others—while rejecting the term feminist. Most acknowledged the important work of the gender studies program and recognized a need to work together. "Men always support other men, but women don't necessarily support other women. I have recently become aware of this and will now vote for women," noted one of the directors. But even the gender studies program, while offering courses, focused on working with community women's groups outside of the university. Actively confronting women's status within the university occupied a seemingly small part of their agenda. In fact, women in positions of power generally took the long view, arguing that gradual change would result in a better life for the next generation of women.

When asked if they included gender issues in their classes, many said no, even though they placed their faith in new values in the younger generation. Some, including the director of the Consejo Universitario, were strong supporters of the gender studies program. The reluctant activists often said that to treat everyone equally was their contribution. One of the quietly subversive directors said she did address women's issues, but more than that she discouraged her mostly women students from marrying too young and encouraged them to stay in school. The director of the computer science department directly dealt with gender issues in her math classes and in seminars for engineering students. The dean of letters taught courses on feminist theory and literature. The gender studies program has recently implemented a master's degree. Negative responses to sexist language was a common form of resistance.

Because the causes of gender inequality were externalized to the society at large and women were typically located in units with high percentages of women, it should not be a surprise that these women had few suggestions for changing the university to make it a better place for women. These women were sufficiently divided in their views of the university that they did not constitute a conscious sub-culture and certainly not a subculture bent on revolutionizing the university. In fact, parallelling the close relationship of the Latin American university to the state, there was in some ways a blurring of lines between the external and institutional levels of culture with respect to women. Women did not leave their private lives at the door when they doned their professional hats.

Already viewing their lives as better than those of the majority of working women, it was difficult for them to envision improvement in the university. Rather than defining themselves as victims of a machista society in which the *doble jornada,* or double workload, weighed heavily on them, they described themselves as strong, capable women who had succeeded in that society. They agreed that changes in the university organization without concomitant changes in societal attitudes would be useless. Sociologist Lynne Phillips's conclusion about her own struggle to interpret Latin American women's responses to their situations seems valid here: "Looking for evidence of women's resistance only in articulated protests . . . I ignored the possibility that their resistance was to be found precisely in their self-constructions" (1991, 100). The response these women forged to their circumstances was to be successful themselves and, by doing so, to improve the lives of the women around them.

Notes

An earlier version of this chapter was presented at the Annual Meeting of the American Educational Research Association, New Orleans, Louisiana, April 8, 1994.

Agradezco muchisimo a Mirta González Suárez, Irma González y Dunnia Morales por haber hecho posible este estudio y también a las profesoras que participaron y compartieron sus vidas conmigo.

References

Aisenberg, N., and M. Harrington. 1988. *Women of academe: Outsiders in the sacred grove.* Amherst: University of Massachusetts Press.

Behar, R. 1993. *Translated woman: Crossing the boarder with Esperanza's story.* Boston: Beacon Press.

Blanco, G., L. Delgadillo, and Z. Méndez. 1989. *Análisis cuantitativo y cualitativo de la participación de la mujer en la Universidad de Costa Rica.* Ciudad Universitaria Rodrigo Facio: Universidad de Costa Rica.

Bonder, G. 1992. Altering sexual stereotypes through teacher training. In *Women and education in Latin America,* ed., N. Stromquist. Boulder, Colo.: Lynne Rienner Publishers.

La Gaceta Universitaria. 1992. University of Costa Rica.

García, A., and E. Gomáriz. 1989. *Mujeres centroamericanas. Tomo 1.* Facultad Latinoamericana de Ciencias Sociales, Consejo Superior Universitario de

Centroamérica, Universidad para la Paz.

González, M. March 1993. Personal communication.

Kuh, G., and E. Whitt. 1988. *The invisible tapestry: Culture in American colleges and universities.* ASHE-ERIC Higher Education Report No. 1. Washington, D.C.: Association for the Study of Higher Education.

Market Data. Costa Rica. 1992.

Méndez, Z., V.E. Davis, and S.L. Delgadillo. 1989. *Informe regional projecto de investigación análisis cuantitativo y cualitativo de la participación de la mujer en las universidades estatales centroamericanas confederadas al CSUCA: Fases cuantitativas.* San José: Universidad de Costa Rica.

Mendiola, H. 1992. Gender inequalities and the expansion of higher education in Costa Rica. In *Women and education in Latin America,* ed., N. Stromquist. Boulder, Colo.: Lynne Rienner Publishers.

Moore, K.M., and M.A.D. Sagaria. 1993. The situation of women in research universities in the United States. Reprinted In *Women in higher education,* eds., J. Glazer, E. Bensimon, and B. Townsend. Needham Heights, Mass.: Ginn Press.

Perreault, G. 1993. Contemporary feminist perspectives on women and higher education. Reprinted in *Women in higher education,* eds., J. Glazer, E. Bensimon, and B. Townsend. Needham Heights, Mass.: Ginn Press.

Phillips, L. 1991. Rural women in Latin America: Directions for future research. *Latin American Research Review* 25:101.

Stromquist, N. (ed.) 1992. *Women and education in Latin America: Knowledge, power, and change.* Boulder, Colo.: Lynne Rienner Publishers.

Tack, M., and C. Patitu. 1992. *Faculty job satisfaction: Women and minorities in peril.* ASHE-ERIC Higher Education Report No. 4. Washington, D.C.:The George Washington University School of Education and Human Development.

Tierney, W., and R. Rhoads. 1994. *Faculty socialization as cultural process: A mirror of institutional commitment.* ASHE-ERIC Higher Education Report No. 93–6. Washington, D.C.: The George Washington University, School of Education and Human Development.

Universidad de Costa Rica. 1992. Oficina de planificación universitaria. *Perfil del funcionario docente.*

Vicerrectoría de Docencia. 1990. *Universidad de Costa Rica.* Ciudad Universitaria Rodrigo Facio: Universidad de Costa Rica.

Chapter Seven
The Political Economy
of Entrepreneurial Culture
in Higher Education
Policies toward Foreign Students in Australia
and the United States

Gary Rhoades and Don Smart

Although the root word is French, "entrepreneur(ial)" is a concept
that in comparative higher education is generally attached to the
United States. U.S. higher education has been cast as the preeminent example of a "market-driven" system, with a large private sector and a weak—by European standards—Department of Education (Ben-David and Zloczower 1962; Clark 1983; Geiger 1986;
Levy 1986; Trow 1984). Faculty, presidents, and institutions have
been described as entrepreneurial, and becoming more so in recent
years (Etzkowitz 1983; Fairweather 1988). In this chapter, however,
we challenge the portrayal of U.S. higher education as the exemplar
of entrepreneurial culture, arguing that, at least in one policy arena,
Australian higher education manifests a very entrepreneurial culture, and the United States does not.

Much of the recent literature on entrepreneurialism in higher
education focuses on academic science. U.S. universities now hold
patents, urge faculty to commercialize knowledge, transfer technology to private enterprise, and form partnerships with business (Olivas
1992; Peters and Fusfeld 1982; Rhoades and Slaughter 1991; Cote
and Cote 1993). Made possible by changes in federal and state laws
(Slaughter and Rhoades 1993, 1994), such activities are promoted
as a means to increase the global economic competitiveness of the
United States, expressing cultural norms that represent a shift from
traditional academic norms. As countries increasingly become involved in regional trading blocs as a way of positioning themselves
in the global economy, there are implications for the flow not just of
knowledge and capital but of students and faculty. As with academic
science, efforts to increase or control the flow of students represent a
shift away from traditional academic norms. Relatively little schol-

arly attention has been directed to entrepreneurialism in recruiting new students,[1] particularly international ones. In this chapter, we focus on the cultural underpinnings of policies toward international students in the United States and Australia.

Historically the social role of higher education, in general, in these two countries has been at variance. In the United States, higher education has provided more open, broad-based access than has Australian higher education, enrolling and graduating considerably larger percentages of the age cohort. If there has been considerable dispute as to whether such access has translated into upward mobility and enhanced status attainment, both parties to the debate believe that higher education's role is to contribute to democratizing the social distribution of wealth in society. By contrast, the social role of Australian universities in the past was to reproduce and legitimate a social and cultural elite. It is only in recent decades that higher education in Australia has come to play a broader function of training and certifying large numbers of students for occupations that will afford some measure of upward mobility. As we shall suggest, that social role is shifting now in both countries with the globalization of the economy and the pressures accompanying each country's position in that economy. The social role of higher education in both countries has become more explicitly linked than before to national corporate capital's globally competitive position.

Capitalism now is more than a global economic system: it is a culture that cuts across national boundaries. Its effect on and presence in higher education is evident in a variety of values, social structures, relations, and conceptions. For example, historically there have been considerable differences between the United States and Australia in terms of their images of students. Compared to the United States, where students have often been cast as individuals from various socioeconomic backgrounds competing to move up the occupational ladder, in Australia they have been seen more as members of a select group being groomed to maintain their elite position. In both countries, however, students have increasingly become commodified as higher education has become more integrated into a global capitalist system. The internal tensions and contradictions embedded in that system have, as we shall see, played out in different ways in the countries. In other words, the social and cultural underpinnings of higher education have been changing, moving perhaps along different paths, but in a similar direction. In language and policy regarding foreign students, the entrepreneurial path, in its earliest and clearest forms, is more apparent in Australia.

We compare the United States and Australia in the 1980s, focusing on public discussions and policies at the national, state, and institutional levels regarding foreign students in higher education. We analyze primary documents at the national level and rely upon secondary sources to discuss state and institutional policies. In Australia, the choice of primary documents is relatively easy given the centralization of higher education and federal policy—the main sources are Dawkins's Green and White Papers. By contrast, the United States lacks a single, clear, identifiable policy regarding foreign students. Given the policy arenas in which foreign students are discussed, we examine National Science Foundation annual reports (the NSF is responsible for scientific workforce issues) and congressional hearings related to workforce and immigration policy. Exploring the language and narratives of policy discourse, we find that the approach to foreign students in Australia shifted in the 1980s from subsidizing foreign students as part of foreign aid policy to characterizing them as products in the global market and charging them fees at full cost plus a profit margin in order to redress the country's (im)balance of trade. Federal policies in Australia have encouraged universities to be entrepreneurial by recruiting overseas students. In the United States, foreign students have been an issue in federal scientific, labor, and immigration policy, discussed in terms of economic dependency, domestic human resources, and national security. In U.S. states, foreign students are seen as part of a cheap labor force, and parochial hostility (and racism) toward low-status foreign workers plays out in policies requiring foreign teaching assistants to demonstrate oral English proficiency.

Our findings contradict functionalism, the prevailing perspective in comparative higher education, which is characterized by the Parsonian tendency of casting the United States as the most advanced, functionally well-adapted society in the world. That may play out systemically and economically, with higher education being marked more by market values and mechanisms than is the case elsewhere (Geiger 1986; Trow 1984), or politically and normatively, through organizational and professional structures (Ben-David and Zloczower 1962; Clark 1983). In either case, functionalists would predict that U.S. higher education would be the most entrepreneurial, given the cultural, economic, and political patterns of the country and of the higher education system.

Our findings are in many ways consistent with those of neo-Marxist scholars who point to a commercialization of (higher) education as it is enlisted in the service of economic competitiveness, with its research, teaching, and service becoming commodities, corresponding to the products and needs of corporate capital (Barrow 1990; Bowles and Gintis 1976; Dickson 1984; Slaughter 1990). Such commercialization has a cultural expression in the way students are portrayed but says little about "entrepreneurialism." Australia and the United States *both* reveal commodification of education and students by global capitalist relations. Foreign students in both countries are regarded in terms of their contribution to the nation's position in the global economy. If in Australia foreign students are seen as trade commodities, in the United States they are seen as cheap, skilled labor in an international market for science and engineering workers. The largest numbers of foreign students are in commercially relevant, high-tech fields central to global economic relations—business, engineering, and the sciences. In Australia, 45.5, 10.4, and 15% of foreign undergraduates and 23.7, 13.1, and 21.3% of graduate students are in these three areas; in the United States, the numbers are 26.6, 15.1, and 13% of undergraduates, and 14.5, 22.7, and 25.3% of graduates respectively (DEET 1993; IIE 1992).[2]

The grand narratives provided by neo-Marxists may not predict or explain the discourse and policies being renegotiated globally and nationally, in all their contested, contradictory complexity. Nevertheless, we believe that macropolitical patterns of military, political, and economic domination and of higher education structures impact and are articulated in cultural patterns of belief and social policy. Certainly there are variations in the way these patterns are worked out in specific policies and practices. Yet the grand narrative of education's increased commodification in a network of capitalist, global economic relations frames such variations. How can this be in a "postmodern" world? Because the most important "post" is the post–Cold War. With the dissolution of the Soviet empire, capitalist reforms in the Communist world, and patterns of privatization in European social democracies, there is no clear alternative to capitalism in this "postmodern" world. Of course, there are different patterns of capitalism and different positions in the global capitalist stratification system. Herein lies part of the key to the different proclivity for entrepreneurial activity in Australia and the United States.

Structural Characteristics

In the next section of the chapter, we discuss some of the general structural characteristics of Australia and the United States, considering their expected influence on patterns of entrepreneurialism in higher education. Ensuing sections discuss each country in more detail, first providing a short overview and then discussing policies toward foreign students at the national, state, and institutional level. We then offer some general conclusions.

General economic malaise in Australia and the United States in the 1980s has led both to reorient higher education toward business, emphasizing its role in reinvigorating the nation's economy. Governments throughout the world have increasingly emphasized higher education's role in (inter)national and state economies and are establishing policies accordingly.[3] There is variation in what technologies, sciences, and industries are identified as critical and in the balance of emphasis on research and training. But the general theme of higher education being a catalyst in global economic competitiveness and of being steered accordingly is prominent and pervasive. In both Australia and the United States, higher education has been encouraged to become not just more efficient but more entrepreneurial, to generate its own revenues and enhance its country's economic vitality. Thus, one would expect both countries to have adopted entrepreneurial policies toward international students.

Australia's political culture and its state socialist structures would lead one to expect U.S. higher education to be more entrepreneurial. In contrast to the United States, the funding of Australian higher education is highly centralized—virtually all university funding comes from the federal government. Until 1987 there were no private universities in Australia, in marked contrast to the strong private sector in the United States. Business is considerably weaker in Australia, which lacks the large, powerful multinational, corporate class of the United States. Australia has a strong Labor party that came to power at the federal level in the 1980s, whereas United States administrations in the 1980s were conservative Republican. Higher education politics is more centralized in Australia, with its national faculty unions and relatively weak states, whereas state, system, and institutional levels of decision making are embedded in the politics and industrial relations of United States higher education. Finally, culturally the United States is marked more by a laissez-faire political culture that is suspicious of the state and that valorizes private institutions.

Australia and the United States also have quite different positions in the world economy and, relatedly, in the foreign student market. Australia's lesser significance as a world power has historically led to a search for military and economic allies. Australia has always looked "overseas," especially to the United Kingdom, Europe, and the United States for economic and cultural support and models. Its traditional suspicion of Asia, from which it stood apart, was reflected in xenophobic fears of invasion from the north ("yellow peril") and in a discriminatory ("White Australia") immigration policy that was abandoned only in the 1950s. Recently Australia has begun to see its destiny as economically and geographically tied to the Asia-Pacific region. In fact, there has been anxiety about the Asian "tiger" economies, an oft-expressed concern that unless it competes more effectively with the emerging economies of the region, Australia will become the "white trash" of Asia.

Despite its significance as a world power, and partly because of its past dominance, the United States's view of the world is similarly anxiety ridden. In the post–World War II era, the United States became the prominent world military power, extending its role of policeman from Latin America to the world. It was intent on fighting Communism and assisting other nations' efforts to cast off colonial yokes. At the same time, U.S. business gained global dominance in a form of economic (and cultural) imperialism. The United States also has been marked by xenophobic views of the East ("yellow journalism") and fears of invasion by immigrants from the South, expressed in state and national policies and laws, from immigration to language (e.g., "English only" state laws). The United States is threatened by emergent economies in the "Pacific Rim." Seeing its position in the world economy declining, the United States has built a regional trading bloc (the North American Free Trade Agreement) and developed policies aimed at creating economic monopolies at home to maintain competitive dominance in the global economy.

Foreign student demand for higher education is related to the country's position in the "knowledge network" of the dominant industrialized societies (Altbach 1989), which is intertwined with other structures of power and resources. Other countries are "scientifically dependent" on the West in general and on the United States in particular, although that may change.[4] Thus, the foreign student body in the United States is more graduate level (48%), whereas in Australia it is overwhelmingly undergraduate (more than 75%). That may, in part, account for different policies toward foreign students: with increased credentialing throughout the world, undergraduates may be more likely to be characterized as commodities and revenues, whereas graduate students are more likely to be considered a source of skilled labor.

The global economic, military, and cultural positions of the United States make it more probable that foreign students would want to study in American universities than in Australian ones. Australia has some advantages in relation to Asia, yet it is still more likely than the United States to actively recruit students from this area. For example, most OECD countries have national funding arrangements to recruit Chinese students: the United States is "so popular with Chinese students that there is no need for a national support program" (Altbach and Selveratnam 1989, 53). Despite the lack of a national program, there are more than eight times as many Chinese students in the United States as in Australia (IIE 1992; Smart and Ang 1993)—about the same as the difference between the countries in the total number of foreign students and of students generally.

Entrepreneurialism, Australian Style

Between 1988 and 1991, Australian higher education underwent perhaps the most radical restructuring in its history, initiated by a socialist Federal Labor government intent on "turning around" Australia's serious international debt and its major economic problems (Birch and Smart 1989). In 1987 John Dawkins (previously minister for trade) was appointed Minister for Employment, Education, and Training (DEET). As minister for trade, Dawkins advocated making Australia the "Clever Country," focusing on high technology and exports and developing a high-skill economy more integrated with Asia and based on an "export culture" (Marginson 1993). He brought those narratives to his new portfolio, redefining higher education's purposes accordingly. Using the political influence of ministerial discussion and policy papers and the federal control of higher education finance as a lever, Dawkins restructured higher education. Organizationally this meant abolishing the "binary" distinction between universities and colleges, creating a national, unitary system of thirty-nine universities (reduced from seventy-one institutions, through mergers). It also involved steering higher education research and training to areas of national need and making the system more competitive. His *Green Paper* (1987) set the terms of discussion, stressing economic imperatives. Ultimately, Dawkins imposed national economic and research priorities and withdrew a portion of universities' operating grants to create an Australian Research Council that funded competitive grants to individual researchers.[5] He pressured institutions to expand degree output, especially in areas of "national economic need" (business, accounting, engineering, and computing), and obliged them to develop teaching and research management plans to be negotiated annually with his department as the basis for operating grants.

Foreign student policy was directly implicated in this higher education policy context. In fact, it was a central part of governmental efforts to make higher education more entrepreneurial contributors to the economy. Institutions were pressured to generate external financial support by actively recruiting foreign students on a full cost (plus profit margin) tuition basis.

Australia's Foreign Student Policy: From "Aid" to "Trade"

From the 1950s through to 1986, Australia's foreign student policy was one of benevolence, prompted by a "foreign aid" stance. Commencing with the Colombo Plan in the 1950s, Australia, like other Commonwealth countries, brought relatively small numbers of (often poor) students from underdeveloped (mainly Asian and African) countries to Australia for a free education as part of its foreign aid contribution. In the early 1980s, "most foreign students . . . came from Asian families with relatively low incomes by Australian standards and relatively low levels of educational attainment" (Chandler 1989). Most such students were selected by their home governments, and many were incapable of privately paying for their own studies. A small number of "private" foreign students originally paid the same government-subsidized tuition as Australian students (when tuition fees were abolished in 1973 for all students, a cap was placed on private-subsidized students). Policy was shaped politically by the Commonwealth and culturally by a colonial language and tradition of obligation (and control), reflecting a British perspective of noblesse oblige and historical links of empire. Accordingly, the social role or function of Australian higher education vis-à-vis international students was defined by its membership in the Commonwealth, by British colonialism.

Britain's imposition in 1979 of full-cost fees for foreign students led to an increased flow of foreign students in the "private-subsidized" category to Australia, which was seen as a cheap alternative—a niche it initially rejected. That same year, responding to concerns about immigration, Fraser's Liberal government set an Overseas Student Charge for private foreign students (Smart 1988), who still grew in numbers, exceeding "foreign aid" (government-sponsored) students. In this context, two committees of inquiry were created in 1982 to address overseas student policy and the aid program. In 1984 the newly elected Hawke Labor government received these committees' conflicting recommendations, which articulated the split and eventual shift in language, rationale, and storyline underlying foreign student policy. The Goldring Committee (1984), chaired by an academic, expressed the traditional values of obligation and cultural understanding and advocated an approach based on providing aid to students. The Committee explicitly rejected a market approach, citing education is not a commodity to be bought and sold. By contrast, the Jackson Committee (1984, 93–94) (chaired by a prominent business leader) stressed that education for foreign students should be developed as "an 'export' industry," and suggested that "institutions . . . be encouraged to compete for students and funds." Calling for the recruitment—without quotas—of foreign students on a full-cost ("trade") tuition basis (Throsby 1985), the Jackson Committee (1984, 93–94) offered stories of economic benefits to be gained from overseas students, including jobs directly and indirectly incurred from educational expansion.[6] The policy shift was a cultural shift, and a shift in the social definition and function of higher education.

The development of an education "export industry," particularly in the graduate field, would benefit the economy directly, and through research it would be linked to the "high tech" and "new tech" industries which Australia so strongly wishes to develop. (Jackson Committee, 93–94)

Following the committee reports and amidst mounting concern about Australia's deteriorating "balance of trade" and escalating international debt, an Australian Government Education Mission was dispatched to Southeast Asia by then Trade Minister Dawkins with the aim of assessing the "export potential" of education services. It concluded that there was untapped potential: Dawkins claimed that exports from education could soon be as valuable as those from manufacturing (Smart 1988).

In 1985 the socialist Hawke Labor government introduced a new full-fee program for foreign students that offered a major incentive for Australia's educational institutions to recruit private foreign students. Fees for such students, unlike for Australians, would go directly to the institution to fund capital expenditures and other costs incurred by serving this population. There was no quota on numbers, and fees were on a full-cost recovery—plus profit margin—basis. In universities, the profit margins were significant, varying by field: 36% in engineering and computer science and 82% in business studies (Marginson 1993). The economic and trade basis of the policy changes were evident in Dawkins's *Green* and *White Papers* in 1987 and 1988. The papers opened by stressing the need for Australia to consider its position in the international economy and discussed overseas students and the "international demand" for Australian higher education courses under the heading of "Commercial Activities." In 1988 the government announced the phasing out of the private subsidized category of students and indicated that although the foreign aid program was to continue, the principal policy was to market services to full-cost recovery students. A new narrative prevailed.

Australia could no longer see itself so much as a donor of education and training services to developing countries, a benefactor, but more as a partner where mutual benefits . . . is the desired outcome. (NBEET 1990, 2)

The global economy's pressure overrode colonial obligations. The language and story of education shifted from servicing poor students and "developing" the Third World to educational services being trade commodities, an industry's product to be sold to Third-World customers at expensive prices.

The outcomes of the policy shift have been dramatic, particularly for universities. Between 1987 and 1992, Australia's full-fee foreign students increased from 1,019 to 30,296, accounting in 1992 for 76.7% of all overseas students (DEET 1993). In 1990, estimates of the Higher Education Council were that higher education institutions in Australia had the potential to gain a 20% market share of the $10 billion global trade in educational services. In 1993, foreign students spent $1.7 billion in Australia, making education one of Australia's major export earners (*The Weekend Australian,* July 30–31, 1994). "By 1991, six higher education institutions were listed amongst Australia's top 500 exporters" (Marginson 1993, 187).

However, the "export" approach is proving politically problematic in at least two ways. First, foreign students and governments routinely protest that Australia should not be "exploiting" foreign students by charging them a profit-based tuition fee substantially higher than Australian students' fees. Such opposition has heightened in the 1990s with the collapse of many private colleges established to teach English and business to overseas students.

In most cases, students were left with neither fees nor tuition. It has been estimated that the commonwealth government spent about $35 million on refunds to overseas students up to March 1991. In November 1990, Dawkins introduced mandatory registration procedures for a four year period, but the damage had been done. (Marginson 1993, 188)

A second problem is that as long as the Australian government has performance-based entry quotas on local student admission to Australia's universities, there will be claims that Australian students are being discriminated against. In 1987 and 1988, 20,000 qualified Australian students were denied places in the universities of their choice (Chandler 1989). The government claims that because of the full-fee charge, foreign students are "add-ons" who do not take university places away from Australian students. Recently there has been a proposal to allow Australian students, beyond the quota, to be enrolled by paying full fees. Education would be for sale, raising other equity issues.

State Policy: Low-Key Reactions to and Modeling of Federal Policy

It is primarily the federal government that sets foreign student policy and generates the associated bureaucracy. As foreign student numbers have escalated, so too has the federal Department of Education's International Division, the entrepreneurial International Development Program in Canberra (a semigovernment organization representing all Australian universities), and Austrade (the Australian Trade Commission), which has an Education and Training Unit. These bureaucracies work with campuses—which pay client service fees—in recruiting overseas students. For the most part, state governments have kept a relatively low profile and have reacted to or emulated federal policy. Many states have been forced by popular opinion and federal government pressure to legislate guarantees protecting foreign students' interests in the event of the financial collapse and closure of private colleges. Several states have modeled their entrepreneurial efforts on those of the federal government. In Western Australia (WA), the state government quickly recognized the "export income" opportunities of attracting foreign students and established education offices (operated by the Department of State Development) in various overseas sites, including Hong Kong and Singapore, to recruit and advise prospective students. The WA Department of Education now has its own Overseas Student Section, and a State Parliamentary Committee of Inquiry has been appointed to make recommendations on foreign student policy developments. The Queensland state government has initiated similar activities, and Victoria's state government has commissioners in various Western countries promoting its education and other export industries. In 1989 the New South Wales state government established an Education Exports Advisory Council to "develop strategies to stimulate the marketing of education services to overseas students" (Smart and Ang 1993, 120).

Institutional Policy: Entrepreneurial Response to Government Stimulus

Many, perhaps most, universities responded rapidly to Dawkins's blunt challenge to get out and recruit foreign students (Smart and Ang 1993). With the government's stimulus, universities have entrepreneurially initiated marketing and recruiting strategies for foreign students. Slow-moving public-sector institutions with few apparent market instincts or skills have created international offices, adopted sophisticated and aggressive recruitment strategies for the Asian region, and provided large incentives for academic departments to recruit foreign students.

Dawkins's policy provided universities the incentive and opportunity to hire new staff and build new buildings with the profit margin provided in the full-fees structure. At the University of New South Wales, which is one of the top "exporters" of higher education services,

there has been an injection of capital funds into the educational system which was virtually bereft of capital funds . . . Full fee overseas students will probably rescue the national capital investment in universities. The University of New South Wales alone will probably accumulate capital in excess of $3 million annually from fees. Prior to this regular capital inflow . . . it had been common to wait a decade for significant capital grants. (Industry Commission 1991, 152)

Foreign students have been a capital windfall for some institutions.

Moreover, foreign students' fee structure strengthened an on-campus constituency that would support the government's policy. The revenue-driven model of foreign student policy in Australia has given increased salience and centrality to international student offices on university campuses. Such offices are generally luxuriously appointed, located within arm's reach of the university's chief executive officer (vice chancellor), and have generous operating budgets and discretionary funds for marketing, travel, recruitment, and public relations. Furthermore, the heads of the international offices and their recruiting plans and activities are typically closely monitored and sometimes even shaped by their vice chancellors. The reasons are clear. For many Australian universities, foreign students' tuition constitutes the biggest single source of income after the federal government's operating grant. For example, Murdoch University, which ranks fourth nationally in terms of its percentage of overseas students (13.4%), had an operating budget of approximately $62 million (U.S. dollars) in 1994. Almost $9 million of this (nearly 15%) was contributed by foreign student fees. More important, the monies from foreign student fees represent perhaps the most discretionary component of the entire budget. No wonder vice chancellors wish to keep their fingers on the pulse of foreign student policy on their campuses and nationally. Although Murdoch is at the high end of the market in foreign student numbers, there are many institutions with more than 7.5% of their students from overseas, including Curtin University of Technology, Monash University, the University of Melbourne, and the University of New South Wales (Marginson 1993).

A key response of universities is the adoption of incentive policies that ensured that those academic departments that recruited foreign students received the lion's share of the full-cost tuition—in some cases, up to 70%. The Industry Commission established by the government to evaluate the higher education "export industry" stressed that universities would need to provide such departmental-level incentives if Australia was to maximize recruitment (Industry Commission 1991, 157–158). Perhaps due to relatively small campus bureaucracies, universities have largely done just that.

The introduction of full-cost-recovery tuition for foreign students has had an impact on institutions that goes beyond those students and the revenues they generate. First, it has been a powerful political lever and rationale for the Hawke Labor government's reintroduction of tuition for Australian students in 1993. Second, foreign student policy has affected the quality of Australian higher education, or the perception of it, in contradictory ways. Universities have responded positively to growing general demands for enhanced teaching quality and support services. That has involved developing a more service-oriented culture on campuses. Foreign students have felt entitled as "full-fee clients" to make such demands. The current promotion of quality and accountability in universities owes something to foreign students' activism and contribution to creating more of a "marketplace" mentality in Australian higher education. The need to market courses and recruit foreign students has forced some Australian academics to review their traditional perspective of students as "captive clients" who must take whatever is "dished up" to them. Yet the market mentality has also adversely affected foreigners' view of Australian higher education's quality. For example, a study in Singapore (Laurie 1992, 42–44) found, "Singaporeans hold widely to the view that we treat overseas students as a 'money-making racket'; their reverence for education clashes with our treatment of it as a commodity item." Moreover, the race for and influx of overseas students may have adversely affected courses' quality and a cultural emphasis on quality in education, in part because faculty adjust grading practices and in part because of the language limitations of the students. In any case, the culture and social role of Australian higher education has substantially shifted, and a surprisingly entrepreneurial culture has emerged.

World Trade, Immigration, and Scientific Labor in a "Free Trade" United States

In the United States, as in Australia, the 1980s have witnessed heightened fears about America's position in the global economy. The growing imbalance of trade and international challenges to and declines in key American industries have led to restructuring, layoffs, and increased unemployment. Governmental deficits at the national and state level and rising costs of health care and corrections led first to declining increases in state allocations to higher education and then to absolute declines for the first time in fifty years. In response to such economic pressures and patterns, colleges and universities in the last six years have been engaged in restructuring. Unlike Australia, that process has been steered not by the federal government, which lacks the direct financial control of higher education, but by institutions and states. Reagan's and Bush's secretaries of education were vocal advocates of privatization, cost containment, quality, and basic values. Most important for higher education, the administrations undertook massive military buildups with a related focus on science and engineering; they also promoted the growth of a high-technology, high-skill economy, urging universities to strengthen ties to business and contribute to local economic growth and global economic competitiveness. The federal and state push for entrepreneurialism has been directed more at research activities than at teaching, and at pursuing niches in student markets. Indeed, some of the strongest criticism of higher education by education secretaries and national figures such as Ernest Boyer (1987) of the Carnegie Foundation has been that institutions have been too entrepreneurial with regard to students, that they have focused more on marketing and recruitment and on securing federal student loan monies than on graduating students and providing them with a good education. In contrast to Australia, foreign students have not figured prominently in policy deliberations about restructuring or entrepreneurialism.

Foreign students are addressed in workforce and immigration policy in relation to higher education. At all policy levels, the focus is on graduate students, as skilled labor in key scientific fields or as teaching assistants. In contrast to the broader culture surrounding undergraduate students, the culture in regards to graduate students is one less of increasing opportunity than of increasing opportunism. There are a combination of conflicting pushes to reduce dependency on foreign students in science and engineering and yet to encourage their immigration given that dependency, along with protectionist, racist reactions to them. Foreign students are seen as cheap, necessary labor, but also as problematic.

National Policy: Foreign Students as Skilled Labor, Immigrants, and as a Threat

At one time, foreign exchange and aid perspectives drove federal policy toward foreign students. Although in some regards, similar to aid-based policies in Australia, they were linked to a culture (and its attendant understanding of higher education's social role) defined not by the Commonwealth but by the aim of promoting United States and international interests in the context of a Cold War. By the 1980s the federal government began to view foreign students as skilled labor, immigrants, and threats to domestic strength. The policy discourse expressed contradictory tendencies to rely upon foreign students in science and engineering, to accord them special treatment as skilled labor immigrants, yet to resent the impact they had on wages and to fear the country's dependency on them.

The aims of cultural and political exchange were evident in the U.S. Information and Exchange Act of 1948, which promoted student exchanges to increase "mutual understanding between the people of the United States and the people of other countries" (ACE 1982, 26), and in the Mutual Education and Cultural Exchanges Act of 1961, which "promote[d] international cooperation for educational and cultural advancement" through student and other exchanges that would "strengthen the ties which unite us with other nations" (ACE 1982, 27). The aim of foreign aid, evident in the Foreign Assistance Act of 1961 (enabling the Agency for International Development—AID), saw training and sponsorship of foreign students in more politically focused terms—concentrating on "less developed friendly countries"—as a way of promoting *other* countries' economic development and our national interest. By the early 1980s, the shift to a more short-term perspective of foreign policy was evident in "scholarship diplomacy," which linked scholarships to Cold War diplomacy:

The U.S. Federal Government has recently created a number of new scholarship programmes, particularly for students from Central America, and the Caribbean and Latin American Scholarship Program (CLASP) and a new Developing Countries Scholarship Act has been proposed in Congress. This reflects growing awareness of the importance of "scholarship diplomacy," since a report to Congress by the General Accounting Office (1984) revealed that the Soviet Union was financing 10 to 12 times as many students from developing countries as the U.S.A. (Woodhall 1987, 122)

Of course, investment in the scholarship race did not equal that in the arms race, nor was it sustained throughout the 1980s. Moreover, the noblesse oblige that marked Australian foreign student policy prior to 1986 was less evident in the United States. In 1982 a higher percentage of foreign freshman than of U.S. students had college educated fathers (60% versus 51.2%) and fathers with graduate degrees (30.8% versus 15.4%). "It appears that American colleges are increasingly educating the children of the upper classes of other nations" (Solmon and Young 1987, 8). Moreover, the federal government sponsors a very small proportion of foreign students, primarily through the Fulbright and AID foreign student programs, support for which declined in the late 1970s and 1980s. In 1982 the U.S. government supported only about 2% of foreign students in the United States, compared to 5% in 1977 (ACE 1982, 28).

In the mid-1980s, a narrative emerged in national policy discourse that suggested another cultural dimension of the United States not unrelated to the Cold War—a sense of decreased economic strength and a fear of economic dependency. A storyline about "the foreign student problem" emerged. There are variations on and dissonant dimensions to this theme. But alarm about dependence on foreign students translated into policies to increase U.S. students' entry into science and engineering rather than into quotas for foreign students.

In the 1986 authorization hearings for NSF before the U.S. House, there are several references to foreign students, virtually always to the problem of inadequate numbers of American students pursuing graduate degrees in science and engineering. The theme is of "dependency," highlighted by NSF's director.

Increasingly, we are dependent on foreign nationals for new PhDs in engineering and in mathematics and physics, the most critical disciplines of a technological society . . . [O]ur overdependence on foreign citizens as a resource that vital should give us cause for concern. We have no control over that resource. It can stop at any minute, as happened a few years ago with respect to Iran, as an example. (NSF Authorization 1986, 10)

The director invokes a language of dependency throughout that can be read in geopolitical (Iran's revolution and taking of U.S. hostages) and economic (the West's energy and economic dependency on Middle Eastern oil) terms. Discourse about science and engineering "manpower" uses the language of "pipelines," the foreign "flows" over which we have no control and that can "dry up," and the domestic flows of which must be "pump primed." An MIT physics professor, who conducted NSF's physic's survey, offers a more explicitly military storyline:

We are heavily dependent on foreign scientific manpower for physics in this country. This is an obvious cause for concern, particularly because these foreign scientists are ineligible to participate in DoD research. (NSF Authorization 1986, 67)

Again, there is a fusion (pardon the pun) of economic/military concerns. The military and technology "national security" narrative is more prominent in a science policy task force report, "Science Support by the Department of Defense."

Over the years, some military officials have complained that the U.S. educational system is not training sufficient numbers of scientific and technically literate generalists and specialists. They contend that this will ultimately jeopardize not only our potential high technology trade, but also our national security. . . . Foreign engineering Ph.D.s even if they remain in the U.S., generally cannot obtain U.S. security clearances and are thus not available for direct DoD employment. . . . [F]oreign doctoral students comprise about 50 percent or more of the doctoral students population in defense related engineering areas . . . (Task Force on Science Policy 1986, 365–366)

Hearings in 1986 reauthorizing the Defense Advanced Research Projects Agency (DARPA) of DoD highlight tensions surrounding dependency on foreign students. The DARPA director noted that in fiscal years 1984–86, DARPA was doubling the number of graduate students supported on research programs in universities. A congressman asked, "Are we training Americans?" The director assured him that the bulk of the support is for U.S. graduate students, except where there is a special interest that can be served by support of foreign students. In 1990 the same issue came up in response to that DARPA director's point that his agency supports nearly half the graduate students in the United States in computer science. Some Congresspersons articulated the language of concerned taxpayers: we should not "subsidize" foreigners.

Given the push of Reagan and Congress to shift the burden of financing higher education to students by altering the balance of grants and loans, and given the big increase in numbers of foreign students (over 100% from 1970 to 1980), why was there no proposal similar to Australia's full-cost recovery policy? The answer is in the reliance of institutions, fields, and science agencies on foreign students. Agency officials and higher education lobbyists tell a tale of dependency, but precisely because of that dependency they do not call for restrictions on foreign students; instead they seek to stimulate an increase of U.S. students in science and engineering.[7] Nevertheless, the annual reports of NSF from 1986 to 1990 foreshadow concern about immigration trends and possibilities.

Questions have been raised among science and technology policy officials as to whether the possible return of foreign specialists to their native countries could pose a threat to the long-term competitiveness of U.S. industries. (NSF 1986, 35)

Discourse surrounding immigration policy reveals another tension in national policy: federal officials pose the threat first of restrictions on foreign students staying in the United States to work and then of their repatriation, whereas the xenophobic, racist sentiment of the Congress and the country speak to a threat of being overrun by immigrants, legal and illegal. In 1986 a report of the Office of Technology Assessment to a congressional Task Force on Science Policy noted disagreement about whether more foreign students should be allowed to stay on to work in the United States. The administration and universities thought they should stay. Congress and professional associations thought not, with the latter complaining about foreigners' negative impact on professional wages because they are willing to work for less than U.S. natives. In later years, an increase in the numbers of foreign students returning home was cast as "the problem." In a 1989 congressional hearing, "Stimulating Investment in R & D," representatives of the Association of Graduate Schools and the Association of American Universities suggested that increasing percentages of foreign degree recipients will return home due to incentives and changing circumstances in those countries—actions by the Korean and Chinese governments are cited in particular. Despite concerns about "importing talent" and "failing to develop our own intellectual resources," by 1990 there was a successful push to alter the emphasis of immigration policy, prioritizing human capital, "skill-based" criteria (job skills in needed areas) over humanitarian, "family-based" ones (refugees, uniting families). At a congressional hearing on "Increasing U.S. Scientific Manpower [*sic*]," a representative of the National Institutes of Health articulated the policy shift and its rationale:

When current U.S. immigration policy was framed in 1965, the human resource concerns I have reviewed this morning did not exist. Immigration streams were relatively low and had little effect on the nation's labor market. . . . Mr. Chairman, I believe that without impeding the humanitarian intent of our current policy, we can enhance this nation's competitiveness and accelerate advances in scientific research through selective reforms in our immigration policy. Adoption of a more skill-based immigration policy for professionals whose skills are in short supply would improve the ability of government, academia and industry to meet their manpower needs. Present immigration laws limit our ability to recruit and retain talented scientists. ("Increasing U.S. Scientific Manpower" 1990, 34–35)

The immigration legislation passed, in large part in the form lobbied for by universities and agencies. Congresspersons' efforts to append a tax on foreign students, with the monies being used for U.S. students, ultimately failed.

Foreign students, then, are addressed at the national level primarily in terms of their impact on the graduate labor market and skilled workforce. In the United States, foreign graduate students are seen by some as valuable human capital and by others as "foreigners" who are a threat to our self-sufficiency, who should not be subsidized, and who are cheap labor that will depress wages. There is little concern with foreign undergraduates, who constitute only 3 to 4 percent of degrees in natural science and engineering.

State Policy: Students as Costs; Foreign Students as Low-Quality Teachers[8]

Higher education and students are seen by state legislators as costs. Most states will not fully bear the costs of nonresidents—that explains differential tuitions for in- and out-of-state students. As costs rise, so do demands for accountability and for evidence of quality. So, too, has emerged a neoconservative political culture of increased questioning of the efficiency, effectiveness, and necessity of public institutions and of social welfare functions of the state. State legislatures and boards have criticized universities' focus on research and called for more attention to and greater faculty involvement in undergraduate education. In the 1980s, foreign students have figured in these issues in terms of residency rules and teaching quality. Both sets of policies, residency rules and teaching quality, are racist. Neither is an entrepreneurial effort to attract foreign students.

Standard state policy, supported by legal precedent (Olivas 1988), is to have differential tuition for in- and out-of-state students, the latter bearing a much higher share of their education's costs. Nonresidents may pay as much as ten times higher tuition than do residents. Such policies reflect state "taxpayers" unwillingness to "subsidize" out-of-state students whose parents have not paid taxes in the state. The language emphasizes costs. For the most part, in terms of tuition, foreign students pay the same as out-of-state students (i.e., as nonresidents).[9] Some states have "good neighbor" agreements allowing students from contiguous states to pay in-state tuition and vice versa. Reciprocity arrangements have also been negotiated by border states such as Arizona and Texas with neighboring states of other countries. Moreover, many states provide exemptions, exceptions, and waivers to residency requirements to various categories of people, including "resident aliens," and thus small numbers of foreign students pay in-state tuition (Olivas 1988). In any case, the aim is not to generate new revenues from foreign students; the rationales and perspectives underlying such arrangements are aimed instead at reducing higher education costs for state residents (e.g., those going to neighboring states) and at promoting mutual benefits of exchange—educational, cultural, and broad, long-term economic.

Yet many states violate law about "resident aliens" that holds states cannot discriminate by "defining a disfavored group as nonresident" and making them pay out-of-state or differential tuition (Olivas 1986, 21).[10]

Legislators often guard their borders ferociously. This tendency is most pronounced in legislative treatment of alienage, where states may exceed their constitutional authority and where foreign policy implications arise. . . . [I]n a recent legislative session in one state, the legislature ignored the attorney general's opinion . . . and failed to correct a state-wide practice concerning resident aliens—even though the United States Supreme Court had definitively ruled on the practice and struck it down three years earlier. A recent study found that nineteen states were not in compliance with the Court's ruling, and seven additional states had major institutions with similarly discredited practices. (Olivas 1988, 270)

Undocumented aliens won a case against the University of California, which required them to pay nonresident tuition and fees despite the fact that they had been residents in California for from three to eleven years (Olivas 1986). Such illegal treatment of foreign students is in many cases connected to the growth in the 1980s of anti-immigrant, racist, and nativistic social movements.[11] It is also sometimes linked to national foreign policy developments.

[I]n the wake of the Iranian disturbances of 1979, a few legislators in about a dozen states introduced various measures to charge foreign students in state-supported institutions significantly increased rates of tuition. Those measures died within the course of the legislative sessions. . . . (ACE 1982, 36)

Policies and practices in the United States about residency and "aliens" offers little evidence of economic or entrepreneurial orientations; rather, they are racist, reactionary efforts to disadvantage, punish, or keep out certain "foreigners."

Throughout the 1980s, the most prominent state public policy development related to foreign students was the promulgation of provisions by legislatures and state boards regarding the oral English proficiency of foreign teaching assistants and faculty. Such policies have been a reaction to a groundswell of criticism from students and parents regarding foreign teaching assistants' (TAs) language skills. One author quotes letters sent in the early 1980s to the University of California president, the governor, senators, members of congress, and the assembly. Two were from parents upset about their childrens' inability to understand foreign TAs: they closed as follows:[12]

[A]s an overburdened taxpayer, I know of no good reason why I should be subsidizing the education of foreign students—send them home. Charity begins at home. (Bailey 1982, 5)

In other words, do not subsidize foreigners when there are needy "Americans."

The sense of threat from "aliens" evident in the reaction to foreign students is expressed in the rash of "English only" laws—making English the official, only legal language of the state—adopted by popular referendum in several states. Most recently, states have translated that sense of threat into a sense of outrage at having to spend state resources on "illegals," suing the federal government to pay for social services states provide them.

The legislation of English has also touched higher education. Seventeen states have Oral English Language Proficiency (OELP) policies, established from the early 1980s to the early 1990s (Monoson and Thomas 1993). Policies ranged from state laws—such as the one Florida adopted in 1983 that mandated nonnative English speaking instructors "be proficient in the oral use of English, as determined by the Test of Spoken English. . . . or a similar test"—to governing board policies to executive orders and other requirements.[13] Most policies affect only international teaching assistants (ITAs)—44%—or ITAs and faculty—44% (12% affect only faculty).

The only dimension of entrepreneurialism evident in language policies has been the response by test-making companies and publishers, which have turned the problem of foreign teaching assistants into a revenue source.[14] The Educational Testing Service has developed tests—Test of Spoken English, Speaking Proficiency in English Assessment Kit (SPEAK), and Oral Proficiency Interview—used by institutions to assess foreign instructors. Collier MacMillan and Prentice Hall Regents now have texts on the subject.[15]

Given the cost perspective of state policymakers, it is surprising they have not implemented a full-cost-plus-profit-margin fee for foreign students. In the absence of other obvious factors, one might explain this in terms of competition among states for students—if one state raises its fees it will lose foreign students to states that maintain lower fees. But most states have been raising tuitions at public institutions dramatically, particularly for out-of-state students. That certainly suggests the predominance of cost concerns and orientations. Yet in the case of foreign students, the racist, antiforeigner sentiment expressed in the implementation of residency and the development of English proficiency policies offers a compelling explanation.

Institutional Policy: Conflicted Responses to Cheap but Problematic Labor

U.S. colleges and universities manifest conflicted responses to national and state policies regarding foreign students and to the students themselves. Such students are critical to institutions' science and engineering profile of graduate students (they are important clients), and they are low-cost labor in undergraduate education (they are employees—as teaching assistants). But foreign students can be problematic for institutions given the restrictions and paperwork embedded in national policy and the particularly parochial, racist impulses evident in state policy.

Institutions, and institutional associations, have lobbied Congress against immigration laws that would restrict or inhibit the flow of foreign students and their ability to work in the United States as postdocs or faculty. They need foreign graduate students to maintain science and engineering programs, and they need them to work not just as postdocs and faculty but as teaching assistants. With some exceptions, there is little evidence that institutions invest much in infrastructure or inducements to realize the educational or entrepreneurial possibilities of increasing the number of foreign students, although this may be changing in some universities. A major factor is the lack of incentives and organizational support provided by the federal government—there is nothing like the tuition incentives and marketing/recruiting supports (through Austrade) in Australia. Where is the incentive for a U.S. university to recruit foreign students when foreign student tuition is identical to that paid by out-of-state American students? Out-of-state fees are increasingly closer to full cost, but there is no profit margin over and above that to cover the need for support services for foreign students. There is no reason for universities to create incentive structures encouraging academic departments to recruit more foreign students. If anything, there is a trend toward making it more difficult for foreign students to enroll, through raising admission standards (e.g., on English proficiency tests) in making financial assistance more difficult to get (Barber 1983; McCann 1986), and in forcing foreign applicants to provide evidence of ability to pay educational expenses.

Of course, there are some institutions that are active and successful in drawing international students. There are also some institutions that draw large numbers of international students with little effort. But two surveys by the Institute of International Education in the early 1980s reveal a low level of interest and investment in foreign students: foreign students are at the bottom of university officials' priority list; institutions (especially publics) are sensitive to legislative pressures regarding foreign students and to issues of economic protectionism and national security; and services and infrastructure for foreign students is generally inadequate and poorly funded (McCann 1986). Although one might expect private universities to be more entrepreneurial in this regard, there is little evidence to that effect. A recent study (Afonso 1990) of 104 Research I and II universities found much variation in involvement in international activities. She created a multivariable index of such activity (including foreign student enrollments, foreign language and area studies enrollments, and number of National Association of Foreign Student Administrators) and found that private institutions did not score higher.

Although foreign students are important clients and cheap, skilled labor to universities, institutions face restrictive, racist pressures at the state level. Moreover, institutions manifest some of these tendencies themselves. Institutions react to and/or resist state policies regarding international students, ignoring or implementing policies in various ways. For example, the "governance pattern" in determining residency and tuition for foreign students varies from state to state: authority may lie in the legislature, coordinating agencies, or institutions (Olivas 1992). In states (seventeen) where institutions have the autonomy to determine residency requirements, there is variation from institution to institution, with some, such as Eastern Michigan University, developing policies to attract international students, and others doing quite the opposite. In states where legislatures or boards determine residence, there is still great variation in the interpretation and administration of the policies (Padilla 1989). Variation is also found in oral English proficiency policies (Monoson and Thomas 1993). In fact, in states with no mandates as to oral English proficiency, many institutions have such a policy, and "four-fifths of the institutions in the Big 10, Pacific 10, and Big 8 Athletic conferences [housing the lion's share of large public research universities in the country] now require an English language proficiency test" (Jacobs and Friedman 1988, 552). Such practices do little to attract foreign students.

Part of the explanation for the lack of entrepreneurialism is that at the graduate level, recruitment and admissions are organized and controlled more by academic units. Given the discourse about the dependency of certain fields on international students, one might expect quite active efforts by departments to increase or at least sustain the flow of foreign students. But for the most part, faculty are more sensitive to quality than to quantity (Evans 1993). Besides, recruiting international students is expensive, and there are disincentives in the form of rules, regulations, and procedures affecting such students, with no incentives in the form of support/resources. There is also risk as to the true language capabilities of such students. Neither the organizational environment nor faculty culture dispose most departments and faculties in most U.S. universities to be entrepreneurial.

Conclusion

International students have long been part of the flow of people, knowledge, resources, and goods from one country to another. For example, the concept of "brain drain" has long characterized apprehension in some countries about the pattern of student flows—that as with natural resources, students were flowing from the less developed to the developed world. In the 1980s the international flow of students increased, and many countries' policies toward such students changed dramatically. Despite a general trend toward more entrepreneurial policies in Australian and United States higher education, only in Australia has foreign student policy epitomized the entrepreneurial commercialization of higher education, treating students as trade commodities in the global economy. In the United States, policy has been driven by conflicted concerns about human capital, immigration, and costs that reflect a culture of education as commodity, but not a culture of entrepreneurialism. Foreigners are skilled students in science and engineering, yet they are suspect as teachers. Foreign and immigrant workers are cheap, skilled labor that is critical yet threatening to the country's economic self-sufficiency.

In our view, two general factors shape the character of entrepreneurial activity in higher education, and the form of foreign student policies: first, the country's position in and stance toward the world political economy; and second, the organizational and financial structures of higher education that determine its place in the national political economy. Each has a fundamental impact on higher education culture, affecting interpretations of what students are and of what the social relationship is between them and higher education institutions. Foreign student policy in Australia was originally embedded in the political economy of the British empire; it has now shifted to a late twentieth century form of economic educational imperialism. Connections to the old empire, via the Commonwealth, have been superseded by regional connections that have created anxiety about Australia's position as a First-World country. The shift in foreign student policy was precipitated in part by a change in Britain's policy, restricting the flow of students there and increasing the flow to Australia. A Labor government saw that pattern as an opportunity, reconceptualized foreign students as trade commodities, and sought to further increase the flow of such students in an entrepreneurial effort to advantageously position Australia in the international economy. By contrast, foreign student policy in the United States has partly remained embedded in the old international political economy of Cold War American imperialism, colored by political aims of training foreigners and inculcating them with American values and infused with parochial and racist anxieties about economic decline and immigration. Apprehension about position in the global economy has shifted the focus from education contributing to *other* countries' economic development to its centrality to the United States's competitiveness. Talk of the global economy has clashed with protectionist reactions in Congress and in conservative social movements against foreign threats. The common ground is that graduate students are seen as a natural resource: the aim is not to increase exchange but to ensure control over the resource by cultivating it internally, stimulating the flow of U.S. students in science and engineering.

Ironically U.S. Republican administrations that promoted a relatively weak federal state, tied to a powerful corporate class, were less inclined to link foreign student policy to the international economy than was an Australian Labor government of a strong federal state with a relatively weak business class. Entrepreneurialism in higher education was more evident in the strong state and public system of higher education than in the market-oriented system with a strong private sector. The state socialist model of Australia, with relatively weak layers between the federal government and the operating units, has enabled the development of powerful incentives for entrepreneurial action at the campus and departmental levels.[16] Australian universities are quite dependent on federal funding, and thus vulnerable and responsive to federal demands. States and campuses generate little revenue, and thus the incentive structure is easy for the federal government to manipulate: the incentive provided by allowing campuses to collect and keep tuition monies from foreign (but not Australian) students is powerful, especially in that foreign student numbers are separate from the annual quota of student places set by the federal government for the institution. Campus bureaucracies are relatively small and not so involved in processing students and in collecting and reallocating monies to academic units—thus, the incentive to attract foreign students is passed along to the department. And in reallocating global campus budgets, administrations have increasingly been allocating to departments in a way that mirrors the Relative Funding Model by which the federal government determines the campus budget (i.e., national per capita costs based on discipline mix).

By contrast, the organizational and financial structure of American higher education, with the strong intervening levels of state politics and finance and of campus central administration, has inhibited the national or local development of incentive structures for attracting foreign students. In other words, a political culture that values decentralized control of education has inhibited the development of an entrepreneurial educational culture in some regards in those decentralized institutions. In public higher education, the state represents a major, often principal, source of funding. Consequently, state legislative concerns about the subsidization of nonresident students (U.S. and foreign alike) and the quality of teaching and undergraduate education impact campus administrators' actions. Most institutions generate substantial revenues from nonfederal sources, from tuition (some of this is federally financed student aid), gifts, and external grants and contracts (most of this is federally funded). Thus campus administrations are major competitors with academic units for resources. Expenditures for administration have increased more rapidly over the past two decades than those for research or instruction (Leslie and Rhoades, forthcoming). Campus administrators reallocate monies from the state and the federal government, weakening the link between student numbers and funding: for example, in research universities, monies are reallocated to units that fare well in the research "marketplace" of federal grants, for this is a major source of discretionary revenues for managers. Academics, too, compete in this marketplace to enhance their resources and position in the academy (Jencks and Riesman 1969). Neither academics (and departments) nor institutions look to foreign students as a major discretionary revenue source. Local cultures, then, do not foster entrepreneurial attitudes and actions toward foreign students.

In short, state socialist structures and actors, in party politics, financing, and organizational arrangements, effected a more entrepreneurial approach or "commodification" toward the treatment of foreign students as trade goods in the global economy than did laissez-faire capitalists. Australia has outcompeted the United States in the global market for foreign students. In 1990 the United States had about 380,000 such students: on the same per capita basis, Australia would have been expected to have about 25,000 foreign students—the actual numbers were closer to 33,000 and were upwards of 41,500 by 1993. The markets in which these two countries are competing are somewhat different—most of Australia's foreign students (over 75%) are undergraduate, whereas nearly half of foreign students in the United States are graduate. Nevertheless, the two cases point to complex links between states and entrepreneurial, "market-oriented" activity. Markets and states are not separate, counterposed domains; they are interconnected entities.

The comparisons we have made apply to foreign student policy: patterns may differ in other domains of higher education. It is possible that given their positions in the international economy of science, institutions and academics in Australia and the United States are working out their respective niches in the marketplace of students and science (the proportions of foreign graduate and undergraduate students in the countries are suggestive in this regard). Moreover, the construction of higher education's links to the global economy, and the restructuring of its financing and organization accordingly, are in flux. Campus bureaucracy is growing in Australia: for example, on average it now levies 35% overhead on research grants. New structures are being created between departments/faculties and campus managers—maybe the fastest growing being the international offices. As with many other higher education systems, Australia may be moving toward U.S. patterns of campus management and bureaucracy, even as the United States is moving toward a model of more centralized federal science and technology policy, similar to the rest of the world (Slaughter and Rhoades 1994; Rhoades 1994).

Finally, the effects of foreign student policy should not be overstated in that their numbers are concentrated in a few fields—business, engineering, and science in both countries. However, such concentration of students and policy discourse says much about what fields of study are seen as critical to the country's competitive position in the global economy and thus will be favored in higher education's future. Regardless of how (in)directly the state seeks to steer higher education, the context of a discourse about global economic competitiveness sets national, state, and institutional priorities and influences choices as to what academic programs will be accorded steerage class or first class treatment in the years to come. As we have seen, such a context also sets courses and shapes choices about foreign student policy in complex, unexpected ways. Seeing overseas students as trade commodities and seeking to redress imbalances of trade, policymakers in Australia structured incentives to encourage departments and institutions to entrepreneurially pursue such students as a key to maintaining first class position in the world economy. By contrast, policymakers in the United States were conflicted, seeing foreign students as key factors of production in the economy—as clients and labor in high technology fields—yet as steerage class immigrants (ironic, given the wealth and education of foreign relative to native students) who threatened the country's self-sufficiency and preeminent world position.

Notes

A special thanks to Larry L. Leslie and Sheila Slaughter, whose experience on a Fulbright semester in Australia dramatized for us the entrepreneurial character of Australian higher education. Thanks as well to Rodger Philpott, who first pointed out to Gary Rhoades the commodification of foreign students in Australia.

1. In part, this may be because the most active institutions in such activities tend to be the least prestigious (e.g., community colleges). Such institutions are not even acknowledged as members of the postsecondary education community—e.g., proprietary institutions in the United States.

2. Certainly an argument could be made that other fields have relevance for global economic relations. However, as currently defined in federal and institutional policy discussions, business, engineering, and science are seen as the engines of economic growth and competitiveness.

3. Generally, such policies are directed toward strengthening the connection between corporate business and higher education's research and training activities. Big science, high-technology fields are targeted as critical contributors to a nation's position in the global marketplace. Higher education's training of school leavers and retraining of workers is portrayed as a central mechanism in transitioning from old, manufacturing industry based economies to new, high-technology, information, and service-based economies.

4. Indeed, the case of Japan presents a challenge to this conventional perspective regarding the relationship between scientific and economic dominance. Moreover, emergent economies are seeking, sometimes successfully, to develop their own higher education systems in ways that are tightly linked to the country's economic vitality.

5. In addition, in 1990 the prime minister announced the creation of fifty Cooperative Research Centers, focused on key Australian economic niche markets and products, fostering cooperation among university, business, and government researchers.

6. Such a policy was originally followed by a Britain with a quite different rationale, to stem the tide of subsidized students (and it succeeded in drastically reducing foreign student numbers): by 1983 Britain was pursuing a modified policy of this sort to regain their market share of foreign students and generate revenue (Chandler 1989).

7. The dependency narrative soon translates into a demographic tale. Given the decrease in numbers of students pursuing science and engineering, there is an increased focus on precollege math and science teaching and on undergraduate science education, evident in the annual reports of NSF from 1986 to 1990. Moreover, given the declining proportion of eighteen to twenty-two year olds who are white males, there is an emphasis on attracting women and minorities into science and engineering.

8. Thanks to Larry L. Leslie, whose comments were particularly helpful on this section and who stressed the simple cost perspective of state legislators.

9. Indeed the largest category of international students, those with F-visas, are "ineligible for consideration [for residency] in all states, consistent with federal law and major U.S. Supreme Court cases on the point" (Olivas 1992, 586).

10. Such inconsistencies between state and federal law are possible, and persist, because of the nature of the American legal system, which requires an individual to file suit claiming that the state law violates federal law.

11. Proposition 187, recently passed in California, which denies governmental ser-

vices to undocumented immigrants, is only the latest expression of the anti-immigrant backlash.

12.   Such sentiments have led many educational professionals working in the area of international education and teaching English as a foreign or second language to suggest that the people who need training are the intolerant students (and parents) more than the international teaching assistants.

13.   The concerns about the English proficiency of instructors has been played out at another level of policymaking, specific to the United States—regional accrediting bodies. The Southern Association of Colleges and Schools has as one of its accreditation criteria a passage related to foreign teaching assistants: "Institutions may appoint graduate teaching assistants for whom English is a second language only when a test of spoken English, or other reliable evidence of the applicant's proficiency in oral communication and speech, indicates that the appointment is appropriate" (Southern Association 1989–90, 29).

14.   Of course, academics working in the area of English as a Foreign Language have also benefited.

15.   See, *The Foreign Teaching Assistant's Manual* (Byrd, Constantinides, and Pennington 1989) and *Communicative Strategies for International Teaching Assistants* (Smith, Meyers, and Burkhalter 1992).

16.   Thanks to Sheila Slaughter who suggested the terminology of state socialism.

References

Afonso, J.D. 1990. *The international dimension in American higher education.* Ph.D. dissertation. Center for the Study of Higher Education, University of Arizona.

Altbach, P.G. 1989. *Foreign students and international study: Bibliography and analysis, 1984–1988.* Lanham, Maryland: University Press of America.

Altbach, P.G., and V. Selvaratnam (eds.) 1989. *From dependence to autonomy: The development of Asian universities.* The Netherlands: Kluwer Academic Publishers.

American Council on Education (ACE). 1982. *Foreign students and institutional policy.* Washington, D.C.: American Council on Education.

Bailey, K. 1982. The foreign TA problem. In *Foreign teaching assistants in U.S. universities,* eds., K. Bailey, F. Pialorsi, and J. Zukowski. Washington, D.C.: National Association for Foreign Student Affairs.

Barber, E.G. 1983. *A survey of policy changes: Foreign students in public institutions of higher education.* New York: Institute of International Education.

Barrow, C.W. 1990. *Universities and the capitalist state: Corporate liberalism and the reconstruction of American higher education, 1894–1928.* Madison: University of Wisconsin Press.

Beazley, K.C. 1992. *International education in Australia through the 1990s.* Ministerial statement. Canberra: Australian Government Publishing Service.

Ben-David, J., and A. Zloczower. 1962. Universities and academic systems in modern societies. *European Journal of Sociology* 3:45–84.

Birch, I., and D. Smart. 1989. Economic rationalism and the politics of education in Australia. In *Politics of Education 1989 Yearbook.* London: Taylor and Francis.

Bowles, S., and H. Gintis. 1976. *Schooling in capitalist America: Educational reform and the contradictions of capitalist life.* New York: Basic Books.

Boyer, E.L. 1987. *College: The undergraduate experience in America.* New York: Harper and Row.

Byrd, P., J. Constantinides, and M. Pennington. 1989. *The foreign T.A.'s manual.* New York: Collier Macmillan.

Chandler, A. 1989. *Obligation of opportunity: foreign student policy in six major receiving countries.* New York: Institute of International Education.

Clark, B.R. 1983. *The higher education system: academic organization in cross-national perspective.* Los Angeles: University of California Press.

Cote, L.S., and M.K. Cote. 1993. Economic development activity among land-grant institutions. *Journal of Higher Education* 64(1):55–73.

Dawkins, J.S. 1987. *Higher education: A policy discussion paper. Green Paper.* Canberra: Australian Government Publishing Service.

———. 1988. *Higher education: A policy statement. White Paper.* Canberra: Australian Government Publishing Service.

Department of Employment, Education, and Training (DEET). 1993. *Selected higher education statistics, 1992.* Canberra: DEET.

Dickson, D. 1984. *The new politics of science.* New York: Pantheon.

Etzkowitz, H. 1983. Entrepreneurial scientists and entrepreneurial universities in American academic science. *Minerva* 21: 198–233.

Evans, L. 1993. *Graduate student recruitment.* Ph.D. dissertation. Center for the Study of Higher Education, University of Arizona.

Fairweather, J. 1988. *Entrepreneurship and the university: The future of industry-university liaisons.* ASHE-ERIC Higher Education Report. Washington, D.C.: Association for the Study of Higher Education.

Geiger, R. 1986. *Private sectors in higher education: Structure, function, and change in eight countries.* Ann Arbor: University of Michigan Press.

Goldring Report. 1984. Mutual advantage: Report of the committee of review of private overseas student policy. Canberra: Australian Government Publishing Service.

Increasing U.S. Scientific Manpower. 1990. Hearing before the Subcommittee on Science, Research, and Technology, July 31, 1990. Washington: U.S. Government Printing Office.

Industry Commission. 1991. Exports of education services. Report No. 12. Canberra: Australian Government Publishing Service.

Institute of International Education. (IIE) 1992. *Profiles: 1991/1992: Detailed analyses of the foreign student population.* New York: Institute of International Education.

Jackson Committee. 1984. Report of the committee to review the Australian overseas aid program. Canberra: Australian Government Publishing Service.

Jacobs, L.C., and C.B. Friedman. 1988. Student achievement under foreign teaching associates compared with native teaching associates. *Journal of Higher Education* 59(5):551–63.

Jencks, C., and D. Riesman. 1969. *The academic revolution.* New York: Doubleday.

Laurie, V. 1992. Learning to export, by degree. *The Bulletin* 14 April:42–4.

Leslie, L.L., and G. Rhoades. Forthcoming. Rising administrative costs: On seeking explanations. *Journal of Higher Education.*

Levy, D. 1986. *Higher education and the state in Latin America: Private challenges to public dominance.* Chicago: University of Chicago Press.

Marginson, S. 1993. *Education and public policy in Australia.* Cambridge: Cambridge University Press.

McCann, W.J. Jr. 1986. *A survey of policy changes: Foreign students in public institutions of higher education from 1983–1985.* IEE Research Report No. 8. New York: Institute of International Education.

Monoson, P.K., and C.F. Thomas. 1993. Oral English proficiency policies for faculty in U.S. higher education. *The Review of Higher Education* 16(2):127–41.

National Board of Employment, Education, and Training (NBEET). 1990. Australian paper for the OECD/CERI conference on higher education and the flow of foreign students: Programs and policies. Hanover, April. Canberra: NBEET.

National Science Foundation (NSF). 1986. *National science foundation annual report, 1986.* Washington, D.C.: National Science Foundation.

National Science Foundation Authorization (NSF Authorization). 1986. Hearing before the subcommittee on science, technology, and space, May 15, 1986. Washington, D.C.: U.S. Government Printing Office.

Olivas, M. 1986. Plyler v. Doe, Toll v. Moreno, and postsecondary admissions: Undocumented adults and enduring disability. *Journal of Law and Education* 15(1):19–56.

————. 1988. Administering intentions: Law, theory, and practice of postsecondary residency requirements. *Journal of Higher Education* 59(3):263–90.

————. 1992. The political economy of immigration, intellectual property, and racial harassment: Case studies for the implementation of legal change on campus. *Journal of Higher Education* 63(5):570–98.

Padilla, R. 1989. Postsecondary residency classifications: The application of complex legislation to the complex circumstances of students. Monograph 89–6. Houston, Texas: University of Houston, Institute for Higher Education Law and Governance.

Peters, L., and H. Fusfeld. 1982. Current U.S. university-industry research relationships. In *University-industry research relationships*, ed. National Science Board. Washington, D.C.: National Science Foundation.

Rhoades, G. 1994. Is the NSF still the "balance wheel" of basic science? Paper presented at the annual meeting of the Association for the Study of Higher Education, November 10–13, Tucson.

Rhoades, G., and S. Slaughter. 1991. The public interest and professional labor. In *Culture and ideology in higher education: Advancing a critical agenda*, ed., W.G. Tierney. New York: Praeger.

Slaughter, S. 1990. *The higher learning and high technology: Dynamics of higher education policy formation.* Albany, New York: SUNY Press.

Slaughter, S., and G. Rhoades. 1993. Changes in intellectual property statutes and policies at a public university: Revising the terms of professional labor. *Higher Education* 26:287–312.

————. 1994. Academic science policy in the Clinton administration. Paper presented at the annual meetings of the Society for Social Studies of Science, October 12–16, New Orleans.

Smart, D. 1988. Recruitment and financing of Candidates to study overseas: the case of malaysia and its implications for Australia. Background paper, Senior Policy Seminar on Financing Education in the East Asian Region, Jakarta, sponsored by Economic Development Institute of the World Bank and the Australian International Development Assistance Bureau.

Smart, D., and G. Ang. 1993. The origins and evolution of the commonwealth full-fee paying overseas student policy, 1975–1992. In *Case studies in public policy: A one-semester workbook*, ed., A. Peachment and J. Williamson. Western Australia: Public Sector Research Unit, Curtin University of Technology.

Smith, J., C. Meyers, and A. Burkhalter. 1992. *Communicative strategies for international T.A.'s.* Englewood Cliffs, New Jersey: Prentice-Hall Regents.

Solmon, L., and B.J. Young. 1987. *The foreign student factor: Impact on American higher education.* New York: Institute of International Education.

Task Force on Science Policy. 1986. *Demographic trends and the scientific and engineering work force.* Science Policy Study Background Report No. 9, report prepared by the Office of Technology Assessment, December 1986. Committee on Science and Technology, U.S. House of Representatives.

Throsby, C.D. 1985. Trade and aid in Australian post-secondary education. Working Paper No. 85/8. Canberra: Development Studies Centre, Australian National University.

Trow, M. 1984. The analysis of status. In *Perspectives on higher education: Eight disciplinary and comparative views*, ed., B.R. Clark. Los Angeles: University of California Press.

Woodhall, M. 1987. Government policy toward overseas students: an international perspective. *Higher Education Quarterly* 41:119–125.

Chapter Eight
Educational Decentralization in Latin America
The Case of Chile

Claudio Figueroa and Marcos Valle

Believing education to be the key instrument in the creation of an economy and a social structure similar to those of developed countries, Latin American governments, both democratic and authoritarian, have responded to political, economic, and cultural demands with the expansion of their formal education systems. Particularly in countries that have experienced political upheaval (Latin America's middle name?), developmental policies inevitably manifest themselves in formal education through reforms that may have any one, or all, of the following features: (a) the elimination of any evidence of ideological characteristics of a previous regime, (b) school enrollment campaigns, (c) increase in the budget allocations earmarked for support of the educational system, and (d) a program of regionalization of education (Hanson 1991). Increasingly, this expansion of the formal education systems takes the form not only of increases in the number of schools and universities but also through a transfer of decision making from the central government to local units, a process called decentralization.

Transfers in decision-making power often imply, albeit subtly, a democratizing process. Therefore, it may appear paradoxical that, given their history in this century, Latin American countries have decentralized their educational systems. After all, in the period immediately following the Great Depression alone, seventeen governments in the continent were toppled through force and replaced with authoritarian counterparts. The post–World War II era was particularly hard on the local democracies; for example, coups d'état overturned governments in Venezuela (1945, 1948, and 1958), Argentina (1955, 1962, 1966, and 1976), Brazil (1945 and 1964), and Chile (1973). Moreover, even when they have resulted from democratic processes, decentralization policies failed to accomplish a shift in the *source* of power, even when they have managed to shift the *locus* of power. How then is one to understand the meaning of decentralization in Latin America?

Our premise is that decentralization of education in Latin America has been a process informed by divergent political logics, having different meanings for different governments, and serving much less educational purposes than it does political ones. In fact, we propose that decentralization processes have never actually resulted in decentralized power, since they have been political strategies, rather than technical ones. To make our point, we explore in this chapter the case of Chile by viewing how two ideologically different governments—Allende's and Pinochet's—advanced the decentralization of Chile's education system to further their divergent political agendas affecting the entire educational system, including higher education. Central to our argument is the importance of understanding the role culture plays in defining the ideological perspectives of each of the governments.

In order to contextualize our criticism of decentralization in Chile as essentially rhetorical, we organize this chapter in the following manner. First, we provide a cultural-political overview in which we include a discussion of what has been called the "centralist tradition" of Latin America, as well as of the roles played by its most prominent social actors in maintaining that tradition. Next, we focus on decentralization and its uses by the Allende government and the military junta of Pinochet to advance their opposing political agendas. We conclude by stating, among other things, that neither project was truly decentralizing, as the ultimate power continued to lie with the central government.

The Larger Cultural Context

"Let us fly to Argentina," the thief or mobster would say to his teary lady friend in many a U.S. gangster movie of the 1940s and 1950s. The backdrop of the smoke-filled setting was a poster depicting Rio de Janeiro, Brazil. The obvious assumption underlying the scene was that in South America, one would be unreachable to the long arm of the U.S. law. The imperceptible suggestion was that one would be rid of *any* law. Indeed, the long-held view of Latin America was that of a lawless conglomerate of indistinguishable "banana republics." Such perception, apparently ingrained in the U.S. collective unconscious, has deterred the common person's understanding of the complexities of that continent.

While the movie industry bears part of the blame for the institutionalization of that prejudiced view, notwithstanding the average U.S. citizen's notorious lack of intellectual curiosity for phenomena occurring in other countries, Latin America does owe a significant part of its reputation to a sequence of dictatorships. In fact, a perception exists in the Northern Hemisphere that (a) authoritarian regimes are the government of choice of Latin Americans, and (b) democracy has no history in the continent.

Contrary to this popular view, several forms of liberal democracy have been attempted in Latin America since the emancipation wave in the eighteenth and nineteenth centuries. The Latin American independence movements and the resulting constitutions were often modeled after the French Revolution and the newly founded United States. Regrettably, the ruling elites of the incipient Latin American democracies did not share the basic understandings on which both the French and U.S. democracies were created. Consequently, they supported independence and constitutionality so long as they furthered their centuries-long privileges.

The democratic ideals that fueled independence movements in Latin America were often imported by ideologically liberal, upper-class, urban individuals who were usually educated in Europe. Out of fidelity to the principles of equality and liberty, but also in search of political power, these political aspirants searched for the support of lower classes. Whereas this alliance furthered independence movements, it proved difficult to enforce when democracy failed to bring about the benefits it had promised to deliver. To survive the instability of this political order, both the elites or the upcoming young liberals would alternatively or successively reach for the support of the Church or the military, institutions characterized by a rigid hierarchy and a strong centralized, authoritarian structure.

The "vertebral centralism" (Véliz 1984) tradition of Latin America has grown from medieval precepts of the Catholic Church that date back to Aristotle and Saint Thomas Aquinas. Among other principles, this framework is based on the belief in a functional social hierarchy and on principles of moral idealism and historical continuity. Latin America's religious tradition is hegemonic, which, in turn, lends it a belief in an ordered and hierarchical universe. It comes as no surprise, therefore, that such notions as the normalcy of inequalities among people and the imperative need for a strong, authoritative state to regulate and govern the diverse and heterogeneous societal groups have powerfully influenced political choices in many Latin American countries over the years.

Outside analysts often fail to comprehend this aspect of Latin America's struggle for liberal democracies because they spend much time trying to identify pressure groups fighting for control of the central state, assuming, erroneously, that the central government in Latin America is as instrumental as in Europe. In reality, in Latin America the "central government is itself the most powerful pressure group" (Véliz 1982).

A homogeneous, authoritarian, and monolithic government is, historically, a very pertinent notion to Latin America. In the past, the king and queen headed the political pyramid. Later, the central state assumed that position, as well as the tendency to control and regulate all that surrounds it, whether corporate, class, or group life. This drive is operationalized through a vast administrative machinery centralized at the nations' capitals. This hierarchy is replicated at the state, municipality, and city levels. Such structure, in turn, replicates the old patriarchal and paternal system and transforms the central administration into sources of control, wealth, jobs, opportunities, contracts, etc. (Véliz 1982). Inevitably, the highly bureaucratized, centralized structure gives rise to opportunism and nepotism, corruption and bribery, not to mention the ability to regulate class structure. It is within this frame of centralism that reform—educational or otherwise—must be comprehended.

To understand Latin America, it is also helpful to think of a permanent state of tension between the central government and its attempts to enlarge the scope of its power and the several groups of social actors on whose power so many alliances depend. Foremost among these groups are the Church and the army.

The conquest of Latin America by the Spanish and the Portuguese was intimately connected to a rationale of religious expansion. The catechetic mission soon evolved into a powerful, political one.

The Catholic Church oftentimes used its "salvation in the hereafter" doctrine as justification for endurance of colonial inequalities. The Roman Catholic Church, a landowner itself, frequently supported the prevailing political order by allying with the oligarchs and the military.

The last thirty years have seen a change in the Church's role, championing the cause of social justice. Particularly in Chile, Brazil, and Nicaragua and notably in El Salvador, the Roman Catholic Church has struggled to expose the life conditions of the poor and to promote social advancement.

The military too has had a long tradition of involvement in Latin American history. Not only was the independence of several Latin American nations brought about by a military general, but the Brazilian Republic was also proclaimed by Army Marshall Deodoro, Brazil's first president. Once poor, uneducated, and unsophisticated, the Latin America militaries are now educated, sophisticated, and the recipients of billion-dollar budgets, thanks to generations of centralist governments whose survival depended on the strength of the armed forces. Not coincidentally, industrialization and economic growth in many Latin American countries have equaled the development of the arms industry, as is the case of Brazil.

Eminently bureaucratic and command dependent, the military leaders in Latin America often feel frustrated by the apparent chaos of democratic participation, as well as by the plethora of ideologies, especially the leftist ones, that have emerged over the decades in the continent. Conservative and order oriented by training, today's military no longer protect solely the interests of the oligarchs but also that which they perceive to be the economic, orderly progress of the country, as well as their own privileges. Educated in exclusive institutions whose curricula are highly technical and doctrinaire, the Latin American military pledge allegiance to the corporation, to order, and recently have aligned themselves with the government bureaucrats and private industry.

During the Stalin years in the Soviet Union, an aide reputedly tried to counsel the leader as to the political power of the Pope and the Holy See. "The Pope?" Stalin allegedly reacted, "How many tanks does he have?" To fully understand the Latin American scenario, one would do well not to overlook Stalin's aide's advice, for, in Latin

America, the Church and the military have often united to oust "subversive, alien ideologies," as the recent history of the continent demonstrates. This is particularly true in the Chilean case.

Decentralization: The Concept

Decentralization is a complex, multifaceted process. Rondinelli and Nelli (1984), for example, distinguish among four kinds of decentralization. Deconcentration occurs where administrative responsibilities are delegated to low levels of the ministry or central agencies. Delegation occurs when responsibilities are transferred to organizations that are outside of the bureaucratic structures, indirectly controlled by the central government. Devolution refers to a transfer made through subnational government unit activities that are outside of the direct control of the central government. Finally, privatization is the transfer of responsibilities to voluntary organizations or private enterprises. These distinctions, of course, assume decentralization to be a process of increasing loss of power by the central state. It tends to benefit the private sector because some responsibilities are transferred to private enterprise.

Surprisingly, the rise of privatization as one of the decentralization policies of choice in Latin America has coincided with the arrival of the second wave of democratic governments in the region. The pre-1970s era of democratic governments, particularly those rooted in socialist ideologies, chose developmental paths that included protection of the incipient national industries and government ownership of segments of the economy. Historically, the most orthodox forms of protectionism were, of course, tariffs and quota systems. Importation of products that might compete favorably with and hurt the local industries was forbidden. As a result, trade treaties with highly industrialized powers, particularly the United States, became obstacles in the foreign policy roads of those nations. The military governments of the 1970s and early 1980s were equally nationalist and protectionist, except for the Chilean military government.

Different from its neighbors, the military in Chile pushed strongly for privatization and the consequent reduction of the role of the state. Subsequent democratic regimes, surprisingly, have followed the same path, with the elimination of most obstacles to imports, the "dollarization" of the economies, the establishment of international trade treaties such as MERCOSUR and NAFTA, and moves to privatize important, previously state-owned, strategic industries.

Rondinelli, Nelli, and Cheema (1984) state that in "Third-World" countries there is a suspicion that the principal mechanism of economic decentralization, i.e., the market, is immoral and anarchic, its operational mechanism impersonal, rewarding a few people at the expense of many. Many neoclassic economists agree that the market in developing countries is working inadequately. An imperfect, selectively rewarding market seems to aggravate the deep discrepancies existing in Latin America, a socially and politically fragmented continent. This fragmentation, as Whitaker (1961) has written about Argentina, differs from pluralism in the United States. Whitaker explains that in Argentina the divisions run very deep with some factions constantly quarreling and fighting or simply not communicating with each other. This situation has lead to a widespread feeling of frustration and loss of direction among many Argentineans that has perpetuated domestic differences and bitter feelings.

These "domestic differences," neoclassic economists claim, could be eliminated, at least at the market-processes level, through the removal of barriers to the workings of the free market. Opposers claim, however, that market imperfections justify the continuation of control and strengthening of central intervention. Economic centralization, in turn, reinforces centralized political control, which brings us back to the centralist culture of Latin America.

We define decentralization as the complex process whereby participation of individuals and social groups in decision making at the peripheral levels of the system is increased as a result of a transfer of planning, decision-making, or administrative authority from the central government to the local administrative units. Put more simply, decentralization entails the transfer of power from one unit to another.

Two caveats must accompany this definition: one is that we do not imply, by using the word transfer, that such change is inevitably the result of an action by an all-powerful, magnanimous government. It may, indeed, result from agency by other instances of power. Second, we think it is important to stress that local units may not be, and in fact most often are not, governmental organizations. Indeed, usually they are field organizations, local administrative units, semiautonomous and parastate organizations, local governments, and nongovernmental organizations. Additionally, decentralization is by no means a monolithic process. Indeed, it may be achieved through three different processes, namely, nuclearization, regionalization, and municipalization.

With regard to education, nuclearization implies grouping schools through a net of services in a specific geographic area. "Geographic" must be understood loosely, for, oftentimes, the area is defined not only by borderlines but also by demographic, topographic, socioeconomic homogeneity, as well as by communication factors (Ministerio de Educación, Costa Rica 1976). A number of Latin American countries have experimented with nuclearization: Peru, Guatemala, Honduras, Costa Rica, Colombia, Nicaragua, Venezuela, Argentina, Brazil, and Ecuador. To date, in-depth studies are still lacking that might explore the accuracy of objectives, consider more convenient processes, and ponder more appropriate strategies to coherently decentralize a system.

Individual countries' differences notwithstanding, nuclearization is generally a policy aimed at: (a) the democratization of the teaching process, (b) the application of a curriculum that is consistent with, rooted in, and relevant to local realities of individual educational nuclei, and (c) the satisfaction of educational and developmental needs of marginal populations (Ministerio de Educación, Costa Rica 1976).

Regionalization refers to a systematic process of adjusting the development of policy to the needs and potentialities of human conglomerates within certain limits. Thus, regionalization is a means of orienting development into a given geographic area (OEA 1981, 7), an attempt at solving the problem of unbalanced national development. Regionalization requires compatibility between national and regional goals.

The following criteria have characterized regionalization in Latin America. First, there is a transference of functions from central organisms to regional administrative units, which, in turn, take the responsibility for the execution of the policies under the coordination and supervision of the central body. Second, there is a regionalization of the supply of education through the creation of specialized organisms, either autonomous or integrated to the system structure, working through sections offices. Finally, there is an identification of possible ways in which regionalization may be designed at the national level, through the experimentation in concrete geographic units with an integration of education and decentralized public service (OEA 1981).

Regionalization attempts to harmoniously distribute development and, specifically, horizontally distribute education services. Thus, its impact transcends mere educational policy limitations. Clearly, it has strong economic, political, cultural, and ecological implications. The economic and the political implications are clear. In Venezuela, for instance, a strategy of delegation and decentralization, central to the national development plan, was implemented after the fall of the last dictator in 1958. This well-outlined policy created eight strong socioeconomic, locally administered nuclei in newly created regions.

Other countries have also experimented with regionalization, either of their own accord, or through projects supported by international agencies. In the 1980s, for instance, the OEA's "Proyecto Multinacional de Regionalización Educativa" sponsored regionalization in Chile, Costa Rica, Ecuador, Nicaragua, Honduras, El Salvador, Guatemala, and Panama. All of these different countries shared the following characteristics: (a) the strengthening of the decentralization processes, (b) the organization and expansion of nuclearization efforts, (c) the implementation of diagnostic research to design communal curricular models, and (d) the institutionalization of regionalization as a new model of planning and administration to foment intersectorial coordination on educational work (OEA 1981, 14).

Municipalization is not, *stricto senso,* a new modality in education reform in Latin America. Traditionally, municipalities have supervised the administration of local schools. In Brazil, for instance, municipalities are typically responsible for the first four levels of the *primeiro grau* education and, in some cases, the next four layers. Increased responsibility on the part of central governments to expand initial schooling has decreased municipalities' concern for education. Its lack of novelty aside, municipalization experienced a boost in the 1980s, when the process was a popular tool in overcoming local barriers to the implementation of decentralization policies. It is, however, a more radical proposition than decentralization proper, for it requires the reform of the traditional municipality role and, as a consequence, brings about a change in the traditional political balance. Further, municipalization requires fiscal and financial reforms to ensure the return of economic and budgetary administrative power to the municipalities and to guarantee effectiveness.

Municipalization assumes that market forces can check the effects of centralization and central planning of public services, which makes it clearly a neoliberal concept. Consequently, it is a virtually ideology-specific policy that belongs in the repertoire of developmentalist, strong governments more than it does in that of socialism-inclined democracies. Because it has been used indiscriminately by both kinds of governments, however, it is fair to claim that decentralization (in any of its manifestations) has been used in Latin America not as a result of technical decisions but, instead, for political reasons, the logic of which is not always constant.

Hevia (1991) identifies four rationales for the growing application of decentralization policies in Latin America. The first is the neoliberal rationality, based on the need to decrease public spending, to privatize the hiring of teachers, or to transfer the schools to the private sector. The second is the "geopolitical" rationality, which sees decentralization of the state's administration as a means to achieve both regional development and the occupation and integration of all regions of the country.

Administrative efficiency is the logic that justifies decentralizing for the purposes of control and making the decision-making process more efficient. Democratic participation, on the other hand, calls for more autonomy of decision making, power, and resources to the lowest level of the system to resolve the problems in the education sector. These different logics can be related to two paradigms that interpret educational phenomena: the liberal-economic paradigm and the critical paradigm (Hevia 1991).

Decentralization and the Liberal-Economic Paradigm

The liberal-economic paradigm is based on a functionalist perspective that ascribes the dynamic of social change to a tendency of internal balance of the forces at work in society. From this perspective, decentralization is a simple and linear change aimed at obtaining more participation of the population in the public sphere. Advocates of this model understand that, in different countries, there is a uniform tendency toward participation. The proponents of the paradigm see the centralized government as homogeneous and monolithic.

The attempt at counteracting the historical centralist nature of Latin America follows a decentralization path for two main reasons: first, to improve the efficiency of the system (i.e., get rid of the bureaucracy) and, second, to diminish the failures of centralized planning (Rondinelli and Cheema 1983). The decentralization path is then pursued by a political determination on the part of the central government to give participation to the communities. Hence, the levels and forms of decentralization will vary according to what is being delegated. Hevia (1991) suggests that delegation of responsibilities may include: (a) responsibility for planning and generation of administrative resources and (b) responsibility for the decision over which institution receives the delegation. Among the institutions vying for a role in the delegation process are: (a) the low levels of the ministry of education, (b) public organizations outside of the regular structures of the ministry, (c) units of subnational governments on regional or local levels, (d) community organizations, (e) private organizations, and (f) specific individuals.

Decentralization and the Critical Paradigm

Advocates of the critical paradigm see decentralization as a process that allows increased participation of individuals or social groups. Specifically, this paradigm proposes that decentralization consists of strategies that aim at resolving issues of distribution, generation, and placement of power within the educational realm. To achieve this goal, power is at times moved from the central to the local government, from a central institution to another, or from the government to the private sector. These transfers represent a shift in the site where power is actualized, but not in the site where it emanates (McGinn and Street 1986).

It is also possible to see decentralization from a critical perspective, as a means to secure broader representation of the legitimate terests in education (Hevia 1991). Accordingly, levels of centralization or decentralization in a given country can be defined by the level of power and social control groups exert over a specific public activity.

In order to corroborate our premise that the process of decentralization has had different meanings under different governments and that it has responded to a political strategy rather than a technical one, we develop a view of decentralization focused on how the ideologically different governments of Salvador Allende (1970–1973) and the Pinochet Military Junta (1973–1989) used almost the same language in their policies to advance decentralization of the Chilean educational system for their divergent political agendas.

Allende's Decentralization Efforts

In order to assure increased participation of individuals and social groups and, therefore, secure broader representation of the legitimate interests in education, the Allende government proceeded to decentralize education in a manner consistent with its ideological positions. Such positions, as stated in the Congress of the Socialist Party in 1967, were as follows:

1. The socialist party, as a Marxist-Leninist organization, establishes the seizure of power as a strategic objective to be achieved by this generation, in order to install a revolutionary state that will free Chile from dependence and economic and cultural backwardness and will initiate the construction of socialism.

2. Evolutionary violence is inevitable and legitimate. It is a necessary result of the repressive and armed character of the class state. It is the only road that will lead to the seizure of political and economic power, and its later defense and reinforcement. Only by destroying the bureaucratic and military apparatus of the bourgeois state can the socialist revolution be consolidated.

3. Peaceful and legal forms of warfare will not, in and of themselves, lead to power. The Socialist Party considers these as limited instruments of action, incorporated into the political process that will bring everyone to armed warfare. Consequently the alliances established by the party can only be justified to the extent that they contribute to the realization of the strategic objectives just noted. (Jobet 1971, 130)

From its election in 1970 to its fall in 1973, the Allende government produced numerous documents concerning the reform of education. One of the earliest documents was a report entitled "Educational Policy of the UP Government: Immediate Measures." The objectives of education were integrated into the general objective of the popular government, which was the transformation of a capitalist society into a socialist society. Within this framework, the general objectives for the educational system were: (a) guaranteed access to school for all children of school age and the opening of the schools to adults to form a system of permanent education; (b) assurance that students would not drop out of the system; (c) achievement of real participation by educational workers, students, parents, workers' organizations, and the people in general in the transformation of the educational systems within the framework of national planning; (d) orientation of the educational systems toward a commitment to the interest of the working class rather than the interest of the bourgeoisie and imperialism; (e) redefinition of the role of the educator in terms of the requirements of the proposed socioeconomic transformation; and, finally, (f) the production of graduates who would be critical and creative, who would feel solidarity with their fellow citizens, and who would "have the disposition and the capacity to contribute to the construction of a socialist society" (Farrell 1986, 61).

Another document produced later—"The General Bases for the Formulation of the 1972 Operational Plan and Frame of Reference for the Six-Year Educational Sector Plan"—also stated general education objectives: (a) democratization of education through expansion of the system and increased local participation in both planning and administration; (b) equalization of educational opportunities; (c) participation of all education workers in the transformation of the educational system; (d) assistance in the process of structural change that was moving Chile toward a socialist society; (e) establishment of a unified and integrated educational system that would be more closely linked to the needs of the society; (f) formation of the "New Man," who would be able to overcome Chile's underdevelopment and cultural, economic, and technological dependency; and (g) establishment of a system of permanent education that would help Chilean workers to surmount their cultural disadvantages (Farrell 1986, 91).

The transformation proposed by Allende was not to be the work only of technicians. Instead, it was to be discussed, studied, decided, and executed by the organizations of teachers, workers, students, and parents, within the general line of national planning. Additionally, the executive direction of the educational apparatus was to have an effective representation of all social organizations integrated in local, regional, and national councils of education (Programa Básico 1970, 30).

To foster this transfer of governance to the hands of the community, two types of educational councils were to be created: one type was to be composed of education workers to direct the technical and professional aspects of schools; the other would be a school community council, composed of parents, students, workers, neighbors, and educators, to critique planning and regulate relations between the school and the community. The principles of diversification and decentralization were also important in the democratization process. Coordinating at all levels to meet local needs was unnecessary to satisfy the requisites of national planning, so technical centers were created at each level to handle research, evaluation, documentation, and planning tasks (Fisher 1979, 68).

The policymakers of the Unidad Popular understood that educational planning and the degree of autonomy for decision making at the local level was a "political road rather than a technical one" (Farrell 1986, 71). Therefore, the connection between policy and ideology was clear. The role to be assigned to local, provincial, and regional units in the overall national planning process was limited. To what extent would they have autonomy to reach conclusions that differed from those already established by the central authorities? The position was clearly expressed by the superintendent of education in a speech delivered to mark the opening of in-service training on February 25, 1971. His theme was "This is the year of Educational Democratization." His interpretation of democratization was as follows:

[Chile,] finding itself at a decisive cross-roads, democratically deliberated and chose a path. This path is oriented toward the liquidation of unjust socio-economic structures, toward the conquest of true national

independence, toward an accelerated development effort and an authentic
democratization. It is a path which has a target: SOCIALISM. (Farrell
1986, 73)

The superintendent added that, since the nation had already
chosen this new goal, education had to reorganize itself to contribute to its realization. "We will have to redefine the aims and objectives of our educational system, we will contribute to forming the
NEW MAN, the citizen who will live socialism." Thus, the goals
had been established already; it was incumbent upon teachers and
other contributors to the national consultation to collaborate in accomplishing them, not criticize them or suggest others (Farrell 1986,
73). The strain between central planning and local control was the
principal problem affecting the educational system. The more there
is of one, the less there can be of the other.

In the same way, the concept of democracy in the educational
system was stated by some of the socialists as "imposing authority,
overstepping legality and not waiting for orders from authorities.
One must make decisions, take the initiative, neither seeking per-
mission nor allowing one's actions to be sanctioned by legal formu-
las" (Farrell 1986, 70).

In short, as the document of the superintendent of education
stated "the education we [Unidad Popular] will build will not be
neutral. . . . The new education will have a political meaning and
orientation" (Farrell 1986, 95).

The Military Government's Decentralization Efforts

In the last year of the UP government, the Chilean society was po-
larized. Strikes and street disturbances, many of them violent, para-
lyzed virtually every sector of the economy and public life. The military took office by a coup.

The Junta's Declaration of Principles stated its fundamental belief
in the spirituality of man, on the "Christian concept of man and
society," a concept that "gave rise to the Western civilization" (Junta
de Gobierno de Chile 1974). The Junta affirmed its belief in man as
a social being, inherently rational, and, by essence, different "in their
desires, duties, and aspirations." Humans could not be regimented.
Happiness must be conquered individually. Human beings had not

been created to serve the state, but, rather, the latter had been created to serve the former.

The rights of the individual and the rights of intermediate social organizations (such as the family or the community) should not be assumed by the state. The new order believed the state to exist merely to carry out those functions that lower level organizations are unable to conduct: national defense, foreign affairs, strategic or fundamental services or industries, and national planning. Other functions fall to the state only when intermediate organizations, which normally assume these functions, fail or neglect to carry them out. In these instances, the principle of the "subsidiary state" applies: the state, in its capacity of ensuring the common good, is endowed with these functions (Junta de Gobierno de Chile 1974, 16–17).

The "subsidiary state" was grounded on a neoliberal economic model, one that opened the country to foreign capital and goods, liquidated unprofitable national industries, reduced the role of the state, and promoted the role of private capital and the free market (Aedo et al. 1985, 163). Additionally, it was oriented by an emphasis on order, austerity, probity, and authority. Among other things, the Junta proposed a long-range and integrated planning effort; an authoritarian, impersonal, and "just" government; a juridical order; accelerated economic progress; respect for human rights; respect for individual merits and efforts; sobriety; and the restoration of an apolitical character in the administration of the government (Kraft and Figueroa 1992).

Merit and impersonality were also present in the justification of the decentralization reform of education. The Junta believed that all individuals have a right to education in two basic aspects: access, and permanence and promotion. The subsidiary aspect of the reform was the argument that the community must participate at the different levels of the system. Further justification for this was that in a centralized government and administration, the central office rules all educational work without proper consideration of the differences existing between regions. An additional principle orienting the reform was lifelong education or "permanent education": "Man should be educated from birth to death" (Plan Nacional Indicativo, quoted in Figueroa 1994, 24). In sum, the general objectives the government established for the educational sector were: to promote equal opportunities, to allow systematic adequacy of the educational system to the needs of the country and its citizens, to promote activities that facilitate the process of lifelong education, and to improve the cultural patrimony of the nation through physical, intellectual, and moral development of the citizens.

When the educational decentralization process described above was applied in Chile in 1982, such implementation occurred at two levels. Ministerial Regional Secretariats of Education were created and given power for human resource management, materials, and financial resources, and schools were provided with autonomy for administration of the curriculum. The application of the decentralization process took place through the municipalization of educational administration. The aim was to achieve better quality of education, higher levels of community and teacher participation, and the making of a more effective and efficient administrative process.

The government's arguments in support of municipalization were several. One was that through municipalization, decentralization is deepened, thereby allowing greater efficiency in the solution of problems. Another argument was that municipalization improved the rationalization of administration by leaving the ministry with only normative duties to fulfill. Third, teachers' salaries would be improved by virtue of more resources being made available to the municipalities. Further, teachers would have increased occupational opportunities, for they would be given the opportunity to select the municipalities they wanted to work for, in accordance with their interests and aspirations (Egaña and Magendzo 1983).

Economic competition was introduced by the government to the world of education. Hoping to increase the efficiency of education and to encourage the private sector to bridge the gap that would create projected further cuts in public resources for education, the government initiated a process of privatization of education. Decentralization of K-12 schools was carried out by transference and per-student subsidy. Government-owned primary and secondary schools were transferred to municipalities under special legal arrangements, and vocational secondary schools were transferred to private, nonprofit organizations (Shiefelbein 1991, 20).

The higher education system was also affected when in 1981,

government-dictated reform transformed the branches of public universities, the University of Chile and the State Technical University, into autonomous universities. The system grew from eight to sixty-two universities, forty of them private (Figueroa 1994, 11). Presently, there are 306 private and public higher education institutions, including 78 professional institutes and 156 technical centers (Consejo Superior de Educación 1991, 25).

Politics and the Language of Decentralization

Impact of changes in political and administrative organizations and, specifically, in the educational system are hardly neutral. Rather, they advance the interest of some groups in society over others. Reform often alters the figures of resource allocation between regions and localities, increases or decreases the magnitude of political influence, and increases or restricts citizens' access to policymakers and to decision-making processes in the system. Chile illustrates the point well: the rhetoric of the Allende reform was one of local involvement, but the national ideology appeared to overwhelm and control local initiatives. The military government decentralized administratively but, again, kept a tight ideological influence on all levels of the educational system.

The rhetoric of educational reform in both governments abundantly referred to participation, local control, empowerment, and decentralization, together with several semantic substitutes. Much was done in the way of announcing a new age and new procedures, of heralding the birth of the "New Man," one who would be permanently taught in an educational environment where there would be equality of opportunity. New offices and structures were created to implement the decentralization policies. The simple creation of decentralized structures and the announcement of new procedures for participation do not guarantee, however, as Cheema (1983) has pointed out, that there will be effective generation of economic growth with greater social equity.

The language of decentralization was semantically multilayered. In the Allende government, participation in (educational) decision making meant more than an administrative strategy for educating the people to the demands and responsibilities of the new society. It also meant the concomitant creation of the very character of the new society. The metalanguage was one of consciousness raising for the continuing evolution of society (see also Fisher 1979).

In the military government, decentralization was promoted as an "opportunity equalizer," a tool to acknowledge regional differences and increase local participation. The social impact of its "equal opportunity decentralization" policy can be measured by the multiplication of private universities in the country. Its record on freedom and "man's" self-realization can be evaluated by the abolition of the democratic elections of local councilors and mayors—so much for local decision making. The government appointed the mayors and the municipalities ceased to be an organ of policy formation to become an executive agency for policies designed at higher levels of the government (Hevia 1982).

Chile offers a particularly good example of how the policies of the dominant political ideology define educational systems in political terms. The educational system has had to redefine itself in new social and political terms appropriate to the circumstances. In order to provide the institutional framework necessary for popular decision making and policy development, the Allende government sought initiatives such as the "democratization law." This law promoted basically several political concessions to assure participation of each party. In terms of its ideology and policies, the "democratization of education" was referred to as open and popular decision making in the educational process. The military Junta's "democratization of education," on the other hand, referred to the extension of basic educational services to all individuals (Fisher 1979).

The rhetoric of permanent education also differed from one government to another. For the Allende administration, it meant there was to be a national system that would provide education from birth to old age. Education was to be understood as "education of the masses, by the masses and for the masses, in a society of the Socialist type" (Farrell 1986, 162). Having appropriated the concept and made it one of its own principles of educational policy, the military government, however, read the concept to mean that "man" can be educated from birth to death.

The two governments' pursuit of decentralization of decision making in the educational system was also marked by vastly different approaches, particularly concerning issues of class. While the

Allende government sought to incorporate the masses, specifically the working class, in the process of decentralization, the military government sought to limit decision making to individuals with advanced technological skills. Allende understood "educators" to mean more than titled teachers and professors. Laborers, campesinos, and community members were also members of the *consejos de Educación* (councils of education), together with other people from all sectors of community and educational life. The military, on the other hand, through the creation of the Regional Ministerial Secretariats, formed a lower echelon of technocrats and bureaucrats to whom some of the decisions were delegated in the process of municipalization.

Conclusion

Fisher (1979) has claimed that the process of social change and its relationship to political ideology and educational reform follow two patterns. One he describes as "the commitment to political socialization as an instrument to promote and sustain dominant ideology and as a means to win and consolidate political power" (68). The second is the influence of external interest groups on the formation and implementation of educational reform.

The Allende government's commitment to political socialization came in the form of education as popular culture. The military, on the other hand, conducted its political socialization tasks neither through national debate nor through local cooperative projects. Instead, its objectives were served through an accurate and methodical control of information and through government-sponsored patriotic displays and demonstrations (Fisher 1979, 68).

The external interest groups that influenced the formation and implementation of educational reform policy in Chile were several: the Church, the private education sector, the educational bureaucracy, and the teaching professionals, among others. The decentralization of education in Chile, then, is a process of social change "based in large part on class interests, but manifest through other institutionalized interests groups" (Fisher 1979). Likewise, we propose it was chosen not for its technical value but also as a strategy where political efficacy is as important, if not more important, than the educational potential of the reform. We argue that the decentraliza-

tion policies in Chile were used by a central minority group to un-
balance the forces in a local community against the dominant central group. Further, as McGinn and Street (1986, 25) suggest, it was
the location of power, not the shares of power, that were changed.

A comparative look at the decentralization policies of the Allende
government and the military Junta in Chile yields a number of important conclusions. The most critical ones for us are, first of all,
that both governments saw decentralization of education primarily
as a mechanism to increase the central government's effectiveness
and ideological control. As could be expected, the processes were
accompanied by elaborate supervision and control mechanisms.

Second, we advance that the main reason why both governments brought about the decentralization process was a political one.
Hence, the decentralization process is an ideological principle where
objectives such as democratic decision making and participation in
the government can be seen as fascinating goals in themselves. Thus,
decentralization is a political decision.

Third, although decentralization is a political decision, one must
acknowledge its potential for the improvement of education. Challenges faced by the educational systems are becoming so complicated that most solutions require that people who are near the problems be actively immersed in developing and implementing adequate
responses.

Fourth is the crucial point of how decentralization may be utilized according to the different—at times conflicting—logic of different governments. In the case of the military government in Chile,
the rationale for decentralization was a combination of three key
elements: neoliberalism, administrative efficiency, and geopolitics.
Neoliberalism justified the economicist privatization practice at the
expense of the public schools. Administrative efficiency justified the
control and shaping of the decision-making process at the local level.
Geopolitics justified the implementation of a municipalization policy
and the involvement of local, politically useful administrative ech-
elons. The Allende government, on the other hand, saw decentralization as an instrument to achieve democratic participation in the
forging of a new, socialist Chile. Thus, the same mechanism can
serve different logics and ideologies, depending solely on the rationale of each government.

Fifth, and now we return to a point made in the introduction, the decentralization of education in Chile came from the highest level of the government. It was a political determination by the governments that allowed the process to unfold. Hence, power and authority were transferred from a major unit of government to a minor unit one. However, direct control and, consequently, direct power was kept in the central government over the now decentralized units. Different strategies ensured that, though power was now shared differently, the main location from which it emanated remained the same. Hence, decentralization does not equate with democratization.

Sixth, triggered by decentralization policies, higher education was affected by a series of important transformations. These changes included not only the number of institutions the system gained but also a reduction in the state's role as financier of higher education, the introduction of competition among universities, and increased differentiation in the level of quality across the existing institutions. Higher education faced uncertain changes as policies shifted from one perspective of decentralization to another; faculty, administration, and students rapidly gained or lost power depending on whose definition of decentralization was dominant.

Finally, the Chilean decentralization process did not bring about the instatement of flexible structures in the education system. In fact, both governments proposed changes that sometimes replaced one rigid structure with another, creating a new bureaucratic system at the lower levels of the system, one that will be just as difficult to modify. Interestingly enough, the power at the local levels and the periphery turned out to be more concentrated than at the center.

In this chapter we have attempted to make the point that educational decentralization in Chile has been utilized by opposing ideological currents for political and expedience reasons, not technical ones. In our comparative analysis of Chile, the cultural context is critical to understanding the context in which the use of the same concept leads to different political outcomes. Now that the U.S. schools brace themselves for a new wave of reform, the pendulum of reform swings in a rather predictable pattern. In the United States, the pendulum will move from an "intensification of the current system," which normally generates results that are "primarily quantitative" and which is marked by intense centralization, to a reaction against "the current system," typically characterized by the opposite features (Passow 1990; Kirst 1990; Bacharach 1990).

The Chilean example, however, suggests a surprising pattern, in that one same strategy was employed by two vastly different ideological models, with similarly articulated rationales, to the construction of dramatically different visions of a nation. More importantly, neither project came to be a truly decentralizing project, for the ultimate power and control continued to lie with the central government. The enigma—and the uniqueness—of the Chilean decentralization experience, and, for that matter, that of the entire Latin American experience as a whole, cannot, we suggest, be understood without consideration of the cultural context of the problem and the development of models that account for what corporatists stress to be the enduring character of Latin American society. We believe that, unless one understands the Latin American tradition and ethos—the authority of the state, the centrality of its interventionist role, the place of the Catholic cultural and philosophical framework, the paternalistic relationships—one will fail to understand Latin America. The region must "be taken on its own terms," be those terms a dictatorship or a populist, socialist democracy. Hence, the perspective of cultural politics of this chapter and book.

References

Aedo, R., I. Noguera, and M. Richmond. 1985. Changes in the Chilean educational system during eleven years of military government: 1973–1984. In *Education in Latin America,* eds., C. Brock and H. Lawlor. Dover, N.H.: Cloom Helm.

Bacharach, S. 1990. Education reform: Making sense of it all. In *Education reform: Making sense of it all,* ed., S. Bacharach. Boston: Allyn and Bacon.

Cheema, G.S. 1983. The role of voluntary organizations. In *Decentralization and development: Policy implementations in developing countries,* eds., G.S. Cheema and D.A. Rondinelli. Beverly Hills: Sage.

Chilean Ministry of Education. 1971. Bases generales para la formulacion del plan operativo 1972 y marco de referencia para la formulacion del plan sexenal del sector educaciónal. Mimeograph. Santiago, Chile.

Consejo Superior de Educación. 1991. *Un año de trabajo.* Santiago: CSE.

Egaña, L., and A. Magendzo. 1983. *El marco teorico politico del proceso de decentralizacion educativa (1973–1983).* Santiago: PIIE.

Farrell, J. 1986. *The national unified school in Allende's Chile.* Vancouver, B.C.: University of British Columbia.

Figueroa, C. 1994. All that glitters is not gold, The role of the state in higher education. The case of Chile. Unpublished manuscript. Eugene, Oregon.

Figueroa, C., and R. Salinas. 1989. *Bases teóricas para la administración del sistema educaciónal Chileno.* Valparais: Playa Ancha University.

Fisher, K. 1979. *Political ideology and educational reform in Chile, 1964–1976.* Los Angeles: UCLA Latin American Center.

Hanson, M. 1991. Decentralización y regionalización en educación: Lecciones del pasado para el futuro. *La Educación* 108–110: 1–8.

Hevia, R. 1982. *Cambios en la administración educacional: El proceso de traspaso a las municipalidades.* RAE No. 2733. Santiago: PIEE.

———. 1991. *Politica de decentralisation en la education basica y media en America Latina: Estado del arte.* Santiago: UNESCO.REDUC.

Jobet, J. 1971. *El partido socialista de Chile.* Santiago: Editorial Universitaria.

Junta de Gobierno de Chile. 1974. Declaracion de principios. Mimeograph. Santiago, Chile.

Kirst, M.W. 1990. The crash of the first wave. In *Education reform: Making sense of It All,* ed., S. Bacharach. Boston: Allyn and Bacon. 20–30.

Kraft, R., and C. Figueroa. 1992. Chilean educational reform. Unpublished manuscript. Boulder, Colorado.

McGinn, N., and S. Street. 1986. La decentralización educatiónal en America Latina: politica nacional o lucha de facciones? *La Educación* 99:20–45.

Ministerio de Educación pública, Costa Rica. 1982. Plan de regionalizacion del sistema educativo. *La Educación* 88:44–87.

———. 1976. Nuclearización educativa. RAE No. 855. San José: Ministerio Educación.

OEA. 1981. Algunas reflexiones en torno a la regionalizacion en America Latina. *La Educación* 87:5–34.

Passow A.H. 1990. How it happened: wave by wave. In *Education reform: Making sense of it all,* ed., S. Bacharach. Boston: Allyn and Bacon.

Programa básico del gobierno de la unidad popular. 1970. Santiago: Horizonte.

Rondinelli, D.A. and G.S. Cheema. 1983. Implementing decentralization policies: An introduction. In *Decentralization and development: Policy implementations in developing countries,* eds., G.S. Cheema, D.A. Rondinelli, 9–34. Beverly Hills: Sage.

Rondinelli, D.A., J. Nelli, and G.S. Cheema. 1984. Decentralization in developing countries: A review of recent experience. World Bank Staff Working Papers 581:93.

Schiefelbein, E. 1991. Restructuring education through economic competition: The case of Chile. *Journal of Educational Administration* 29, 4:17–29

Véliz, C. 1982. Centralism and nationalism in Latin America. In *Politics and social change in Latin America: The distinct tradition,* ed., H. Wiarda. Amherst, Mass.: University Press.

———. La tradición centralista de America Latina. Barcelona: Ariel.

Whitaker, A. 1961. The Argentine paradox. *Annals* No. 334:107.

Chapter Nine
Private and Public Intellectuals in Finland

Jussi Välimaa

University life can be seen as a monastic vocation for individuals who step outside society to escape it. In the Finnish tradition, this kind of understanding of the social role of universities and intellectuals does, however, describe only the academic devotion to intellectual life. The other dimension is secular, more political and social. In Finland, this secular tradition has an equally long history as that of sacred tradition. In the following, I will describe how this dichotomy has developed historically and how it influences the understanding of the social role of universities in the present society.

My essay is not intended to be a historical narrative but rather an analytical description based on historical evidence. As I will discuss, at one point in the history of Finland, universities were seen as critical arbiters in the development of Finnish culture and in the construction of the nation. At present, however, academe's importance is increasingly defined in terms of the economy. The constituents of a university and the degrees they obtain are empowered by the economy either through scientific breakthroughs and their subsequent development, or the value of their degrees in the workplace. I argue here that the national identity (knowing who we are as a nation) created by Finnish intellectuals is the heart of cultural, political, and economic systems in Finland because it is a part of national knowledge, when knowledge is understood as a social product (see Tierney in this book). Consequently, I will examine the social role of higher education from the perspective of intellectuals. The concept "intellectual" is a crucial analytical tool because it provides a viewpoint from which higher education can be analyzed as a cultural phenomenon. I argue that "intellectual" is a socially constructed term that depends on the social and cultural contexts in which intellectuals reside.

Since the task of analyzing the relationship between intellectuals and society is far too extensive for one essay, I will use Finland as a case study for discussing the interaction between intellectuals, universities, and society at the higher education system level. I refer to two theoretical frameworks useful for analyzing the Finnish situation and society. First, in the sociological tradition, Finland can be taken as an example of a "small" nation compared to "big" nations (Alapuro 1988). This theme, in turn, relates to the social role of Finnish higher education in the debates about the differences between big countries and small countries. From this perspective, one can ask how universities and intellectuals have interacted with the cultural, political, and economic processes in a small nation. Second, to be able to conceptualize these processes, and the role of intellectuals in them, I refer shortly to the systems theoretical approach introduced by Niklas Luhmann (1987). As research questions, these issues can be translated as follows: how has the cultural understanding of universities developed historically, and what is the role of intellectuals in explaining the social role of higher education in Finland?

I begin with the definition of organizing concepts, followed by some historical background information on Finland with regard to higher education. The historical section is succeeded by a discussion of intellectuals and nationalism with an illuminative example taken from teacher training. In the third section, I discuss the Fennoman tradition of intellectuals that leads to creating and distinguishing between public and private intellectuals. Finally, I discuss the prestige of higher education and the interconnectedness of the theoretical approach to the themes of this chapter.

Academics, Professionals, or Intellectuals?

"Academic," "professional," and "intellectual" are terms interconnected with each other, but they refer to different traditions in the analysis of intellectual life. "Academic" is reserved for persons educated in higher education institutions. In Finland, this perhaps the most value-neutral term of the three since it refers to education only, not to social dimensions. "Professional," in turn, is a social category introduced by Durkheim into social sciences to describe the position of highly educated academic groups such as lawyers and doctors in modern society. For Durkheim (1964), and especially for Parsons (1964), professionals are a group whose social rules and norms are not set by the relationship with the employer but with their colleagues as a group (Konttinen 1989, 15–40). "Intellectual" and "professional" are debated terms in social sciences. Thus, "intellectual" is not a social category nor a position in the society defined by education, but a combination of the two. According to Parsons, intellectuals can be characterized as persons primarily concerned with the articulation of cultural symbols (Nettl 1970, 58). Sociologically speaking, intellectuals can be defined as persons with cultural positions who have opinions that they want to make public (Rahkonen and Roos 1992). To complete the definition of intellectuals, I refer to Jacoby (1992, 3–13) and state that the difference between intellectuals and academics is that academics work in universities without the ability to write to "normal" audiences. Jacoby (1992) introduces the term "public intellectuals," which means intellectuals who occupy the media with their ideas, as compared to "private intellectuals," who are academics who publish in specialist journals. These references point out that intellectuals are members of society in need of an audience with whom to share their ideas. In this sense, intellectuals are defined publicly in relation to their audience.

I also refer to the term "intelligentsia" to analyze historically intellectuals and the consumers of their ideas as a social group. According to Sadri (1992), this group is based on hierarchical classification of intellectuals and intelligentsia. In this Weberian tradition, intellectuals can be defined either as seekers of pure knowledge or as committed intellectuals: leaders, liberators, and saviors. In both categories "intelligentsia will be found more willing than intellectuals to view ideas instrumentally" (Sadri 1992).

When analyzing the social role of higher education and that of intellectuals, we can either assume that local traditions and the mission of the university are a decisive explanatory factor in the production of knowledge as suggested by Tierney (1991), or we can assume that international disciplinary backgrounds are the most powerful explanatory elements in academic behavior, as suggested by Becher (1989). In an American context, it seems rational to assume that the mission of an institution is, in part, to explain the production of knowledge (Tierney 1991). In the European context, this kind of assumption is, however, much harder to prove because the European system is not as competitive and market oriented as the American higher education system (Dill 1992). In Europe, universities resemble each other, whereas in the United States higher education institutions differ according to their missions and their structures (Välimaa 1994a). In Europe, it is possible to have national higher education policies inside the territorial national states, whereas in the United States, the dynamics of higher education institutions are directed to a greater extent by market forces and differentiated by state. For this reason, in the European context, the historical role of universities can be of central national importance. This is especially true in Finland.

The questions concerning knowledge production, whether national, institutional, or disciplinary based, are, in turn, related to issues of identity: how do intellectuals understand themselves, and how does this understanding change over time? In another paper (Välimaa 1994a), I have argued that the identity of Finnish academics is influenced more by local traditions than international disciplinary culture when analyzing the attitudes of academics toward assessment. When analyzing Finnish academics as a group, I assume they are a homogenous group. Of course, this assumption is a generalization and not valid because there are clear differences according to institutions and disciplines (Välimaa 1992, 1994a). The assumption, however, contains an important point that serves my purpose. Namely, by contending that Finnish academics are a group, I assume that national traditions, history, and language, and the conditions of a small country create an identity that separates Finnish academics from those in other countries. In the following, I also argue that these national traditions have influenced both the self-understanding of academics and the relationship between the universities and intellectuals. In this sense, my approach is nationalistic more than an international perspective that would focus on uniting disciplinary cultural elements in academia.

Finland and the Development of Higher Education

Both culturally and politically, Finland belongs to Scandinavia. As a consequence of this relationship, Finland has had a traditionally weak feudal class structure and a strong tradition of independent peasants leading the way to modern society with an emphasis on social and democratic ideas (Alestalo and Kuhnle 1984). Geopolitically Finland is a small nation situated between Western and Eastern Europe that has one dominant language group. Historically this geopolitical position has caused political dependencies with the stronger neighboring nations. Finland was ruled by the Swedish kings from the twelfth to the nineteenth century. During the Napoleonic wars, the country was invaded by the Russian Empire in 1809. At that time, Finland was understood more as a geographical than a political concept. For the development of Finland as a political unit, it was important that the invaded area was granted the political status of an imperial grand duchy with an independent internal administration in governmental, financial, and religious matters. Autonomy lasted for about 100 years, during which Finland developed from an "incidental byproduct of wars between Sweden and Russia," as Thaden (1984, in Alapuro 1988, 19) puts it, into an independent national state that reached political independence in 1918 after World War I (Alapuro 1988; Jutikkala and Pirinen 1962). The role of higher education was essential in this cultural "nation-building" process, as I shall show later.

Today, Finland is the seventh largest country by area in Europe (338,000 square kilometers) and is inhabited by approximately 5 million people. The citizens are served by twenty-one higher education institutions scattered throughout the country.

Higher Education from the Seventeenth to the Nineteenth Century

The history of Finnish higher education is the history of one university (referred to as the National University) until the beginning of the twentieth century. The foundations of Finnish national higher education were laid during the seventeenth century when Finland was part of the Swedish Kingdom. At that time, Sweden wanted to enhance the intellectual capacity of the kingdom by strengthening the existing universities and by founding new institutions. One of these new institutions was the Royal Academy of Åbo founded in 1640 in the capital of Finland, Turku (known by its Swedish name Åbo). The university consisted of four disciplines: theology, philosophy, law, and medicine. Originally, its main purpose was to educate Lutheran clergy and civil servants for the Swedish Kingdom, the Protestant superpower of the time (Klinge et al. 1987, 12–107). According to the founding statutes of the university, the main purpose of the new institution was defined as follows:

WE CHRISTINA, Queen of Sweden . . . declare that . . . through education, good administration and order in society, good knowledge of the true God leading to the realization of honorable, virtuous and Christian life will be attained . . . and . . . we desire to promote the better cultivation of liberal arts in order to increase the fame and beauty of the Finnish Grand Duchy . . . (Klinge et al. 1987, 82–84 translated by author).

This manner of characterizing the role of universities and university magistrates can be seen as the starting point for a historical continuum in defining the relationship between the state and the intellectuals as a relationship based more on loyalty to secular authorities than on academic traditions. It is also culturally significant that the founding of the Royal Academy was based on an ideology whereby education socializes ordinary people to become the members of civil society in the way Norbert Elias has described this historical process (Klinge et al. 1987, 65–67). It was culturally important that under the Swedish rule the Royal Academy provided a "cultural basis" to combine Finnish local patriotism with cultural nationalism. However, the eighteenth-century Finnish academics, such as Juslenius and Porthan, developed their cultural ideas without political purposes, as argued by Lehtinen (Lehtinen 1989).

The role of the Royal Academy of Åbo changed at the beginning of the nineteenth century when Russia invaded Finland during the Napoleonic wars. The situation of the university on the western coast of Finland close to Sweden proved problematic for the rulers of Finland both in a cultural and political sense. The rulers of Finland, both Finnish civil servants and Russian officials, interpreted the small student unrests in the 1810s and the 1820s as a political threat to Finnish autonomy. The political situation of the university changed, however, when Turku was destroyed by the great fire of 1827. Using the damage caused by the fire as an excuse, the czar moved the university to Helsinki, the new capital of Finland, and renamed it the Imperial Alexander University. Reforms were made to the academy when the location of the university was changed. As incentives for the academics, university structures were redesigned following the German Humboldtian ideas that emphasized the critical scientific approach, the uniformity of teaching and research, and the autonomy of the universities. Furthermore, the resources of the university were increased and developed. This, in turn, secured the loyalty of the academics to the czar and kept hidden the increased political control that was the leading motive behind moving the university (Klinge et al. 1989, 76–105).

By the time the university reopened in Helsinki, there were about 400 Finnish male students. The language of instruction, nevertheless, continued to be Swedish until the end of the nineteenth century (Strömberg 1989, 291–307). Up to that time, the upper estates of the society considered Finnish as a language with poor cultural traditions. Influenced by conscious Swedish policy, Finnish was a language mainly used by peasants and lower classes. This state of affairs was, however, changed during the nineteenth century by a group of Finnish nationalists residing at the National University. As a result of this nationalist ideology, many Swedish speakers supporting the nationalist "Fennoman" movement learned Finnish and even translated or changed their family names into Finnish. A good example is provided by Professor Y.S. Yrjö–Koskinen (formerly Forsman), who was one of the leaders of the Fennoman movement. He learned Finnish and published the first doctoral dissertation in Finnish on the history of Finland in 1858 (Suolahti 1974).

At the beginning of the nineteenth century, the Lutheran Church and the national university performed important political functions. The university educated the priests, and the Lutheran Church, through parish congregations, was responsible for the rural government as well as for public education (Alapuro 1988, 27). This situation changed, however, during the nineteenth century. In the 1860s, the national legislation began the process by which local government was divorced from the parish administration and the educational system was divorced from the Church.

Higher Education in the Twentieth Century
The twentieth century has been characterized by the expansion of

higher education as part of the Finnish educational system. Historically, three different periods of expansion can be traced. The first extends from the beginning of the century until 1930. During this period, six higher education institutions were founded. Student enrollment more than doubled from about 3,000 students to more than 7,000 students (Nevala 1991, 28). The second period (1931 to 1957) was defined by minor expansion and willingness to maintain the status quo. The third period (1958–1993) has been the most rapid period of expansion in the history of Finnish higher education. The number of higher education institutions has increased by fourteen, and the number of students has grown from 21,000 to 126,000. The number of academic teachers reached 7,900 in 1992. This figure does not take into account the number of researchers funded by the Finnish Academy (929) and by other sources (1,189). As mentioned above, there are twenty-one higher education institutions with 126,000 students scattered around the country (Ministry of Education 1994). Theoretically, the phase of "massified" higher education (making it available to the masses) was reached in the early 1970s when over 15% of the student age group entered higher education (Ahola 1993).

Traditionally, the expansion of Finnish higher education during the twentieth century has been explained, first, by external forces such as industrialization that contributed to the foundation of three technical universities and three institutions of economics. Second, political debates between Swedish speakers and Finnish speakers have, in turn, resulted in the foundation of two universities in Turku as well as the Business School for Swedish speakers during the 1910s and the 1920s. Third, from the 1960s onward, the process of establishing provincial higher education institutions was encouraged, in part, with the help of the regional policy principle, in Finnish *aluepolitiikka,* (Kangas 1992; Nevala 1991). In fact, the last period of expansion was an essential part of the national "welfare-state-building project," because providing equal educational opportunities, including higher education, in all parts of the country was one of the essential aims of the welfare state policy (Panhelainen and Konttinen 1994). Moreover, building the welfare state created jobs for academics in the expanding public sector of society. Politically, the dynamics of the welfare-state-building process have been driven mainly by the regional equality principle based on the political, economic, and academic activities of regional interest groups. Thus, the expansion of higher education, as well as the political conflicts concerning the expansion, were solved through founding new institutions rather than strengthening the existing ones (Välimaa 1994b).

From the higher education perspective, the building of a Scandinavian welfare state has also reshaped the social role of higher education. The problems of the expansion ended, however, with budget cuts in higher education at the beginning of the 1990s because of Finland's economical problems: the growing national debt and an unemployment rate of about 20% (in 1993). Being part of the public sector, all higher education institutions are suffering from reduced budgets (Välimaa 1994b). Jolkkonen (1993) has even noted that the welfare state has become the destiny of academics because cuts made in the public sector after 1992 have hit the nontenured faculty and academic professions, especially women working in social and educational professions.

If we define higher education policymaking, however, as a process where the needs of society meet the needs of academe, we are, in fact, analyzing the relationship between the universities and society. In Finland, this process is historically rooted in the making of the Finnish nation, in that the symbolic mediators between the university and society and the leading Finnish intellectuals have been professors working at the National University in Helsinki. To be able to analyze the model of interaction between academics and the people, I will examine the role of the National University, historically, as a social arena for ideas and persons.

Nationalism, National University, and Intellectuals

I will define nationalism as a "civic religion" for a modern territorially centralized state. It is a "set of motivations in the citizens that gives them a primary and overriding sense of obligation toward state and eliminates the various other obligations they feel toward other groups and centers within or outside the territory" (Alapuro 1988, 86–87). This ideological perspective is an interesting attempt to unpack the concept of nationalism into various forms of social relations and social coherence. In addition, this kind of a definition makes it interesting for the understanding of Finnish nationalism. It is fruitful to assume that "nationalism is not the awakening of nations to self-consciousness but rather the inventing of nations that never existed" (Alapuro 1988, 86). In the Finnish case, this directs the attention to the conscious efforts initiated and implemented by Finnish nationalists. This group can also be defined as intelligentsia in the sense that social stratification existed between the leaders and the organizers of the movement (Sadri 1992). Historically this social grouping was initiated at the National University.

The spokesman of the Finnish nationalistic movement, J.V. Snellman, professor of philosophy at the Imperial Alexander University and later senator in the national government, formulated the ideological aims of the nationalist cultural movement in the spirit of the Hegelian tradition developing the "spirit of history" into the concept of "national spirit" (Wilenius 1982). According to Snellman, the development of a nation will be fulfilled through the state (Alapuro 1987, 458). The ideology of "without a language there can be no nation" was both culturally radical and politically significant. It was a radical cultural statement because practically all the educated people (including Snellman) had Swedish as their mother tongue. This notion also laid the foundation for the development of this culturally initiated ideology into the nationalist political movement, Fennomania, in the nineteenth century. Culturally the Fennomans had two goals. First, they promoted the education of the nation, and second, they wanted to nationalize the educated (Rommi and Pohls 1989).

From a higher education perspective, it was socially significant that many of the leaders of the Finnish-speaking intelligentsia, of the Fennoman movement, and their opponents, as well, worked at the National University (Rommi and Pohls 1989). In this sense, the University provided a social forum, in fact the first public forum, for different views and different persons to debate with one another. During the second half of the nineteenth century, the role of the professors and students was even vital in maintaining the political debate during the periods when conventions of the estates-based parliament were closed (Alapuro 1988, 28; Klinge 1992). Moreover, Klinge has argued that the student associations provided models for Finnish political parties, because the student nations became the nuclei of the later party organizations (Klinge 1992). Further-more, and here I am expanding the approach to the development of a civil society, Klinge (1992, 37) has maintained that "it was in the academic setting that the idea of civic activity outside the bureau-cratic system, i.e., in associations, the free press, and parliamentary politics, finally emerged and developed."

As was the case with postsecondary institutions in other coun-tries at the time, those who studied there were mainly from the ruling class. In Finland it was socially important, however, that the National University was practically the only regular form of social mobility during the nineteenth century before industrialization was initiated (Waris 1940). Especially during the last half of the century, the Na-tional University was opened increasingly more to sons and daughters of peasants and workers as well (Konttinen 1991). Klinge et al. (1989, 171–172) has even argued that the increase in the number of higher education students began earlier in Finland than in other parts of Europe and Scandinavia. Specifically, in the mid-1910s the number of students per 100,000 inhabitants was 94 students in Finland, 88 in Denmark, 87 in Sweden, and 67 in Norway (Elovainio 1971).

As I have tried to show above, the National University has been both politically and culturally an important place in the making of Finnish national identity. This has strengthened the high social sta-tus of universities in general and higher education degrees in par-ticular in the Finnish society. The National University was also the cradle of the Finnish intelligentsia. Thus, this nation building ben-efited the rising group of Finnish speaking intellectuals who, as a social group, emphasized the importance of education and the Na-tional University.

One of the main goals of the Fennomans was the nationaliza-tion of the people. But what did this actually mean besides publish-ing newspapers and books? In order to reach the practical (and lo-cal) level of nationalizing the people, I will approach the issue from the perspective of elementary school teachers, because I believe that education was one of the most important channels in the cultural nation-building process.

Nationalism and Rural Intellectuals

One of the essential cultural and political goals of the Fennomans was to educate the people to strengthen the cultural basis of the Finnish-speaking civilization (Rommi and Pohls 1989, 85). At national level, this aim materialized in 1866 in the law of compulsory elementary education for all children. In practice, the elementary-school teachers were responsible for the process of educating the people. For this reason, it was important to educate Finnish-speaking teachers in a nationalist context.

All new teachers for the primary schools were trained in the teacher-training seminars (or colleges) during a four-year training span. The first seminar was founded in Jyväskylä in 1863 and the second one in Sortavala in 1880. In 1920 there were several teacher-training colleges located all over the country. The pedagogical goals of the teacher-training colleges were religious in the Lutheran sense, moralistic following the Victorian sexual mores, and patriotic in the sense of Finnish nationalism (Isosaari 1989). Furthermore, the teacher-training seminars were boarding schools with tightly regulated curricula and separate departments for male and female students. I do not believe, however, that teachers could be called intellectuals based on this training. Academically speaking, primary-school teachers were not defined as intellectuals at the end of the nineteenth century nor at the beginning of the twentieth century.

The definition changes, however, when we analyze the social roles of teachers in rural areas. The Sortavala Seminar described school teachers in rural areas as "candles of the people" (Isosaari 1989). Normally the teacher, the pastor of the parish, and the doctor were the most learned men in the community. Isosaari (1989) noted that teachers were active in all social fields in the rural community, especially in the rural areas of the central and eastern parts of Finland. Depending on the form of activity, teachers participated in or initiated cultural, political, and civil societies and associations, especially from the 1890s to the 1920s (Isosaari 1989, 118–120). In this sense, teachers were clearly considered as intellectuals in the country. Socially and culturally, school teachers were often seen as forerunners of modern times, as *rural intellectuals*. Thus, through the national schooling system, the cultural impact of higher education spread around the countryside because teachers were trained at institutions inspired by nationalistic enthusiasm. This national enthusiasm was basically a cultural attitude, but it could easily be translated into political language in the fight for the national independence of Finland. From this viewpoint the teachers were implementing the "nation-building project" as part of the Finnish-speaking intelligentsia. Thus, historically, Fennomania seems to have been a cultural movement that enabled a hierarchical structure to support intellectuals residing at the National University and in rural areas.

Fennoman Model of Intellectuals

The word "intellectual" is a problematic term in Finland because it has negative social connotations both as a concept and as a social group. Namely, in a study on Finnish intellectuals in the 1980s by Finnish sociologists, one of the first reactions to the questionnaire was: are there any Finnish intellectuals at all (Rahkonen and Roos 1992, 114)? Similar opinions were repeated in an interview with students at the University of Jyväskylä (Piskonen 1993). These reactions reflect social values in the Finnish society. Alapuro (1987) has defined the social and cultural position of Finnish intellectuals as "state intellectuals," signifying persons who usually have an academic education and hold a civil servant position either in the universities (all professors are civil servants as defined by their relationship to the employer) or in public administration. This definition, in turn, relates the Finnish state intellectuals to the European tradition of intellectual politicians who want to do their duty to the nation more than only interpret (or change) the world (Rahkonen and Roos, 1992, 108–109).

There are two facts to be remembered when analyzing the position of state intellectuals. First, Finland is a small nation with a relatively small population of restricted labor markets for academics. This situation is strengthened by the fact that Finnish is spoken only in Finland. These facts create limited possibilities for intellectuals to be employed by other than the public sector. Second, the model of interaction between intellectuals and the people developed mainly during the nineteenth century as a byproduct of the nation-building project. According to Alapuro, since the times of the Fennomans, Finnish intellectuals have longed for solidarity between ordinary people. This identification with the people is based on moralistic pathos and on an idealized picture of the people as well as on the feeling of serving the people. Simultaneously, it aims at a unified nation with intellectuals as its leaders (Alapuro 1987, 476–478). I call this the "Fennoman model of intellectuals."

The Fennoman tradition functions in a twofold way. On the one hand, it has strengthened the national self-understanding of the Finnish intellectuals. Morally and ethically it is based on a willingness to serve the "ordinary people," to help the people. On the other hand, it is socially reflected in the unwillingness of the Finnish intellectuals to call themselves intellectuals, something above the ordinary people. Politically this Fennoman model of interaction has signified, however, a model where academic people are expected to act as leaders of the nation and of the ordinary people (Alapuro 1987). In fact, politically this model of interaction with the people is elitist, even though morally it claims to be democratic. Actually, in both aspects, the Fennoman model of intellectuals is based on superiority compared to the "ordinary people." It is perhaps due to this moral and political contradiction that the concept "intellectual" has never been socially accepted in social democratic Finland with its Scandinavian egalitarian traditions.

This moral attitude has influenced the behavior of the Finnish intellectuals during the twentieth century as well. According to Alapuro, the willingness to serve (and to lead) the nation was reflected in the right-wing political movement of students during the period between the two world wars, called AKS (Academic Karelia Society) and in the left-wing political movement of the 1970s (Alapuro 1987). Both student movements were morally justified by the conviction to teach "ordinary people," although these two student movements did not define "ordinary people" in the same way. Following the Fennoman tradition, the right-wing movement defined "ordinary people" as independent peasants, whereas for the left-wing students "ordinary people" consisted of workers.

Alapuro also suggests that this tradition has brought the people and the state intellectuals together in the "welfare-state-building project" from the 1960s onward. However, this last great national project is no longer expanding because of the economic recession in Finland in the 1990s. From the perspective of academics, it means decreasing labor markets. From the perspective of intellectuals, the audience and the media have changed, setting new demands on the intellectuals who occupy the media with their ideas, as has been suggested by Jacoby (1992) and others (Rahkonen and Roos 1992).

Intellectuals and the State

The new situation has caused new challenges, especially to traditional state intellectuals, because the economic crisis has created a demand for national visions and mission statements. Traditionally, national visions have been created by state intellectuals residing at the University of Helsinki. However, at the moment this tradition seems be both practically and conceptually in a crisis because no one has been able to create a national vision. This state of affairs is, in turn, related to the nature of the postmodern society that is no longer constituted from one center, but from many centers. Instead of "state intellectuals," we should examine the changed role of intellectuals, and of higher education, from the perspectives of "private intellectuals" and "public intellectuals." From this point of view, we can also examine the cultural role of higher education in the differentiated society.

Jacoby makes the distinction between private and public intellectuals on the basis of the audience: public intellectuals are (or used to be) persons who can discuss important issues in "normal media" with a wide audience, whereas private intellectuals are those who are experts only in their small academic fields (Jacoby 1992). Jacoby's concepts describe, in fact, the relationship between intellectuals and society. In Finland, I suggest that this kind of distinction is historically rooted in the concepts of state intellectuals and rural intellectuals. Traditional state intellectuals have been professors of the National University occupying the nationwide media with their visions and ideologies. In this sense, they have been and are close to the definition given by Jacoby as public intellectuals. The position of state intellectuals (as public intellectuals) normally residing at Helsinki University, as Rahkonen and Roos (1992, 117) have suggested, has not been challenged by historical changes, whereas that of private intellectuals can be defined differently. Following the definition of intellectuals given earlier in this paper, I could argue that school teachers as rural intellectuals were in fact private intellectuals. The route from rural intellectuals to private intellectuals is a tempting vision, especially from the perspective of the audience: both are considered "silent intellectuals" at the national level. It is not, however, rooted in the historical experience because rural intellectuals used to be local intellectuals, whereas the modern private intellectuals are not defined by geographical locations but according to their academic specialist audiences. The analysis of this change requires discussion on the new "silent intellectuals."

I begin by claiming that in Finland the change concerning public and private intellectuals is connected to the opening of the higher education system to the masses. With the emergence of the "mass education" university, the number of academics (both M.A.s and Ph.D.s) has significantly increased. However, the number of public intellectuals has not followed this trend; in society today we have only sixteen intellectuals belonging to the "hit parade of intellectuals," with eight academics in the list (Rahkonen and Roos 1992, 115–117). To draw attention to this contradiction, I could refer to the postmodern philosophers who argue that changes of media have affected the nature of public intellectuals requiring new communicative intellectual skills (Rahkonen and Roos, 1992). While drawing attention to the changes in the media, this assumption does not, however, throw light on the internal processes of academia creating or exploiting the use of "active silence." Are private intellectuals not even interested in participating in public debates, as Jacoby (1992) has suggested?

A fruitful view on the internal life of private intellectuals is to analyze how "silent academics" are made in Finland. Typically, they are recruited from local graduates. In the five largest Finnish universities, the number of staff recruited from their alma mater is as high as 79%, and the corresponding average in all the higher education institutions (excluding the art academies) is as high as 66% (SVT 1993:2, 58–65). When these facts are combined with the socioeconomic factors in a small nation, we can explain the processes related to the silence of private intellectuals. First, there are only limited possibilities available for the younger generations interested in an academic career. Second, the mobility of academics is restricted by the recruitment model preferring graduates from one's own institution. Socially this means that you "stick to your post," since there are not many possibilities available. It also means that both "public intellectuals" and "private intellectuals" are loyal to the state by employment and to academic world by the local social ties. In this sense, the dynamics of smallness are directed toward securing a future in the near environment (Häyrynen 1987, 227). Socially it leads to closed social and intellectual circles. From the perspective of the intellectuals, these dimensions in the social dynamics of a small nation do not encourage the rise of new public intellectuals because the social role reserved for private intellectuals, that of an expert or a professional, is much less demanding. Concentrating on a field also helps to secure an academic future, as Jacoby has noted (Jacoby 1992). In Finland these processes seem to support each other.

Economists as Public Intellectuals?

In Finland the 1990s have been characterized by economic difficulties. Besides causing problems for the universities, the new situation has also challenged public intellectuals to debate civilization, taking into account technical and economic perspectives (von Wright 1993). This, in turn, reflects the social reality, where the dominant way of seeing society, and the value of higher education, are embedded in economist's language. As to higher education, the dominant themes are related to the efficiency of education and the service function of higher education institutions.

The first arguments demanding more efficiency and societal relevance for higher education were published by industrial societies at the beginning of the 1980s (Korkeakoulut ja metsäteollisuus 1983). Inspired by the strategy of self-regulation, similar argumentation was found in the policy papers of the Ministry of Education, stating that higher education institutions should be managed more efficiently and that they should also be more sensitive to the needs of society (Higher Education Act of 1986). This viewpoint has become even more dominant with the economic problems of Finland in the 1990s. At the national level, economically formulated understanding of higher education in society is apparent in many policy papers published by the government, where the national survival strategy of Finland is based on knowledge and expertise (see, e.g., Tiedon ja osaamisen Suomi 1993). The same attitude is reflected in the official background paper prepared for the OECD evaluation of Finnish higher education policy. According to the report, "the long-term policy is to make Finland a country of knowledge and expertise, promoting education and research as part of a national strategy of survival" (Ministry of Education 1994, 127). More precisely, it means that "1) Finnish higher education will be measured up to the highest standards; 2) contacts between higher education, business and industry will be cultivated; 3) higher education intstitutions, together with the Academy of Finland, will produce centers of excellence which hold their own in international competition; and, finally 4) teaching and research in the institutions of higher education will be directed towards supporting the development of Finnish industrial structure, entrepreneurship and internationalization" (abbreviated translation from Ministry of Education 1994, 127–128).

On the basis of these policy statements, it is evident that, for the makers of the national development strategy, the value of higher education is seen as part of the nation building of Finland. In the present society, it does not, however, lean to nationalist ideologies but emphasizes the economic aspects of higher education in the internationalized world market situation. This kind of understanding of the national mission is quite different from the previous cultural and social views in defining the role of higher education. In fact, it is related to defining national identity from an economic perspective. Thus, higher education is still considered important in the "nation-building project," because of the economic potential in higher education institutions and not because of the cultural potentials. Under these social conditions, the debates on higher education are dominated by economic values as well.

In this kind of changed cultural environment, the role of public intellectuals has also changed. It is even possible that private intellectuals as experts in their special fields enjoy higher social status than public intellectuals with their more general opinions. In this cultural environment, it is more than natural that economic pamphlets, analyses of actual problems, and interviews of economists have significantly increased during the years of recession (Niiniluoto 1994, 18–21). It appears that, in this sense, economists have come closer to being public intellectuals than private intellectuals due to their treatment of economic issues that are believed nationally important.

Conclusion: Higher Education at a Social Crossroads

As apparent in the official documents, the social status of higher education is esteemed highly in the present Finnish society. This social fact is reflected in at least three ways. First, ever since the 1960s there have been more applicants and examinees to the higher education institutions than have been accepted by the institutions. As an example, in 1992 there were 85,384 applications, 53,768 examinees, and 20,552 accepted students. Second, university professors (together with the prime minister and the bishop) have been ranked as the highest positions in the professional status scales on the basis of national questionnaires (Alestalo and Uusitalo 1978). Third, in 1993 the prime minister nominated a committee consisting of intellectuals (mainly university professors and researchers) to analyze the mental status of Finland and to develop visions for our future (Niiniluoto and Löppönen 1994).

I maintain that this surprising political act can be seen as a continuation of the Fennoman tradition. In addition, the nomination of the committee provides an example of how Fennoman traditions meet the traditional academic values that defend the right of a scholar not to interfere with political life. Namely, the main arguments presented by the opponents of the committee were that academics should not interfere with social matters, but they should concentrate on analyzing the trends in society as academics and not as politicians (Jallinoja 1993). Thus, academics should not be public intellectuals! The members of the committee maintained that this is exactly the distinction that should not be made (Niiniluoto 1994, 246–248). The head of the committee, a professor of theoretical ethics at Helsinki University, claimed that academics should take part in the discussion as citizens. In fact, he seems to be saying that academics should feel a national responsibility, that they should be public intellectuals! In Finland this feeling of responsibility can be seen as a continuation of the Fennoman tradition where the role of an intellectual is easily seen as that of a state intellectual loyal both to the homeland and to academia, whereas the tradition supporting private intellectuals is rooted in the traditional academic values of academic freedom. However, this is not the place to review the social interplay between disciplinary differences and academic values in Finland (Välimaa 1992).

Historically the change from state versus rural intellectuals to public versus private intellectuals can be explained by the change from a hierarchical and stratified class-based society to a fragmented postmodern society. At the beginning of the twentieth century, the connecting link between state intellectuals (on the national level) and rural intellectuals (on the local level) was the ideology of nationalism. Today, however, no apparent uniting national ideology seems to exist between private and public intellectuals and with society. This, in turn, reflects the differentiated social reality where society no longer has only one center but many. According to Luhmann (1989), the new society can be understood as consisting of different, horizontally simultaneous systems interacting with each other. In this analytical framework, higher education can be defined as one of the few meeting points of the different social systems in society. As to Finland, higher education has provided an opportunity for debate by the various representatives of many interest groups: political, cultural, religious, and economic. In this sense, higher education as a social system has a double meaning: it is part of society, but it is also separate from society. At the beginning of the twentieth century, the borderline between society and academia was crossed by cultural acts, creating a national vision for the emerging nation. Nowadays, the borderline from economy to the political system, and to education, is crossed by money (Luhmann 1989). Historically this indicates the change in the direction of interaction. During the making of the Finnish national identity, the intellectuals residing at the National University defined the nature of the civil society. At that time, it was natural that university professors acted as ministers in the government, as Klinge (1992) has stated. Nowadays, the civil society, in turn, defines the nature of higher education.

As I have tried to show, national traditions have guided the self-understanding of Finnish academics. From this point of view, Finnish intellectuals are linked to the process of producing national knowledge. When saying this, I do not intend to negate the value of academic traditions to seek the truth. What I wish to emphasize is that the national parameters to produce nationally relevant knowledge have been set by politically and culturally defined ideological nationalism and not by academic traditions. Furthermore, the social role of intellectuals has also been defined in national terms as that of state intellectuals. In this national context, the differentiation of society and that of the academic world has increased academic freedom of private intellectuals. Thus, from this perspective, the inability of the national committee to create a unified national vision reflects a social situation where Finland, like other small nation-states, is no longer defined as a purely national entity. The lack of one center in society causes confusion for unified national goals, which, in turn, causes problems for creating a unified national vision. It seems that public intellectuals are not able to create national visions, and private intellectuals are not motivated to try.

References

Ahola, S. 1993. Diversification and the mass higher education system in Finland: Martin Trow revisited. In *Korkeakoulutuksen kriisi? [Higher education in a crisis?]* Articles from the Fifth Symposium on Higher Education Research held in Jyväskylä, August 19–20 1993, eds., H. Jalkanen and L. Lestinen, 41–54. Jyväskylä: Institute for Educational Research.

Alapuro, R. 1987. De intellektuella, staten och natio–nen. *Historisk tidskrift för Finland* 72 (3):457–479.

———. 1988. *State and revolution in Finland.* Berkeley: University of California Press.

Alestalo, M., and S. Kuhnle. 1984. The Scandinavian route: Economic, social, and political developments in Denmark, Finland, Norway, and Sweden. Research Reports no 41. Helsinki: University of Helsinki, Research Group for Comparative Sociology.

Alestalo, M., and H. Uusitalo. 1978. Occupational prestige and its determinants: The case of Finland. Research Reports 20. Helsinki: University of Helsinki, Research Group for Comparative Sociology.

Becher, T. 1989. *Academic tribes and territories: Intellectual enquiry and the cultures of disciplines.* Bury St. Edmunds: The Society for Research into Higher Education and Open University Press.

Dill, D.D. 1992. Administration: Academic. In *The encyclopedia of higher education, Vol. 2,* eds., B.R. Clark and G. Neave. Oxford: Pergamon Press.

Durkheim, E. 1964. *The division of labor in society.* London: The Free Press of Glencoe, Collier–MacMillan Ltd.

Elovainio, P. 1971. Opiskelkjakunnan suuruus ja rakenne Suomen korkeakoulululaitoksessa [The size and structure of the student population in the Finnish higher education system]. *Sosiologia* 5: 262–276.

Heikkinen, A. 1983. *Perinneyhteisöstä kansalaisyhteiskuntaan.* Koulutuksen historia suomessa esihistorialliselta ajalta itsenäisyyden aikaan. [From traditional society to civil society]. Jyväskylä: Institute for Educational Research.

Häyrynen, Y.P. 1987. The life contents and social types of Finnish intellectuals: on the basis of a longitudinal study of students of the 1960s. In *Intellectuals, universities and the state in western modern societies.* eds., R. Eyerman, L.G. Svensson, and T. Söderquist. Berkeley: University of California Press.

Isosaari, J. 1989. *Seminaarista yhteiskuntaan.* Sortavalan seminaarista vuosina 1884–1940 valmistuneet kansakoulunopetta–jat maamme kulttuuri–, yhteiskunta– ja talouselämän vaikutta–jina [From Seminar to Society]. Hämeenlinna: Suomen Kouluhistoriallisen ran julkaisu–ja.

Jacoby, R. 1992. *The last intellectuals: American culture in the age of academe.* 3rd ed. New York: The Noonday Press.

Jallinoja, R. 1993. Tutkija ja päättäjät. [Researcher and Decision makers]. *Yliopisto— Acta Universitatis Helsingiensis* 24:46.

Jolkkonen, A. 1993. Hyvinvointivaltio akateemisten kohtalona [Welfare state as the destiny of academics]. In *Korkeakoulutuksen kriisi?* [Higher education in a crisis?]

Articles from the Fifth Symposium on Higher Education Research held in Jyväskylä, August 19–20 1993, eds., H. Jalkanen and L. Lestinen. Jyväskylä: Institute for Educational Research.

Jutikkala, E., and K. Pirinen. 1962. *A history of Finland*. London: Thames and Hudson.

Kangas, L. 1992. *Jyväskylän yliopistokysymys 1847–1966*. [The university question 1847–1966: A study of the foundation of the Jyväskylä Institute of Pedagogics and its development into a university]. Jyväskylä: Studia Historica Jyväskyläensia, No. 44.

Klinge, M. 1992. Intellectual tradition in Finland. In *Vanguards of modernity*, ed., N. Kauppi and P. Sulkunen. Jyväskylä: Publications of the Research Unit for Contemporary Culture.

Klinge, M., Knapas, R., and A. Leikola. 1987. *Kuninkaallinen turun akatemia 1640–1808* [The Royal Academy of Åbo]. Helsingin yliopisto I. Helsinki: Otava.

———. 1989. *Keisarillinen aleksanterin yliopisto 1808–1917* [The Imperial Alexander University]. Helsingin yliopisto II. Helsinki: Otava.

Konttinen, E. 1989. *Harmonian takuumiehiä vai etuoikeuksien monopolisteja?* [Quarantees of social harmony or monopolies of privileges? Functionalist and neo–weberian approaches in the sociology of professions]. Jyväskylä: University of Jyväskylä, Publications of the Department of Sociology.

———. 1991. *Perinteisesti moderniin: Professioiden yhteiskunnallinen synty Suomessa* [Traditional way to modernity]. Tampere: Vastapaino.

Korkeakoulut ja metsäteollisuus [Universities and forest industry]. 1983. Foundation for Research in Higher Education and Science Policy. Report 33. Rauma.

Lehtinen, E. 1989. Suomalainen patriotismi ja kansallistunne ruotsin kaudella [Finnish patriotism and nationalism under Swedish rule]. In *Herää Suomi*, eds., P. Tommila, P. Pohls, and M. Pohls. Jyväskylä: Gummerus.

Luhmann, N. 1987. *Soziale systeme. Grundriss einer allegemeinen theorie*. Nordlingen: Suhrkamp.

———. 1989. *Ecological communication*. Polity Press: Padstow.

Ministry of Education. 1994. *Higher education policy in Finland*. Helsinki.

Nettl, J.P. 1970. Ideas, intellectuals, and structures of dissent. In *On intellectuals: Theoretical studies, case studies*, ed., P. Rieff. New York: Anchor Books.

Nevala, A. 199 . *Mittavat murrokset—pienet muutokset. Korkeakoulupolitiikka ja opiskelijakunnan rakenne Suomessa 1900–luvulla*. [Remarkable reforms—Small changes]. Licentiate thesis in philosophy. University of Joensuu.

Niiniluoto, I. 1994. Suomen henkinen tila ja tulevaisuus [The mental status and future of Finland]. In *Suomen henkinen tila ja tulevaisuus*, eds., I. Niiniluoto and P. Löppönen. Juva: WSOY.

Niiniluoto, I., and P. Löppönen. 1994. *Suomen henkinen tila ja tulevaisuus* [The mental status and future of Finland]. Juva: WSOY.

Panhelainen, M. and R. Konttinen. 1994. International network for quality self-evaluation in Finnish higher education. *International Network for Quality Assurance Agencies in Higher Education* 5:20–24.

Parsons, T. 1964. *The social systems*. London: The Free Press of Glencoe.

———. 1970. "The intellectual": a social role category. In *On intellectuals: Theoretical studies, case studies*, ed., P. Rieff. Anchor Books: New York.

Piskonen, H. 1993. *Opiskelijoiden kulttuuripääoma ja tiedekulttuurit*. [Cultural capital and disciplinary cultures among students]. Publications of the Department of Sociology 54. Jyväskylä: University of Jyväskylä.

Rahkonen, K., and J.P. Roos. 1992. The field of intellectuals: the case of Finland. In *Vanguards of modernity*, eds., N. Kauppi and P. Sulkunen. Jyväskylä: Publications of the Research Unit for Contemporary Culture, No. 32.

Rommi, P., and M. Pohls. 1989. Poliittisen fennomanian synty ja nousu [The emergence of the political Fennomania]. In *Herää suomi*, eds., P. Tommila and M. Pohls, 69–119. Jyväs–kylä.

Sadri, A. 1992. *Weber's sociology of intellectuals*. Oxford: Oxford University Press.

Strömberg, J. 1989. Ylioppilaat. In *Keisarillinen aleksanterin yliopisto 1808–1917* [The Imperial Alexander University], eds., Klinge et al. Helsingin ylipoisto II. Helsinki: Otava.

Suolahti, G. 1974. *Nuori Yrjö–Koskinen* [Young Yrjö–Koskinen]. Keuruu: Otava.

SVT. 1993. Official Statistics of Finland, Science and Technology 1993:2. Helsinki.

Thaden, E.C. 1984. *Russia's western borderlands, 1710–1870*. With the collaboration of Marianna Foster Thaden. Princeton, N.J.: Princeton University Press.

Tiedon ja osaamisen Suomi. 1993. *Kehittämisstrategia* [Knowledge and expertise in Finland]. Helsinki: Valtion tiede– ja teknologianeuvosto.

Tierney, W.G. 1991. Academic work and institutional culture: Constructing knowledge. *The Review of Higher Education* 14:199–216.

Välimaa, J. 1992. Faculty cultures and innovations: A case study. In *Current visions and analyses on the Finnish higher education system*, ed., P. Hakkarainen, P. Jalkanen, and H. Määttä. Jyväskylä: University of Jyväskylä, Institute for Educational Research.

————. 1994a. Academics on assessment and the peer review: Finnish experience. *Higher Education Management Journal* 3:391–408.

————. 1994b. A trying game: experiments and reforms in Finnish higher education. *European Journal of Education* 29 (2):149–163.

Waris, H. 1940. Yliopisto sosiaalisen kohoamisen väylä–nä. Tilastollinen tutkimus säätykierrosta Suomessa 1810–67 [University as Way for Social Mobility]. *Historiallinen Arkisto* 47:199–272. Helsinki: Suomen Historialli–nen Seura.

Wilenius, R. 1982. Filosofisen luomisen aikaa 1840–1842 [The period of philosophical reflections]. In *J.V. Snellman, teokset II*. Jyväskylä: Gummerrus.

von Wright, G. H. 1993. Viimeisistä ajoista. Ajatusleikki. [On the last times. Mind games]. *Yliopisto—Acta Universitatis Helsingiensis* 24:4–15.

Contributors

Varaporn Bovonsiri is an associate professor in the Department of Higher Education, Faculty of Education, Chulalongkorn University, Bangkok. She has served as a researcher in the Office of the National Education Commission, Office of the Prime Minister, and at the Regional Institute of Higher Education and Development Bank in the Philippines. Her research in Thailand is focused on systems of higher education, vocational and technical education, the role of women in education, and education and rural development. She is the author of numerous articles, monographs, and books on higher education in Thailand.

Claudio Alejandro Figueroa is professor of educational policy and management, and director of the Latin American Center for Development, Education, and Culture (CENLADEC), Playa Ancha University, Valparaíso, Chile. At Playa Ancha he has served as director of the Educational Department and chair of the Specialist Program in Educational Administration sponsored by the Organization of American States. He has published a number of articles on educational administration, been a visiting professor at several Chilean universities, and lectured in numerous other Latin American institutions.

Gerald Fry is professor and director of International Studies, University of Oregon. He recently completed a year residence at the Teacher Development Center, University Institute in Laos, where he assisted in the development of the nation's educational system. He is a former Ford Foundation officer in Thailand and has published widely on educational, political, and economic development in Thailand and Southeast Asia.

Ken Kempner is associate professor of Higher Education and Research at the University of Oregon. He specializes in comparative and higher education with a focus on culture and the social role of higher education institutions. He is a former Fulbright scholar to Brazil, a Yamada scholar to Japan, and has been a visiting professor at the Universidad de Las Americas, Puebla, Mexico. His recent writing addresses comparative reform efforts in higher education and includes a book published in Japanese with Misao Makino on U.S. education.

Rollin Kent is associate professor, Center for Advanced Studies, Mexico City. As a sociologist, his research is focused on institutional and academic culture in Mexican universities. He recently headed the Mexican research team associated with the Latin American Comparative Higher Education Policy Group. His current work addresses institutional change, policy analysis, and the transformation of the research establishment in Latin America.

Misao Makino is professor of international education at Meiji University, Seijo University, and Aoyama Gakuin University. He serves additionally as Chairman of the Yamada Scholarship Foundation, board member of Kudan Medical Clinic Hospital, and chairman of AEA Continuing Education of Japan (affiliated with ETS). He is the author of numerous books on the teaching of English and coauthor and translator with Ken Kempner of *Cultural and Historical Perspectives on U.S. Education.*

Gary Rhoades is associate professor of Higher Education at the University of Arizona's Center for the Study of Higher Education. His recent work focuses on the restructuring of academic labor and higher education institutions.

Don Smart is associate professor of education and former Dean of the College of Education at Murdoch University in Western Australia. His work focuses on the politics and restructuring of higher education.

William G. Tierney is professor and director of the Center for Higher Education Policy Analysis, University of Southern California. He is the author of several books, including *Building Communitys of Difference: Higher Education in the 21st Century, Official Encouragement, Institutional Discouragement: Minorities in Academe—The Native American Experience,* and *Naming Silenced Lives* with Daniel McLaughlin. He is widely published in the area of higher education culture, leadership, and equity. Tierney is a former Peace Corps volunteer in Morocco and recently served as a Fulbright Scholar in Central America.

Susan B. Twombly is associate professor and chair of Educational Policy and Leadership at the University of Kansas. She spent the 1992–1993 academic year as a visiting researcher at the Institute for Improvement of Costa Rican Education, University of Costa Rica. In addition to academic women, her other research interests include higher education curricula.

Pornlerd Uampuang is Senior Development Officer, Asian Institute of Technology, Pathumthani, Thailand. His current research includes a UNICEF-sponsored project on the status of teachers in Southeast Asia. He is also a member of the National Education Commission's Committee for Higher Education Development and the Committee for Evaluating the Seventh National Higher Education Development Plan.

Jussi Välimaa is researcher at the research group for Higher Education Studies, Institute for Educational Research, University of Jyväskylä, Finland. Prior to coming to the Institute he served as a faculty member in European History and was also information Secretary for the University of Jyväskylä. He has published a number of books and articles on Finnish and European History in Finnish, Swedish, and Italian. His most recent work pertains to innovation and change in academic cultures.

Marcos Valle is a teacher of English as a second language who has taught in his native Brazil and the United States. Currently he is an ESL community college instructor and a supervisor of Spanish student teachers at the University of Oregon, where he is also a doctoral candidate in educational policy and management. His research interests include the politics and sociology of schools and schooling, gender and race in education, power issues in the classroom and society, adult education, and the transmission of culture.

Index